ECW'S BIOGRAPHICAL GUIDE
TO CANADIAN POETS

ECW's Biographical Guide to Canadian Poets

ECW PRESS

CANADIAN CATALOGUING IN PUBLICATION DATA

Main entry under title:
ECW's Biographical guide to Canadian poets

Includes bibliographical references and index.

ISBN 1-55022-152-3

1. Poets, Canadian (English) – Biography.* 2. Canadian poetry (English) –
History and criticism.* I. Lecker, Robert, 1951– . II. David, Jack, 1946– .
III. Quigley, Ellen, 1955– IV. Title: Biographical guide to Canadian poets.

PS8081.E28 1993   C811'.009   C91-095033-4
PR9186.2.E28 1993

The illustrations are by Isaac Bickerstaff.

ECW's *Biographical Guide to Canadian Poets* has been published with the
assistance of grants from The Canada Council and the Ontario Arts Council.

Design and imaging by ECW Type & Art, Oakville, Ontario.
Printed and bound by Hignell Printing Limited, Winnipeg, Manitoba.

Distributed by General Publishing Co. Limited, 30 Lesmill Road, Toronto,
Ontario M3B 2T6.

Published by ECW PRESS, 1980 Queen Street East, Toronto, Ontario M4L 1J2.

CONTENTS

Charles Heavysege 7
Charles Sangster 15
Charles Mair 24
Isabella Valancy Crawford 39
William Wilfred Campbell 45
Charles G.D. Roberts 48
Bliss Carman 55
Archibald Lampman 61
Duncan Campbell Scott 65
E.J. Pratt 70
W.W.E. Ross 74
Raymond Knister 78
F.R. Scott 84
Robert Finch 88
A.J.M. Smith 93
Earle Birney 99
Leo Kennedy 103
Ralph Gustafson 108
A.M. Klein 115
Dorothy Livesay 121
Anne Wilkinson 126
Irving Layton 131
P.K. Page 138
Miriam Waddington 145
Margaret Avison 149
Louis Dudek 155
Al Purdy 160
Raymond Souster 164
Eli Mandel 168
Milton Acorn 176
James Reaney 182

Robert Kroetsch 188
Phyllis Webb 197
D.G. Jones 213
Jay Macpherson 216
Alden Nowlan 220
Joe Rosenblatt 229
Leonard Cohen 232
George Bowering 236
John Newlove 243
Margaret Atwood 247
bill bissett 250
Patrick Lane 255
Dennis Lee 260
Gwendolyn MacEwen 264
Daphne Marlatt 267
Michael Ondaatje 271
bpNichol 278

Charles Heavysege (1816–76)

GEORGE WOODCOCK

ALL THE ACCOUNTS AGREE on the date when Charles Heavysege was born: 2 May 1816. But clearly none of those who have ventured on his biography has seen an actual birth record, for there is a sharp difference of opinion on the place where he was born. J.C. Stockdale, in the *Dictionary of Canadian Biography*, states that it was Huddersfield, Yorkshire;[1] Solly Bridgetower, in Robertson Davies' highly satirical *Leaven of Malice*, declares that, on the day we all agree on, ". . . Charles Heavysege first saw the light of day in Liverpool."[2]

In my view the weight of evidence, slight as it is, supports the jester rather than the *DCB*. The American novelist and poet Bayard Taylor, who sought Heavysege out in Montreal and wrote a sympathetic article on him in *The Atlantic Monthly* in 1865,[3] gave his birthplace as Liverpool. Later, in correspondence with another American writer, Charles Lanman, who discussed him in the

Washington Weekly Chronicle, Heavysege agreed that Taylor's article was "generally correct," though he also said that his "ancestors on the paternal side" came from Yorkshire.[4] The first mention of Huddersfield as a possible birthplace actually came late, when Theodore H. Rand made it in *A Treasury of Canadian Verse*, published in 1900. But Rand was somewhat cavalier with his facts and gave the date of Heavysege's death as 14 July 1879, three years late.[5] So, on balance, it seems best to accept Bayard Taylor's account, of which Heavysege approved, and to take it that he was born in Liverpool, probably of a Yorkshire family from Huddersfield.

Altogether, the information that can be scraped together regarding Heavysege's life is scanty, as it is for other writers who were his contemporaries, like Charles Sangster and Isabella Valancy Crawford, and it consists largely of information that he himself gave to Bayard Taylor orally and to Charles Lanman in letters; little regarding his life before he came to Canada is supported by external evidence.

Such as it is, the information reveals to us a boy born into a poor family and forced to leave school at the age of nine, which was not unusual in the 1820s; he returned to school only for a brief period in later years. There seems to have been a touch of shabby gentility in the family's pretensions. Heavysege told Lanman that there had been a "patrimony," which his father on coming to age had "from a romantic idea of justice . . . sold, and divided the proceeds amongst his relatives."[6] As for the maternal side, one of his daughters remembered "talk about my Father's Mother being a descendant of nobility, or almost royalty,"[7] and Heavysege himself asserted that his maternal grandfather had "wasted a small fortune in the indulgence of a too gay and hospitable disposition, which eventually brought him to end his days in an inferior position."[8] No records have been found of any landholding Heavyseges in England during the early nineteenth century, and I am inclined to believe that, as among so many Victorian English working-class people with a little education and a sense of superiority to their neighbours, all this talk about patrimonies, fortunes, and noble descent among the Heavyseges may have been family myth generated to relieve a shame at not being able to achieve prosperity in a society where poverty itself was a stigma. Certainly, in later years, after Chartism and similar movements had given a certain dignity to proletarian values, Charles Heavysege declared himself proud to belong to the working class.

Heavysege was apprenticed to a wood-carver, presumably in Liverpool, since he later set up his own woodworking business there, and worked from ten to thirteen hours a day all through his later childhood. Apart from this early subjection to long hours of work, that childhood may have been a joyless one, for his family — probably Wesleyan if one can judge from the fact that he attended the Dominion Square Methodist Church in Montreal in later years — appears to have been evangelically Puritan in its attitudes. "I was," he told Lanman, "what is usually styled religiously brought up, and . . . taught to consider not only the theatre itself but dramatic literature, even its best examples, as forbidden things." However, his mother seems to have been more indulgent in this respect than his father, and he managed to persuade her to give him "covertly . . . some few pence weekly for a cheap edition of Shakespeare that was then being issued in parts."9

Yet — as does not seem surprising when one reads Heavysege's own poetry — Bayard Taylor gained the impression that Milton was "the first author who made a profound impression upon his mind" and that he had also been especially devoted at school to Gray's "Elegy." "Somewhat later," says Taylor, "he saw 'Macbeth' performed, and was immediately seized with the ambition to become an actor . . . ."10 That ambition was only to be achieved once, under peculiar circumstances I shall later explain, but it must have been after seeing *Macbeth* that he talked his mother into giving him the money to buy Shakespeare's plays. If one adds the Bible, which must have been constantly present in such a household as his, one probably has the sum of Heavysege's childhood literary influences. It was the kind of self-education that sustained a whole lineage of English working-class dissenting writers from John Bunyan onwards.

In 1843 Heavysege married Mary Ann Oddy, and by her he had seven daughters, but none of the sons who might have helped him sustain his business. At one time, in Liverpool, he apparently employed several hands in his own workshop, but he had neither business ability nor the ambition to make a fortune, and by his thirties he had certainly begun to divert his energies to writing poetry, for his first work, of whose composition we have no knowledge, was published in 1852. This was *The Revolt of Tartarus*, an epic in the Miltonic tradition, and it appeared, under Heavysege's name, in his own town of Liverpool and also in London.

The next year he immigrated to Canada. An unnamed "gentleman" had invited him to Montreal, and there he took up life again as a journeyman wood-carver, working for the firm of J.W. Hilton, cabinetmakers and upholsters. He had not given up his literary ambitions, though he seems to have combined his two occupations, for the poet John Reade, who met him in 1858 when he was living on Saint Constant Street in Montreal, recorded that

> Heavysege told me that he was accustomed to compose while he was engaged at work, the occupation of his hands not interfering with the efforts of his mind. Speaking especially of *Saul*, he said that in this way he had elaborated some of the liveliest scenes.[11]

In 1855 he published anonymously a revised version of *The Revolt of Tartarus* and in the same year, also in Montreal, a volume entitled *Sonnets*, of which not a single copy appears to have survived.

But the work to which Heavysege devoted most of his energies at this time was his massive verse drama, *Saul*. The first edition appeared in 1857, again in Montreal and again anonymously. Much of his later life was to be devoted to working over this massive play for subsequent editions; the second appeared in London as well as Montreal in 1859; and a third, under his own name, was published by Fields Osgood in Boston in 1869 and was reprinted in New York in 1876, the year of his death.

Saul brought Heavysege a measure of success and even some celebrity, outside Canada more than at home. Emerson and Longfellow admired the play when copies first appeared in Boston sometime about 1860, but a copy reached Nathaniel Hawthorne, who was United States Consul in the poet's hometown of Liverpool, even before then, and Hawthorne, duly impressed, showed it to the British poet Coventry Patmore, who in 1858 anonymously wrote a laudatory notice in *The North British Review*, which described it as "indubitably one of the most remarkable poems ever written out of Great Britain."[12]

For the time being, Heavysege basked in the attention he was receiving. Bayard Taylor, visiting Montreal, sought him out at his place of work in 1860 and left the only description that tells us what Heavysege looked like:

Here, amid the noise of hammers, saws, and rasps, in a great grimy hall smelling of oil and iron-dust, we found the poet at his work-bench. A small, slender man, with a thin, sensitive face, bright blonde hair, and eyes of that peculiar blue which burns warm, instead of cold, under excitement . . . .[13]

New works appeared in steady succession, though their reception did not equal that of *Saul*. A second play, *Count Filippo; or, The Unequal Marriage*, which Heavysege brought out at his own expense, was published in 1860; astonishingly to modern readers, it seems to have been somewhat too sexually explicit for Victorian tastes.

In the same year, 1860, Heavysege left his carver's bench, and, at the urging of some of his friends who thought it would be a more congenial occupation for a poet, he became a reporter on the *Montreal Daily Transcript*. He remained there only a short time, returned for a brief period to wood carving, and then joined the staff of the *Montreal Witness*, of which he became city editor; he remained at the *Witness* until 1874, two years before his death.

It was an unhappy choice, which the more perceptive of his friends regretted. John Reade remarked, "I never saw him spending his intellectual strength in that way without feeling how lamentable his choice had been,"[14] and G.H. Flint, who also appears to have known him, said in an address he gave on Heavysege in 1889 that, instead of stimulating his poetic activity, "the endless grind and routine almost ruined it."[15] Heavysege himself told Charles Lanman: "You will know that to be the reporter and local editor of a daily newspaper does not permit of the seizing of those inspired moods, which come we know not how, and leave us we know not wherefore."[16] A rather sad glimpse of Heavysege at this time, attempting to reconcile the demands of poetry and journalism and withdrawing from his family in the process, is given in the recollection of one of his daughters, who remembered that he played the violin as "a sort of safety valve for pent-up feelings" and that "he would join our little family concerts for a few moments, throwing in his rich, deep voice in rolling abandon, then would slip away again to his writings and proof-sheets."[17] Apparently Heavysege's day at the *Montreal Witness* did not end until eight or nine o'clock in the evening, so that to do his own writing he had to work far into the night; when his wife remonstrated that he would harm his health, he apparently answered that he would prefer to shorten his life rather than cease to write. When he did give up his drudgery and retire to devote himself to his writing, it seems to have been too late, for he died two years later of what was described as "nervous exhaustion."

Why Heavysege continued in such an uncongenial occupation is uncertain. Burdened with a large family, he got little financial advantage from it, for when in 1869 the third edition of *Saul* was published, at his expense, he did not even have enough money to pay his debt to the publishers and had to borrow it from his fellow poet George Martin, to whom he still remained indebted at his death. Clearly he can have earned very little from his writings during his life, and what he earned from journalism was consumed in living expenses. Sandra Djwa has suggested that the real reason for Heavysege's burying himself in ill-paid and exacting work on a minor newspaper was social rather than financial: that ". . . in Victorian Canada, newspaper work was considered 'genteel' and the manual labour of woodworking was not" (Djwa, p. xiii). This would certainly fit in with the pretensions Heavysege displayed in giving a fanciful gentility to his forbears. Taking up work as a reporter would have been seen, in a favourite phrase of the time, as "bettering oneself."

Given the frustrations of this later period of his life, it is not surprising that Heavysege's production of new works should have slowly diminished after the completion of *Saul* and *Count Filippo*. As well as revising *Saul* painstakingly for its later editions, he seems to have spent some time preparing an acting version of the play, which the American actress Charlotte Cushman talked of producing, but nothing came of it; it may have been this abridgement that Heavysege read publicly in March 1862 at the Nordheimer's Hall in Montreal, the nearest he ever came to fulfilling his childhood aim of becoming an actor.

In 1864 Heavysege published two poems, *The Dark Huntsman (A Dream)*, a narrative of just over 160 lines produced by the

Witness Steam Printing House, and *The Owl*, a poem of 25 stanzas of which no copy seems to have survived. On 23 April 1864, at the Shakespeare Tercentenary in Montreal, he delivered an "Ode," whose complete version has also vanished; some lines from it, published in the *New Dominion Monthly* in September 1876, after Heavysege's death, are uninspiring.

In the following year, his worst work, a novel called *The Advocate*, and one of his best, the long narrative poem *Jephthah's Daughter*, were published, the latter in both Montreal and London. It was accompanied by a group of sonnets, some of them revisions of the lost *Sonnets* of 1855 and others written since that time. The last of Heavysege's works to be published was another narrative poem, "Jezebel," which appeared in the *New Dominion Monthly* in January 1868, but had to wait more than a century before it appeared in volume form, published in 1972 by the Golden Dog Press.

During those last years, Heavysege almost certainly wrote other poems, for he is said to have burnt a number of his unpublished manuscripts out of discouragement. There is no doubt the lack of an appreciative readership in Canada and the quick extinction of the interest in him that *Saul* had aroused elsewhere combined with the drudgery of his working life to sap the great energy with which Heavysege had written during his first years in Montreal, and he would sometimes speculate on how different his life might have been elsewhere. "I often think," he said to Charles Lanman, "that if fortune had guided my steps towards the States, say Boston, when I left England, the literary course of my life would have been influenced for the better."[18] Yet there seems little doubt that growing discouragement and ill health were accompanied in Heavysege by a burning out of talent and imagination long before the poet's little-regarded death.

NOTES

[1] J.C. Stockdale, "Heavysege, Charles," *Dictionary of Canadian Biography*, X (1972).

[2] Robertson Davies, *Leaven of Malice* (1954; rpt. Toronto: Clarke, Irwin, 1964), p. 187.

[3] Bayard Taylor, "The Author of *Saul*," *The Atlantic Monthly*, Oct. 1865, pp. 412–18.

[4] Charles Heavysege, letters to Charles Lanman, 2 Oct. 1865 and 12 Oct. 1860 respectively, in Lawrence J. Burpee, "Charles Heavysege," *Proceedings and Transactions of the Royal Society of Canada*, 2nd ser., 7 (1901), sec. II, 53–54.

[5] Theodore H. Rand, *A Treasury of Canadian Verse, with Brief Biographical Notes* (Toronto: William Briggs, 1900), p. 393.

[6] Heavysege, letter to Charles Lanman, 2 Oct. 1865, in Burpee, p. 55.

[7] Quoted from a letter of Mrs. Harriet Pettigrew [daughter of Charles Heavysege] to Mrs. Clara Groves Gould, 13 July 1933, in Sandra Djwa, Introd., *Saul and Selected Poems, Including Excerpts from* Jephthah's Daughter *and* Jezebel: A Poem in Three Cantos, by Charles Heavysege, Literature of Canada: Poetry and Prose in Reprint, No. 19 (Toronto: Univ. of Toronto Press, 1976), p. xliii, n. 7. Further references to this work appear in the text.

[8] Heavysege, letter to Charles Lanman, 2 Oct. 1865, in Burpee, p. 55.

[9] Heavysege, letter to Charles Lanman, 12 Oct. 1860, in Burpee, p. 53.

[10] Taylor, p. 413.

[11] John Reade, quoted in Burpee, p. 21.

[12] [Coventry Patmore], "The Modern British Drama," *The North British Review*, No. 29 (Aug.–Nov. 1858), p. 143.

[13] Taylor, p. 414.

[14] Reade, quoted in Burpee, p. 21.

[15] "Charles Heavysege" [summary of a paper read by G.H. Flint to the Society of Canadian Literature, March 1889], *The Dominion Illustrated*, 27 April 1889, p. 266.

[16] Heavysege, letter to Charles Lanman, 2 Oct. 1865, in Burpee, p. 54.

[17] Mrs. Middlemiss [daughter of Charles Heavysege], letter to Lawrence J. Burpee [1901], in Burpee, p. 52.

[18] Heavysege, letter to Charles Lanman, 2 Oct. 1865, in Burpee, p. 55.

Charles Sangster (1822–93)

W.D. HAMILTON

CHARLES SANGSTER was born on 16 July 1822, at the Navy Yard at Point Frederick, near Kingston, Upper Canada, the youngest of five children of James and Ann (Ross) Sangster. He was given the Christian name of his paternal grandfather, Sergeant Charles Sangster, a native of Fifeshire, Scotland, who fought in the American revolutionary war under General Burgoyne and later settled as a Loyalist in Prince Edward Island. The poet's father and mother both grew up on the Island and married there before migrating to Upper Canada during the first decade of the nineteenth century. James Sangster, a ship's carpenter with the Navy Department on the Great Lakes, died following a sudden illness, at Penetanguishene, in 1824, when his son Charles was only two years old.

Sangster's mother was left with a large family, which, he wrote, "she honorably brought up and provided for by the labor of her hands."[1] Though, as he also recorded, he "went to school many years and learned to read and write, if nothing more," it is not surprising he lacked "the advantage of a classical education." "All that I possess mentally," he stated, "has been acquired by careful reading of the best authors (chiefly fiction), properly directed thought, and a tolerable share of industry." This self-education, however, did not take place in childhood: "I would have read more in my younger days, but books were not to be had. The Bible, and the 'Citizen of the World' in two volumes, constituted my library for very many years."

In 1837, at fifteen years of age, Sangster left home to help support his widowed mother. His first job was in the laboratory at Fort Henry, Kingston, where he filled cartridges for use against William Lyon Mackenzie's rebels. In 1839 he was transferred to the fort's ordnance office, where, in his own words, he "ranked as a messenger, received the pay of a labourer, and did the duty of a clerk." For ten years in this position, he struggled for a promotion that never came. "I left the department in the summer of 1849," he said, "having lost ten of the best years of my life pursuing a myth." It was during his spare time while employed at Fort Henry, though, that Sangster acquired his basic self-education and began to write in earnest. His lengthy poem "The Rebel," for instance, was begun in 1839, and some of his shorter pieces are said to have appeared in Kingston newspapers in the 1840s.

When he left the imperial service, Sangster embarked on the newspaper career at which he earned his livelihood for nearly twenty years. During the summer and fall of 1849, he was editor of the weekly *Courier* in Amherstburg, Canada West; and, when that paper failed because of the death of its publisher, he joined the staff of *The British Whig*, a Kingston daily. His title with the *Whig* was subeditor, but his duties were those of a bookkeeper and proofreader. He did not find the work at all congenial, but the eleven years that he spent with *The British Whig* were by far his most productive years as a writer.

Sangster made his national literary début in the December 1850 issue of *The Literary Garland* with two innocuous little verses entitled "Bright Eyes" and "The Orphan Girl," and in 1855 he published samples of his best work in *The Anglo American Magazine*. At this time, he was at work on his first volume of poetry, *The St. Lawrence and the Saguenay and Other Poems*, issued in June

1856 by the printing firm of John Creighton and John Duff, of Kingston, and simultaneously, by subscription, through the firm of Miller, Orton and Mulligan, of Auburn, New York.

On 16 September 1856, at Saint James Anglican Church, Kingston, Sangster, age thirty-four, married Mary Kilborn, age twenty-one, but unhappily, only sixteen months later, his youthful wife contracted pneumonia and died. This was only one of a number of personal tragedies to befall Sangster during his lifetime that gave focus to his natural tendency towards melancholy and depression.

Sangster's second wife was Henrietta Meagher, the seventeen-year-old daughter of a Kingston physician, whom he married in October 1860. In the same year, he had *Hesperus and Other Poems and Lyrics* published at his personal expense through the Montreal publisher John Lovell, and, in a London edition, through Trübner & Co., Paternoster Row.

Both of Sangster's volumes were warmly praised by reviewers, but for reasons that have yet to be fully explained, his writing career came to a virtual halt in the 1860s. His literary activity in the 1860s and 1870s can be briefly summarized: the preparation of a revised and expanded version of "The St. Lawrence and the Saguenay" (which was never published), and the submission of some two dozen poems (chiefly minor and occasional verses) for publication in *The British American Magazine*, *The Saturday Reader*, *Stewart's Literary Quarterly Magazine*, *The Canadian Monthly and National Review*, and *Belford's Monthly Magazine*.

In 1864 Sangster joined the staff of Kingston's *Daily News* as a reporter. Then, in 1868, through the patronage of Alexander Campbell, of Kingston, Postmaster-General in Prime Minister John A. Macdonald's cabinet, he was appointed to a clerkship in the Post Office Department in Ottawa. He welcomed this appointment as a release from the "depressing mental and monetary conditions" of his life,[2] but his health proved unequal to the drudgery of the position from the start, and he suffered a complete breakdown in the early months of 1875. Some light is cast on his condition in an unidentified newspaper editorial from the period.[3] ". . . Mr. Sangster," stated the author, "was performing his official labors under very great difficulties, resulting in an almost complete loss of voice from nervous weakness . . . ." According to the editorial, doubts were entertained in 1868 about his capacity to accept a Post Office appointment, and "he has never fulfilled" the duties of his position. Sangster himself stated that he was "in danger of paralysis," and that his workload would have killed him within a year if it had not been lightened.[4] The Post Office Department responded to his illness by appointing him private secretary to the deputy postmaster-general. He retained this position for ten years, but it is to be doubted that he ever enjoyed full health while in Ottawa. It was another "nervous collapse" in 1885 that precipitated his retirement from the civil service in 1886, following a six-month sick leave.

The principal source of information on Sangster's last years is a collection of fifteen letters that he wrote to W.D. Lighthall between 1888 and 1893.[5] The correspondence began when Lighthall requested copies of Sangster's books from which to make selections for his anthology *Songs of the Great Dominion*. In his letter of 15 November 1888, Sangster expressed deep bitterness over the years he spent with the Post Office Department:

> When they get a man into the Civil Service, their first duty is to crush him flat, and if he is a fool of a poet, or dares to think of any nonsense of that kind, draw him through a knot or a gimlet hole a few times, pile on the agony of toil, toil, toil until his nerves are flattened out, all the rebound knocked out of him, and then — superannuate him on what he can squeeze out of them thro' friends or enemies, and tell him he should be thankful for small favors of the most microscopic pattern.

His letter of 8 July 1888 offered an explanation of his literary inactivity during the previous twenty years:

> I have written comparatively nothing for the past 20 years — I might say positively nothing. I came back to this my native city in September 1886, having been compelled to leave the P.O.D. at Ottawa on a superannuation allowance owing to the breaking down of my nervous system, after 18 years of steady desk work. I took the MS of a third volume on my leaving here at the request of the Hon. (now Sir) A. Campbell, down to Ottawa, put it aside when I assumed my labors at the desk, and left it laid on the shelf for those 18 years, but found no time either to publish, or add anything to it for all that time,

so steady were my duties, and so much did they unfit me for any, even the slightest, literary endeavour.

"The King of France, with twice ten thousand men,
Marched up the hill, and then marched down again."

And that was the case with my MSS. I took them to Ottawa — I brought them back to Kingston!

Two years elapsed in Kingston before he was able to set about his work again and belatedly ready his unpublished poems for publication. His letter of 8 July 1888 to Lighthall continues: "Since coming back I have gained considerably in health — 50 per cent or thereabouts, but it is only now that I feel that I dare use my brain, to set my papers in order, which I am now doing slowly to the best of my ability."

Sangster soon came to regard Lighthall as his literary executor. In his letter to him of 15 November 1888, he stated, "In looking these MSS over I find there is about — well between 3 or 4 thousand lines, very much in need of a publisher, and I must get this mass off my hands before I can do aught with the 2nd ed. of the other 2 vols. . . . . There is too much for one volume, so I think of dividing it into two . . . ." He revealed his thinking in detail in a letter dated 12 March 1889:

Not only had I to defer a reply until now but to cease copying from my MSS the new volume I was preparing (2 vols., in fact). A sudden attack of rheumatism in my right arm and hand compelled me to desist. I am endeavoring to fight back the enemy, but I suppose that warmer weather must come, and the snow and moisture leave, before I can dislodge him. All I can do is to patiently await the result of my endeavors to gain the victory. Then I will go on with copying until the 3rd volume is complete. After that I will have to copy the remainder of my MSS which will make a 4th volume about the size of Hesperus. I can do nothing with volumes *one* and *two* until all this is done. The "slashing" and "passing thro' the crucible" is pretty much done already. There will when all this is completed be four volumes viz:

1. *The St. Lawrence, etc.*
2. *Hesperus, etc.*
3. *Norland Echoes & Other Strains*
4. *The Angel Guest & Other Poems.*

> You see there will be a good deal of work for me to do, and I must not be in a hurry.

Between 1889 and 1891 Sangster deposited all of his manuscripts and the proposed revisions of his published works with Lighthall. "When I concluded to send you the MSS," he wrote on 14 July 1891,

> my idea was to save them, not to the world, but to "this Canada of ours," which, as you know, has occupied much of my thoughts in the rhyming way for many years. I knew that you were inclined to harp on a similar string at times, and that begat a fellow feeling, which urged me on to make you a kind of literary executor, as it were . . . . I did not send them with a view to publication in the near future, but for safety, and for fear of my suddenly collapsing . . . .

The chapbook *Our Norland*, which was issued by the Copp Clark Company, Toronto, about the year 1896, would seem to have been the only publication to result directly from Lighthall's role as Sangster's literary executor.

Less is known of Sangster's domestic existence during his later years than of his literary activity. While the tradition has come down in Kingston that his second marriage was not a happy one, it remained intact, at least, for more than twenty years. Four children were born between 1865 and 1879, one of whom — Charlotte Mary — died of diphtheria three weeks after the family left Kingston in 1868. Sangster's wife was still living with him in 1883, but not in 1886. She predeceased him, probably between these dates. After his return to Kingston (and during a brief residence in Niagara in 1891–92), Sangster sometimes had one or more of his children at home, but at the end he would seem to have been alone. It must be to the summer of 1893 that Wallace H. Robb, of Kingston, refers in the following reminiscence:

In Pittsburgh Township, south edge, Lot D in the 1878 Atlas, is the Sibbit home, an old limestone manor-house still occupied by my neighbours, Ed and Ross Sibbitt [sic]. In 1950, their eldest brother, the late Ex-Reeve John Sibbit, gave me his recollections of Sangster, who boarded for a while one summer with their widowed mother. From my notes, let me reconstruct our conversation:

> Remember Charlie Sangster? Yes, indeed, very clearly — he was an odd duck. It was between 1890 and 1893. Sangster was very old — looked it, with long, flowing hair and beard. He used to wander alone on the shore and through all the nearby countryside. . . . He had the odd habit of never coming back from a ramble empty-handed; nearly always a great armful of dry sticks from the woods. And he would sit on the woodpile, or anything, by the back door, for long periods, quietly thinking, watching who knows what? Birds, men at haying, boats on the river — not seeming to see anything. Sometimes he would sit with mother in the kitchen, silent — a queer bird. He seemed to believe in some kind of spirits; he sometimes complained in the morning that they had kept him awake. Charlie Sangster was a nice, old fellow; he seemed weary and downhearted — a sad and lonely old man with soft, darkish eyes and patriarchal beard like Father Time. We liked him, but couldn't understand him.[6]

Charles Sangster died in Kingston on 9 December 1893, at the home of his nephew, William Sangster, 398 Barrie Street, and was buried in Cataraqui Cemetery, where a small gravestone reads simply: "Charles Sangster POET."

The Week of 2 February 1894 carried the following editorial comment:

> Charles Sangster, the poet, is dead. . . . It is not too much to say that among all the life-histories of English bards who battled with unpropitious fortune, poverty, and neglect, there is scarcely one who has had a rougher or steeper path to climb, or faced unfriendly fate with a braver heart than he. . . . He

has for years past kept so much in the shades of retirement that many of the younger generation of readers will ask, who is Charles Sangster?

Who indeed was Charles Sangster? In life he was obscure. He never held an important position; he joined no movements; he belonged to no associations (except briefly to the Royal Society of Canada); and he was on intimate terms with few, if any, prominent persons. His works were praised when they were published, but his readership was pathetically small; his books sold poorly, and during the last thirty years of his life his name faded even from the literary scene. In death, he was greatly neglected until the general rejuvenation of interest in Canadian literature occurred after World War II. It was not until the early 1970s that a book-length study of his life and work was undertaken,[7] or until the late 1970s that the manuscript poems that he deposited with W.D. Lighthall nearly ninety years previously were published.[8] Although his preeminence among Canadian poets of the pre-Confederation era has never been seriously questioned, a definitive assessment of his artistic achievement and the significance of his contribution to the cultural development of the country is still awaited.

NOTES

[1] Charles Sangster, McGill Univ. Library, Charles Sangster Collection, autobiographical fragment. Except as otherwise noted, Sangster's words are quoted from this document.

[2] Lorne Pierce, *An Outline of Canadian Literature (French and English)* (Toronto: Ryerson, 1927), p. 65. Pierce observed that Sangster was corresponding with William Kirby at this time, and four of Sangster's letters to Kirby were later published by Pierce in his biography, *William Kirby: The Portrait of a Tory Loyalist* (Toronto: Macmillan, 1929), pp. 387–89, 407–08.

[3] McGill Univ. Library, Charles Sangster Collection, unidentified newspaper clipping.

[4] Charles Sangster, letter to David Gibson, 24 Nov. 1875, Public Archives of Canada, Charles Sangster Papers, MG29, G16.

[5] Charles Sangster, letters to W.D. Lighthall, 1888–93, McGill Univ. Library, Charles Sangster Collection.

[6] Wallace H. Robb, "Charles Sangster, Canada's and Kingston's Poet," *Historic Kingston: Transactions of the Kingston Historical Society*, No. 11 (1963), p. 34.

[7] W.D. Hamilton, *Charles Sangster*, Twayne's World Authors Series, No. 172 (New York: Twayne, 1971).

[8] Charles Sangster, *Norland Echoes and Other Strains and Lyrics*, ed. and introd. Frank M. Tierney (Ottawa: Tecumseh, 1976); Charles Sangster, *The Angel Guest and Other Poems and Lyrics*, ed. and introd. Frank M. Tierney (Ottawa: Tecumseh, 1977).

Charles Mair (1838–1927)

FRED COGSWELL

CHARLES MAIR was born in Lanark, Upper Canada, on 21 September 1838, the youngest of six children, all but one of whom were boys. His parents, James Mair, Sr., and his wife, Margaret Holmes, had immigrated in 1831 to join his grandfather, William Mair, who had come over from Scotland to the Ottawa Valley in 1824. Mair's father engaged in the timber trade and operated general stores in Lanark and in Perth. The milieu in which Mair grew up was predominantly Scottish. Its goals were God-fearing respectability achieved by hard work and material gain. They were inculcated in the young by the example of the older members of the family and by a system of education that dealt in "blacks" and "whites" (textbook facts and school regulations were the "whites," and all departures from them were "black" and were met with summary punishment, regardless of the feelings of those concerned). These attitudes were further reinforced by the homogeneity of the adult community. It is true that Native people, French

Canadians, and Irish settlers who did not conform were also present in the Ottawa Valley, but, for Mair's milieu, these were outsiders, suffered by necessity, and scorned as examples of vice and folly.

Given such an education, such a community, and the general malleability of the human race, it is hardly surprising that the narrow-minded bigotry it produced was almost universal, innate, unselfconscious, and self-perpetrating. Only an exceptional few could develop the will to resist it, and of those who did, even fewer possessed the means to put that will into effect. Charles Mair is a case in point. From an early age, he hated school and was punished time and time again for playing truant. From his early poems and from his play, *Tecumseh*, it is evident that Mair was drawn both to the natural forms of beauty in the Ottawa Valley and to the lives of those — like soldiers and Natives — who lived not by inside work in stores and offices but by exercising in the open air the manly arts of war and hunting. Part of this was no doubt owing to his father's softheartedness:

> . . . the father evidently too often gave in to the boy's wishes and allowed him for days on end to live with the timber men in their "chantiers" and to ride with them on their "drives" down the tributaries of the Ottawa, even down to Quebec itself.[1]

Another wider world was opened up for Mair by his mother. His later correspondence indicates the preponderant weight that Mair attached to her social and cultural heritage. Between mother and son was a particular bond, a common love of literature, that his mother was assiduous in forging and maintaining. Mair writes,

> After the fairy tales of childhood, she gave me Spenser's *Fairy Queen* in Charles Knight's excellent edition for a boy, in which the finest stanzas were connected by descriptive prose, and never wearied me. Other books followed: *Robinson Crusoe*, of course, *Gulliver's Travels*, *Pilgrim's Progress* . . . . When I was old enough I read . . . *Morte d'Arthur*, Chapman's *Odyssey*, and a good many of *Shakespeare's Dramas* . . . . I always thought *Tom Jones* our greatest novel, *Rob Roy* the next, and *Jacob Faithful* one of the best.[2]

Thanks to the sustained pressure of the French revolutionary and Napoleonic armies upon Europe for nearly three decades, the nineteenth century was to become, more than any corresponding period in world history, the century of nationalism. Not only did nationalistic concepts alter the political structures and boundaries within Europe but they spread to America, where their most conspicuous manifestations were the paring off from Spain and Portugal of the Latin American states and the notion of manifest destiny which shaped the growth of the United States. Upper Canada was not immune from these developments. Its nationalism was deflected, however, from its natural outlet in a retrograde direction, colonialism. A large number of its earliest settlers had been United Empire Loyalists, who had preferred exile to the nationalistic experiment of self-government undertaken by most of Britain's North American colonies. The War of 1812–14 had further strengthened their determination to remain British by adding to it a sense of pride and local patriotism and deep feelings of suspicion and prejudice against the United States. This patriotic colonial ethos was added to by the immigrants, many of them discharged British veterans, who came to Upper Canada in the decades following the close of the Napoleonic wars. Charles Mair may have differed from his Lanark neighbours in his keen interest in observing nature, reading and writing poetry, and seeking the company of outdoor types, but he was one with them in his pride in Upper Canada's past, his faith in her future, and his attachment to the mother country. Throughout his life, he was proud to have been named after an uncle who had given his life for Britain during the Peninsular War.

There were, then, conflicting tendencies in Mair and contradictory elements in his make-up. During ordinary times of family life and routine work, one may carry such and keep them separate in one's head. Only in prolonged times of crises and stress do they affect actions enough to force one to self-examination and then often too late to alter consequences. This process can be seen at work throughout Mair's career and accounts in large part for both his failures and his achievements in two widely separated areas. There was nothing, though, during the first three decades of his life to interrupt or disturb the habitual balance he had arrived at with the different facets of his nature.

Stoutly built, strong and energetic, and possessed of an excellent constitution, Mair managed to complete high school at Perth and to attend Queen's College in Kingston during the 1856–57 session pursuant to his father's desire that he become a doctor. After only one year, he returned from Queen's to Lanark to help his father and brothers with their timber and merchandising business, which was, at that time, undergoing a period of financial crisis. He remained in Perth and Lanark for ten years, working with his family and dividing his spare time among outdoor expeditions, reading, and writing poetry, which, as well as reviews, he began publishing in local newspapers and magazines. His father having died, and having settled the family business on his brothers, Mair registered in Queen's College Medical School in 1867 and, having successfully completed his first year, seemed well on his way to becoming a doctor. Since the family finances could now permit it, Mair determined to publish a book of his own poems and set off for Ottawa to see his fledgling efforts through the press. One result was to be *Dreamland and Other Poems* (1868). The other was Mair's meeting with four young men: Henry J. Morgan, a clerk in the office of the Secretary of State for the newly formed government of Canada; William Alexander Foster, a Toronto barrister; Robert Grant Haliburton, son of Thomas Chandler Haliburton and a prominent Halifax lawyer and businessman; and George Taylor Denison, a Toronto lawyer and Commander of the Governor General's Body Guard. Out of this meeting was formed the Canada First party, an association that was to affect radically both Mair's future life and the course of subsequent Canadian history.

In 1868, when Mair arrived in Ottawa, the Dominion of Canada was about to celebrate its first anniversary. It was far from being a nation in more than name. Canada had come about, not as a result of pressure from its peoples, but rather through a clever deal engineered by the politicians of Upper and Lower Canada to solve the constant deadlock that had persisted in their assembly and which threatened to paralyze the machinery of self-government. To this end, Canadian delegates had attended the Charlottetown conference in 1864, and persuaded the Maritime delegates to enlarge their projected federal system to include all the British colonies in North America. The result of their labours was the passing, in 1867, of the British North America Act. Only four provinces took advantage of the federal opportunity and two of these, New Brunswick and Nova Scotia, with considerable reluctance. Newfoundland, Prince Edward Island, and British Columbia remained outside the federation, and by far the largest territorial area of British North America remained under the suzerainty of the Hudson's Bay Company. Moreover, not only did the British parliament show no enthusiasm over the new project but public opinion in the United States was so aroused by it that there was serious talk of annexation. Canadian politicians were divided as well in the direction they felt the new nation ought to go. They were agreed, however, that if Canada were to retain its independence of the United States, it must become commercially viable. To be so, it must expand and grow and persuade the other colonies to join it. British Columbia could be enticed into the Dominion by promise of a railway link with the East. But before such a promise could be made, its practicality had to be ensured. The Canadian government therefore applied to Great Britain to arrange the transfer of most of the Hudson's Bay Company's lands in North America to the Dominion. With these, the new nation could have a rich source of agricultural land for development, could bribe capitalists to build a railway to open it up for settlement, and could persuade British Columbia to enter the federation.

This, certainly the greatest single development in Canadian history, was no doubt in the minds of some politicians when Mair and his friends met in Ottawa, and it certainly would have received their approval had they known of it. All five were united in their belief in the new nation's future; all were agreed as to what its objectives should be; and they formed themselves unofficially into an association to work, either directly or indirectly, to see that their objectives were fulfilled. Their aims were threefold: the destruction of the provincialism of outlook that divided Canadians, Canada's geographic expansion through a policy of commercial and territorial imperialism, and the achievement of greater autonomy within the framework of the British Empire. To achieve these ends, they must foster both education and the creation of a rich Canadian artistic and literary milieu, on the one hand, and material progress, on the other. Separately, as private citizens, the members of the Canada First party were pledged to support these goals; politically, they were to hold their fire until a crisis came in which these factors were involved and then, at the decisive moment, throw their full weight into their support.

Mair was not long in putting into practice his patriotic resolutions. During his visit to Ottawa, he had made the acquaintance of the Honourable William McDougall, then Minister of Public Works. McDougall was so impressed by Mair that he put him to work in the Parliamentary Library to help prepare materials to defend the Canadian government against possible litigation on behalf of the Hudson's Bay Company should that company's claims stand in the way of Britain's transfer of the North-West to the Dominion. Mair executed this task so promptly and well that McDougall offered to take him to Britain as his secretary in the negotiations that followed. Mair accepted the appointment but, unable to leave at the proper time, was sent westward instead to act as paymaster and accountant on the Fort Garry Road.

In the autumn of 1868, Mair arrived in Fort Garry to find himself in a divided community. On one side were those opposed to the impending annexation of the Hudson's Bay Company's territories to Canada. These were the Hudson's Bay Company officials; the American settlers, who were in favour of annexation to the United States; the Roman Catholic priests, who saw their role as establishers of French culture and Roman Catholic faith threatened by an influx of Protestant settlers from Ontario once the transfer was made; and the majority of Métis under their leader, Louis Riel. Opposing these were the British army pensioners, the free traders, some of the Métis, and most of the settlers from Upper Canada and Great Britain. The most committed of this latter group were the free traders, who resented the monopoly of the Hudson's Bay Company and felt that a transfer of sovereignty would open the West to free competition, a competition in which they would enjoy the signal advantage of being already on the spot. Since one of their foremost members, Dr. John Christian Schultz, was already a personal friend and since the views of Schultz and his friends coincided with those of Mair's Protestant Ontarian upbringing and the Canadian imperialism he felt obliged to support, he not only consorted chiefly with Schultz and his associates but took their side in the numerous arguments then going on about the future of the West. This by itself would have made him unpopular in Fort Garry. Added to it was the opprobrium that he brought upon himself by his self-ordained task as correspondent for *The Globe* [Toronto].

Initially Mair's letters to *The Globe* were acts of patriotism designed to encourage support for the government's attempts to annex the territory and designed also to persuade Eastern Canadians to immigrate to it. To accomplish these ends, Mair depicted the potential of this new West in the most glowing terms, which were the more believable in that he wrote as an actual eyewitness and interspersed his account with detailed anecdotes written in vivid prose. Unfortunately, at the same time, Mair indulged his Eastern prejudices in these letters and attempted by ridicule to discredit those elements of Western society that were opposed to his views:

> After putting up at the Dutchman's hotel . . . I went over and stayed at Dr. Schultz's after a few days. The change was comfortable, I assure you, from the racket of a motley crowd of half-breeds, playing billiards and drinking, to the quiet and solid comfort of a home. I was invited to a dinner-party at Beffs [sic], where were the Governor's brother-in-law, a wealthy merchant here, Isabister, and other Nor' Westers. Altogether, I received hospitalities to my heart's content, and I left the place thoroughly pleased with most that I had met. There are jealousies and heart-burnings, however. Many wealthy people are married to half-breed women, who, having no coat of arms but a "totem" to look back to, make up for the deficiency by biting at the backs of their "white" sisters. The white sisters fall back upon their whiteness, whilst the husbands meet each other with desperate courtesies and hospitalities, with a view to filthy lucre in the background. (Quoted in Shrive, pp. 70–71)

Whether or not, as he afterwards claimed, Mair had sent the letters to his brother for the latter's private amusement with instructions to forward only public matter to *The Globe*, their impact was damning when copies of *The Globe* reached Fort Garry. To most of its inhabitants, it was plain that Mair had broken two codes of honour. He had accepted Western hospitality and then had held his hosts up to Eastern ridicule. He had written publicly and outrageously about ladies. His host, Alexander Begg, was to take a cruel revenge a few years later when he savagely caricatured Mair in his novel *"Dot It Down": A Story of Life in the North-West* (1871). The women of Fort Garry exacted a much more immediate and smarting revenge. One lady pulled Mair's nose; another boxed his ears; a third gave him a tongue-lashing; and a fourth, Mrs. Bannatyne, the wife of one of the town's leading citizens, publicly horsewhipped him before a large crowd in the town post office.

As a result, Mair's social contacts were confined to the homes of Dr. Schultz and his more rabid Canadian friends and work parties on the Fort Garry Road, a project now under increasing difficulty through Métis hostility aggravated by the actions of a survey party of the Canadian government led by Colonel John S. Dennis. He did, however, find time and opportunity for romance, for on 8 September 1869 he married the nineteen-year-old Eliza (Elizabeth Louise) McKenney, who had come west with Dr. Schultz's bride the preceding year. "At this time," wrote Mair, "a great happiness had come into my life."[3] He was not, however, to enjoy it uninterruptedly. While yet on his honeymoon, Mair joined William McDougall, the newly appointed governor of the North-West Territories, at St. Paul, Minnesota, on 28 September 1869. On October 30, at the border village of Pembina, on their way to Fort Garry, McDougall, Mair, and party were barred from entering the territory by Métis acting under the orders of Louis Riel, who in the interregnum between the abdication of the Hudson's Bay Company's jurisdiction and the transfer of authority to the Canadian government had occupied Fort Garry and established a government of his own. The Red River Rebellion had begun.

On the pretext of winding up his affairs there, Mair was allowed by the Métis to return to Fort Garry. His role during the ensuing events was consistently intrepid, strenuous, and altogether devoted to Canadian interests as he saw them. He was captured in the siege of Dr. Schultz's house, was imprisoned in Fort Garry, sentenced to be executed, but escaped and made his way to Portage la Prairie. From there Mair was one of the leaders in an expedition of British Canadians attempting to recapture Fort Garry from the Métis. Foiled by the desertion of the Kildonan settlers, the expedition was captured by the Métis on its retreat towards Portage la Prairie. Mair, however, escaped and, leaving his wife with friends, set out in February 1870 by dog-team with John J. Setter for St. Paul. After an epic journey of nearly four hundred and fifty miles, on foot and by dog-team, Mair and his companion reached St. Paul, and on March 30 Mair boarded the train en route to Toronto.

Mair's heroic march was not a retreat but a change of tactics. He had come to realize that the British settlers in the West did not possess the resources and expertise necessary to dislodge the Métis. Only military help from Canada on a large scale could do that. He realized also that time was of the essence. How long might it be before Riel would be forced by the logic of the situation to throw in his lot — and that of the West — with the United States? Men like himself, possessed of the necessary firsthand knowledge, writing skills, and crowd appeal, could rouse public opinion and compel the prime minister to use military force. Mair and his friend Schultz, who joined him in Toronto, and the other members of the Canada First party intervened in this first crisis in Canadian history. By their writings and speeches, they so fomented the Canadian public that the government was compelled to dispatch the military expedition under Colonel Wolseley that recaptured Fort Garry and put an end to the rebellion. However much Mair's rash actions may have precipitated the conflict, he played a large role in the principal service the Canada First association was to pay to the young nation.

Once order was restored, Mair returned to the territories, now Manitoba, and settled with his wife and child — whom he had not seen — at Portage la Prairie in 1870. There he bought a store and engaged in the profession he knew best, merchandising. In the early days of the West, the keeper of a general store was guaranteed a virtual monopoly of the business of his immediate locality and, if he attended to business, a slow growth in competency and independence. During his seven years in Portage la Prairie, Mair achieved this slow growth and its rewards, aided by land speculation. He became a leading citizen and added four children (three girls and a boy) to his family.

During these seven years, however, Mair underwent important changes in his views. Although a lifelong Canadian patriot and supporter of the Canada First association, he came more and more to identify himself with the Canada that was the West and not the Canada that was Ottawa. He became critical of federal delays in opening up the land to settlers and of the Eastern apathy towards speeding up the building of the much-needed railway link. He came, too, to see virtue in the Métis and in the Native way of life, which had altogether escaped him during his early Fort Garry days. He came to realize that, although the old way of life on the prairie was doomed by settlement, there was much more that was good in it than he had once conceded. He evidently determined in an oblique way to made amends by a great work of literature that would pay tribute to the genuine virtues of a passing race. Given his family commitments, however, he could not put himself in a position to do so adequately without first engaging in even more crass commercialism. He had to get rich quick, and the only way to get rich quick in the West was to become on a large scale a land speculator.

What was needed to become a successful Western land speculator was to be located, at the beginning of a settlement, on rich agricultural land through which at least one railroad was expected to be built; if there were prospects of two railroads, so much the better. Seven years' experience had taught Mair that the already established Portage la Prairie was not the place, but, during his winter travels, he had encountered the predominantly British hamlet of Prince Albert on the North Saskatchewan River, which, according to his judgement, promised to be the ideal spot. It was surrounded by good land. Although it was a few miles north of the projected Canadian Pacific Railway, it lay directly in what Mair and others considered to be the best possible route of a branch railway to Churchill on Hudson Bay, from whence he felt the rich prairie harvest must ultimately be shipped. What Mair and few other Westerners realized was that no interests in Eastern Canada were likely to favour a commercial venture in which a trade already profitable to them would be completely bypassed. Mair accordingly set up a store in Prince Albert and established his family there.

The boom that followed a few years after Mair's arrival brought him a considerable degree of affluence and a corresponding social position in the community. By 1882 he was able to put his literary dream into effect. He bought a house in Windsor, Ontario, and moved his family there to further his children's education. In 1884 he himself moved to Windsor and there, interrupted only by a few months humdrum soldiering as a volunteer during the second North-West Rebellion, devoted the next two years to composing his poetic drama, *Tecumseh*, which he finished around the middle of December 1885 and which was published in Toronto by Hunter, Rose in the following year.

Tecumseh, into which Mair incorporated the best of what he felt and believed with all the technical skill he possessed, was to have been his greatest literary bequest to posterity. Immediately, its publication brought him a modest commercial success and reviews enthusiastic enough to sustain his literary reputation in Canada for at least four decades. Mair himself estimated "that the years of writing had cost him ten thousand dollars . . . and his return had been but five hundred" (Shrive, p. 195). Mair's estimate was all too modest in the light of subsequent events.

To buy time in which to write *Tecumseh*, Mair had exhausted his surplus capital and neglected his business interests at Prince Albert. Although for a time he seemed to have restored his old prosperity and although he did succeed in 1890 in the town's fight to have a connecting line with Regina built and profited by the brief boom that followed, he and his fellow citizens became increasingly disillusioned by the scarcity of immigrants, by the federal government's failure to promote Western immigration, and by the growing realization that the railway to Churchill would never materialize. In 1891 a depression struck:

> . . . long-established families were moving out . . . . Some of them sold businesses for what they could get; others closed shops to await better times; others left their share of the eighty thousand bushels of wheat no one would buy. And Mair, now over fifty years old, was stricken with a fear he had not known before, the fear of poverty. (Shrive, p. 214)

After short-lived ventures into storekeeping at Kelowna, Benvoulin, and Fort Steele in British Columbia, Mair was finally saved from the worst extremities of poverty by a government appointment in July 1898 to a minor clerkship in Winnipeg. Because the salary was not in itself enough for the Mairs to live on and pay the taxes on their holdings in Prince Albert, they were both forced to work, and because they were unable to find employment in the same locality they were compelled to live apart until 1903, when Eliza Mair was finally able to rejoin her husband at Lethbridge together with their youngest daughter, Elizabeth.

What happened immediately after Mair's employment in Winnipeg is a matter of the deepest irony. Clifford Sifton, the new Minister of the Interior, was able, through his energy and policies, to accomplish within five years the population growth in the West that, had it occurred ten years before, would have made Mair a wealthy man. Mair himself, as a poorly paid clerk initially, put all his energies at Sifton's disposal. His career as a public employee has been summarized as follows by Norman Shrive:

> For almost twenty-five years — until he was in his eighties — Mair served his department well. He conducted settlers to their new homes in Manitoba, Saskatchewan, Alberta, and British Columbia; he escorted deputations of officials from the United States, Great Britain, and Europe who had been sent to investigate immigration possibilities in a great new country. When not travelling he prepared descriptive pamphlets, wrote articles for newspapers and magazines, and handled the foreign correspondence for the several branch offices to which he was attached over the years. After five years in Winnipeg he was placed in charge of the office at Lethbridge. Shortly afterwards he was moved south to Coutts and then west, as an inspector, to Fort Steele, British Columbia. In this latter post he retired in 1921, an old man of eighty-three. (Shrive, p. 227)

The struggle for family and financial survival between 1885 and 1898 and the bureaucratic tasks that occupied him from then until 1901 left Mair with little means or energy for literary tasks and, until 1901, with little means by which to furnish the outlay that publishers in those days required as a *sine qua non* for publication. Late in 1901, however, William Briggs published *Tecumseh, a Drama, and Canadian Poems*, a reissue with revisions and a few omissions of Mair's two earlier volumes together with a small sheaf of poems written during the intervening years. The critical response to this volume, although favourable, was far less than Mair's work had hitherto received.

In 1899 Mair was sent as English Secretary of the Scrip Commission to the Mackenzie River basin to negotiate treaty rights for this area with the Natives, and he contributed letters giving an account of the region and its inhabitants to *The Globe* [Toronto]. These letters formed the basis for Mair's *Through the Mackenzie Basin: A Narrative of the Athabasca and Peace River Treaty Expedition of 1899*, published by Briggs in 1908 jointly with *Notes on the Mammals and Birds of Northern Canada*, by Roderick MacFarlane. The book not only sold out its print-run of two thousand copies but was generally regarded by critics as useful, informative, and readable.

Much of Mair's time during this stage in his life was taken up with family matters. He was saddened by the death, through typhoid fever, of his daughter Elizabeth in 1905 and the further death, two years later, of his wife, Eliza, by a brain haemorrhage. Mair was estranged from a daughter in a quarrel over an early sale of property in Kelowna, and his son, Cecil, after a promising beginning, became a ne'er-do-well, a sponger, and a constant source of grief and embarrassment to his father.

In his old age, Mair was greatly consoled by the growth of Canada as a nation — a growth of which he was extremely proud; he was equally gratified by his conviction that he had played an important part in that process. He did, however, have two important reservations, which, in 1925, at the age of eighty-seven, he expressed in an unpublished manuscript, "A Message to the Youth of Canada." He first admonished Canadians not to forget

> that we are made of two great races, and that the Frenchman's love for this country is not second to our own. We should make the union between us stronger than it has ever been in the past, till the tie of kinship is not less than brotherhood. They have been co-workers, co-builders with us through all the centuries, and our interests are identical. I should like to see the French language taken up in the primary grades of every school throughout the Dominion, for to understand the language of a people is to understand that people's soul. And soul must speak to soul if we would build for God and Canada. (Shrive, p. 254)

And of apprehension concerning the United States, Mair writes,

> . . . let us not take second place to the United States. We have a bigger country than theirs. Our resources have hardly been

touched yet — timber, minerals, water power. Our wheat fields feed the world. . . . But do not let us permit the exploitation of our resources by any other country than our own. They are our heritage, sacred to us by the life and death of our ancestors who just as surely as those who lie in Flanders Fields have passed us the torch that we may "carry on." (Shrive, pp. 254–55)

However flawed at times by self-conceit and limitation of outlook in the days of his young manhood, Charles Mair's life is more many-faceted and wonderful than any poem that this nation has yet produced. His prejudices were not sharpened and embittered by disappointment and loss. In his old age, Mair exemplified the patience and charity that was part of his innate being but which had at crucial times in his life been clouded by the prejudices of his upbringing.

One final absurdity remained. In 1915, thirty years after its publication, *Tecumseh* was "discovered" by the stockbroker and amateur "man of letters" John W. Garvin as "the greatest piece of literary work by a Canadian" (Shrive, p. 260). Garvin's subsequent correspondence with Mair and his actions proved that he also regarded Mair as the country's greatest poet and the true father, rather than Charles G.D. Roberts, of Canadian literature. With Garvin, to believe was to act. He gave a fulsome address on *Tecumseh* before the Canadian Literature Club in Toronto, organized a newspaper controversy as to the parentage of Canadian literature, and championed Mair as its first real parent. Not content with this, he approached the Toronto publishers in an attempt to persuade them to publish Mair's complete poems. Unable to find a publisher who would undertake such a task, he formed his own company, the Radisson Society, and published *Tecumseh, A Drama, and Canadian Poems*; *Dreamland and Other Poems*; *The American Bison*; *Through the Mackenzie Basin*; *Memoirs and Reminiscences*, with an introduction by Robert Norwood, as Volume XIV of *Master-Works of Canadian Authors*, in April 1927. Mair had a chance to reread his complete works, together with a fulsome introduction extolling his poetic and dramatic merits, and to admire the maroon binding and gold tooling of a handsomely produced, if somewhat amateurish, book. Fortunately, he died a few months later without knowing that the book's critical reception was negligible, that it never did sell, and that his would-be benefactor was financially ruined by the cost of its production.

NOTES

[1] Norman Shrive, *Charles Mair: Literary Nationalist* (Toronto: Univ. of Toronto Press, 1965), p. 15. Further references to this work appear in the text. The writing of this biography, undertaken when I was in residence at the University of Edinburgh, has been handicapped to some degree by a lack of access to secondary sources. On that account, I owe a greater debt than normal to Norman Shrive.

[2] Charles Mair, "Memoirs and Reminiscences," in *Tecumseh, a Drama, and Canadian Poems; Dreamland and Other Poems; The American Bison; Through the Mackenzie Basin; Memoirs and Reminiscences*, introd. Robert Norwood, Vol. XIV of *Master-Works of Canadian Authors*, ed. John W. Garvin (Toronto: Radisson Society, 1926), p. lv.

[3] Mair, "Memoirs and Reminiscences," p. xxvi.

Isabella Valancy Crawford (1850–87)

ROBERT ALAN BURNS

WE KNOW VERY LITTLE about the life of Isabella Valancy Crawford. In a letter written to *The Week* [Toronto] in 1885 or 1886, she indicated that she had been born in Dublin, Ireland, the sixth child of Stephen Denis Crawford, M.D.[1] Crawford's mother, Sidney Scott, survived all of her children except for her son Stephen Walter. Although there is no record of Isabella's birth, there is a strong tradition that she was born on 24 or 25 December 1850.[2] All, or all but one, of her older siblings had apparently died before the family emigrated to Wisconsin, where Isabella's younger sister, Emma Naomi, was born in 1854.[3] The son, Stephen Walter, was born in 1856 or 1857. His birthplace is variously given as Ireland and Dublin, Ireland, suggesting that Crawford's mother may have returned to Ireland before emigrating to Paisley, Canada West, in 1857 or 1858 (Livesay, p. 8).[4] There is also a possibility that another sister, named Sidney after her mother, died while the Crawfords were living in Paisley (Petrone, pp. 14–15).

The only detailed account of Crawford's life during the Paisley years is an unsubstantiated narrative written by Mrs. Annie Sutherland for the *London Free Press* [London, Ont.] in 1927.[5] Quoted extensively in an article by Dorothy Livesay, Mrs. Sutherland's sketch reads more like popular sentimental fiction than biography.[6] Several sources indicate, however, that like the Traills and the Moodies, the Crawfords brought gentility and cultivation to the Canadian wilderness, but frontier rigours proved too great for the physician and his family. By 1862 or 1863, the Crawfords are reported to have left Paisley and were staying at an inn north of Kingston when they were discovered by Robert and Lakefield Strickland, sons of Sam Strickland and nephews of Catharine Parr Traill and Susanna Moodie. Robert, who was leaving for a visit to England, offered to allow the Crawfords to stay in his vacant house in the village of Lakefield. Dr. Crawford accepted and became Lakefield's first resident physician (Livesay, p. 8, and Petrone, p. 20).

While in Lakefield the Crawfords are said to have cultivated a circle of genteel friends, among whom were Catharine Parr Traill and her daughter Kate. Tradition has held that Kate and Isabella were the same age and close friends, but Dorothy Farmiloe has shown that Kate was in her twenties and Isabella barely a teenager, so that ". . . it is unlikely the two were close . . . ."[7] The Crawford children were educated at home, where Isabella, according to her biographers, learned Latin, French, and English and read widely in the classics, the Bible, and European literature (Petrone, pp. 15–17). She loved music and is said to have played the piano very well. The first indication of her writing comes from the Lakefield period and includes manuscripts of her first fairy tale and a precociously witty familiar essay.[8] Once, when Mrs. Traill and Kate came to tea, Isabella remarked that she was writing a book that she planned to call "Lavender and Old Lace."[9]

Unfortunately, the Crawfords fared no better in Lakefield than they had in Paisley. Dr. Crawford had a drinking problem that was widely enough known to damage his practice seriously, and there is evidence that his skill as a surgeon could not be relied upon (Martin, p. 393). In 1870 or 1871, when the doctor was in his late sixties, the family moved to nearby Peterborough, a much larger community than Lakefield, where the doctor hoped to be able to expand his practice.

The Crawfords had been very poor while they lived in Lakefield, and in Peterborough their circumstances did not improve (Petrone, pp. 24–26). By 1873 the family may have been in deep financial difficulty, for it was in this year that Isabella's stories and poems began to appear regularly in a weekly publication known as *The Favorite*.[10] Tradition has it that 1873 was also the year that she won a $600-prize short-story contest, but the sponsoring company failed after paying the first $100.[11] On 24 December 1873 her poem "The Vesper Star" was published in *The Mail* [Toronto], and several of Crawford's biographers indicate that it was around that time that she began publishing fiction in Frank Leslie's popular American tabloids.

There is no extant verse published by Crawford in the year following her father's death on 3 July 1875. In view of nationwide economic difficulties and the persistent tradition that Dr. Crawford left his family penniless, there is little to suggest anything but unrelieved desolation for the Crawfords during this period. By the time of Emma Naomi's death on 20 January 1876, it is believed that Crawford's brother, Stephen Walter, had left home to find work (Livesay, p. 9). Her biographers make vague and evasive references to a quarterly allowance from an uncle in Ireland. This, in addition to some small support from Stephen Walter, may have forestalled starvation for Isabella and her mother during the winter of 1875–76. By July 1876 mother and daughter had left Peterborough and were living in Toronto (Petrone, pp. 29–30).

In the decade of her residence in Toronto, Crawford and her mother are known to have lodged at two different addresses (Martin, p. 395). They lived quietly but not reclusively. Their friendship with the Donald Urquhart family gave them opportunities to visit frequently in a genteel middle-class home, and Isabella was a member of the Mechanics Institute and so had access to that organization's excellent library and to the regular lectures that were given at the institute by some of the most distinguished minds in Canada (Petrone, p. 29).[12] Crawford's imagination was deeply engaged by the political, religious, philosophical, and scientific issues of her era, and her mature work, published over the last eight years of her life, provides a record of her intellectual and artistic development.

The only volume of Crawford's verse published in her lifetime was *Old Spookses' Pass, Malcolm's Katie and Other Poems*, printed at her own expense in 1884 by James Bain and Son of Toronto. While the collection was well reviewed in Britain and Toronto, its first issue sold poorly. A second issue in 1886 apparently fared better, but she did not attain the recognition she sought (Petrone, pp. 33–38). Of the three posthumous publications of Crawford's verse in book form, only Glenn Clever's edition of *Hugh and Ion* (1977) is textually dependable. The "Anthology" section of Katherine Hale's *Isabella Valancy Crawford* (1923) features abridged selections of poems that had appeared in John Garvin's *The Collected Poems of Isabella Valancy Crawford* (1905). Garvin's edition has provoked sufficient critical discussion of its textual accuracy to more than justify fresh editorial scrutiny of the corpus of Crawford's poetry.

As Crawford grew older, there is evidence that she became embittered by the neglect of those she referred to as "the High Priests of Canadian Periodical Literature."[13] Her lack of professional fulfilment may have contributed to her increasing preoccupation with the dark side of human nature and experience. The most mature expression of this concern is to be found in the dark undercurrent of "Malcolm's Katie" and in Ion's pessimism in *Hugh and Ion*, both of which were written in the mid-to-late 1880s, a time of disillusionment and fragmentation in Canadian society. The decline of the hope that had buoyed the nation in 1878 is reflected in "The Pessimist," the last of Crawford's poems to be published in *The Globe* [Toronto]:

> Build slightly, builders, in the modern fashion,
>   Your temples and your homes;
> Build no fine vigour of the builder's passion
>   In with your sills and domes.
>
> Build slightly, builders — as the quick wind rearing
>   The towers of leaping spray;
> Build slightly, with swift laughter, swift despairing —
>   Your work is for a day![14]

Coincidentally, Crawford's final message has two sides, darkly ironic in "The Pessimist," but brightly ebullient in "The Rolling-

Pin," published in *The Evening Telegram* [Toronto] on the same day that *The Globe* carried "The Pessimist." Since "The Rolling-Pin" appeared in the evening, one could claim that Crawford's final note is the bright, happy one, itself an ironic contrast with the stark vision of "The Pessimist." Only once more in her lifetime did Crawford's verse appear in the Toronto newspapers. Just one week before her death, *The Evening Telegram* reprinted "The Rose of a Nation's Thanks" by special request.[15]

NOTES

[1] Letter to *The Week* [ca. 1886], MS, Mount Allison Univ. Archives, Sackville, N.B.

[2] See John W. Garvin, "Who's Who in Canadian Literature: Isabella Valancy Crawford," *The Canadian Bookman*, 9 (May 1927), 132; and Ethelwyn Wetherald, Introd., *The Collected Poems of Isabella Valancy Crawford*, ed. John W. Garvin (1905; rpt. Toronto: Univ. of Toronto Press, 1972), p. 15.

[3] Dorothy Livesay, "The Life of Isabella Valancy Crawford," in *The Crawford Symposium*, ed. and introd. Frank M. Tierney, Re-appraisals: Canadian Writers (Ottawa: Univ. of Ottawa Press, 1979), p. 8. Further references to this work appear in the text.

[4] See also Penny Petrone, "The Imaginative Achievement of Isabella Valancy Crawford," Diss. Alberta 1977, p. 14. Further references to this work appear in the text.

[5] Antrim [Mrs. Annie Sutherland], "Old Paisley Landmark Once Writer's Home," *London Free Press* [London, Ont.], 2 July 1927, p. 6.

[6] Dorothy Livesay, "Tennyson's Daughter or Wilderness Child?: The Factual and the Literary Background of Isabella Valancy Crawford," *Journal of Canadian Fiction*, 2, No. 3 (Summer 1973), 161–67.

[7] Dorothy Farmiloe, *Isabella Valancy Crawford: The Life and the Legends* (Ottawa: Tecumseh, 1983), p. 28.

[8] "The Waterlily, a Fairy Tale," and "The Grasshopper Papers," Mss., Lorne Pierce Collection, Queen's Univ. Archives, Kingston, Ont.

[9] Mary F. Martin, "The Short Life of Isabella Valancy Crawford," *Dalhousie Review*, 52 (Autumn 1972), 392. Further references to this work appear in the text.

[10] Penny Petrone, "In Search of Isabella Valancy Crawford," in Tierney, ed., *The Crawford Symposium*, pp. 12–13, nn. 6, 7.

[11] Maud Wheeler Wilson, "Isabella Valancy Crawford," Part I, *The Globe Magazine* [*The Globe*] [Toronto], 15 April 1905, p. 8.

[12] See also Katherine Hale, "Biographical," in *Isabella Valancy Crawford*, ed. Katherine Hale, Makers of Canadian Literature (Toronto: Ryerson, 1923), p. 13.

[13] Editorial, *Arcturus* [Toronto], 19 Feb. 1887, p. 84.

[14] *The Globe* [Toronto], 29 May 1886, p. 14.

[15] Crawford died on 12 February 1887.

William Wilfred Campbell (1858–1918)

GEORGE WICKEN

THE SECOND OF SEVEN SONS, William Wilfred Campbell was born on 1 June 1858 to the Reverend Thomas Swainston Campbell, an Anglican minister, and the former Matilda Frances Wright. Campbell was born in Berlin (now Kitchener) in Canada West, but his father's vocation necessitated a number of moves during Wilfred's boyhood. The family moved from Berlin to Farmersville (now Athens, Ontario), then to Stafford, near Pembroke, to Meaford, and finally to Wiarton. Amid these moves, Campbell appears to have found stability in the family unit and in the family's encouragement of art. "I was a child nurtured among the finer influences of music, culture, thought and learning," he recalled in later years.[1]

Upon completing high school in Owen Sound, Campbell taught for a year in a country school at Zion, near Wiarton. In 1880 he enrolled at University College at the University of Toronto, transferring to Wycliffe, the university's Anglican divinity school, in 1882. Though he did not graduate from the University of Toronto, Campbell did publish his first poems, fifteen in all, in the student

45

newspaper *The Varsity*. In 1883 Campbell journeyed to Cambridge, Massachusetts, where, in addition to studying at the Episcopal Theological School, he continued to write poetry. Campbell befriended Oliver Wendell Holmes at Cambridge, and Holmes aided him in getting his poetry published in *The Atlantic Monthly*. Campbell subsequently published work in such American magazines as *The New England Magazine, The Independent, The Century*, and *Harper's*.

Wilfred Campbell was ordained to the diaconate in 1885 and to the priesthood in 1886. With his wife, the former Mary Louisa De Belle of Woodstock, he lived in West Claremont, New Hampshire, serving Union Church from 1885 to 1888.[2] In 1888 Campbell sought a transfer and was posted to Trinity Church, Saint Stephen, New Brunswick. In the fall of 1890, he asked for another transfer, and the Campbells moved to Southampton, Ontario. Their stay in Southampton was short, however, for Wilfred Campbell resigned from the ministry in early 1891. He and his wife moved to Ottawa, where Campbell began a career that would last a quarter of a century in the civil service. At various times, he worked for the Department of Railways and Canals, the Department of the Secretary of State, the Department of Militia and Defence, the Privy Council Office, and the Archives. It was in Ottawa that the Campbells raised their family: a son, Basil, and three daughters, Margery, Faith, and Dorothy.

Campbell published his first two books of poetry while he was in the ministry; *Snowflakes and Sunbeams* appeared in 1888 and *Lake Lyrics and Other Poems* in 1889. The Ottawa years were extremely productive. As part of the literary circle that included Archibald Lampman and Duncan Campbell Scott, Wilfred Campbell gained prominence as a lecturer, as a member of the Royal Society of Canada, and as a newspaper columnist. With Lampman and Scott, he wrote "At the Mermaid Inn" for *The Globe* [Toronto]. The column, which ran from 6 February 1892 to 1 July 1893, provided these poets with a forum for their views on literature, music, painting, sculpture, architecture, and a variety of other topics. During the 1890s, Campbell published two books of poetry, *The Dread Voyage* (1893) and *Beyond the Hills of Dream* (1899), and a book containing two poetic dramas, *Mordred and Hildebrand: A Book of Tragedies* (1895).

In Ottawa, Campbell formed friendships outside literary circles. Sir Wilfrid Laurier, William Lyon Mackenzie King, and the former Governor General, the Duke of Argyll, were among the men Campbell knew well. Argyll, the head of the Campbell clan, was a friend greatly valued by Campbell for, at the turn of the century, the poet was writing a number of works celebrating his Scottish ancestry. Campbell became a spokesman for British imperialism in the decade or so before World War I, and he was well known for his association with this philosophy both in Canada and in Britain. Between 22 August 1903 and 24 June 1905, he wrote a column entitled "Life and Letters" for *The Evening Journal* [Ottawa]. He published two more books of poetry, *The Poems of Wilfred Campbell* (1905) and *Sagas of Vaster Britain: Poems of the Race, the Empire and the Divinity of Man* (1914); to his two earlier poetic dramas, Campbell added *Morning* and *Daulac* and published all four in *Poetical Tragedies* (1908).

Fiction and travel books also occupied the poet's attention. He drew on Scottish history for his first work of fiction, *Ian of the Orcades; or, The Armourer of Girnigoe* (1906), and upon Canadian history for his second work, *A Beautiful Rebel: A Romance of Upper Canada in 1812* (1909). Campbell collaborated on two lavishly produced travel books, as well. *Canada* was published in 1907 and *The Scotsman in Canada* in 1911. Without a collaborator, he wrote *The Beauty, History, Romance and Mystery of the Canadian Lake Region*. The book was published in 1910.

As editor, Campbell prepared the patriotic volume *Poems of Loyalty by British and Canadian Authors* and *The Oxford Book of Canadian Verse*, both in 1913. He gave poetry readings and delivered lectures in England and, on one occasion, was presented to King Edward VII and Queen Alexandra. At the end of December 1917, Campbell contracted influenza; pneumonia set in, and he died in his Ottawa home in the early hours of 1 January 1918.

NOTES

[1] William Wilfred Campbell, quoted in Carl F. Klinck, *Wilfred Campbell: A Study in Late Provincial Victorianism* (1942; rpt. Ottawa: Tecumseh, 1977), p. 23.

[2] Campbell, quoted in Klinck, p. 266.

Charles G.D. Roberts (1860–1943)

FRED COGSWELL

DURING THE NEARLY eighty-four years between his birth on 10 January 1860 in the tiny hamlet of Douglas, New Brunswick, and his death at Toronto on 26 November 1943, Charles G.D. Roberts lived a full life.[1] He also produced an enormous quantity of creative work.

Publicly, Roberts was, in turn, schoolteacher, college professor, editor, and freelance writer; privately, he was, in turn, an established husband and father, then a footloose bohemian. Throughout World War I, despite his advanced age, he was a soldier. Whatever he was in public or in private life, he somehow found time for both male and female friends, for letter writing and convivial conversation, for reading, for athletics and woodcraft, and for advancing in practical ways the individuals and causes that interested him.

There is a very close relationship between the activities of Roberts, the man, and Roberts, the writer. He was not born rich, nor was he paid exorbitantly for his work. It was, therefore, to support his personal obligations and interests that the vast edifice of his creative work was raised. During his lifetime, twelve volumes of poems and chapbooks, three volumes of selected poems, and six privately printed chapbooks were published. His prose works include one volume of translation, two guide books, three histories, five volumes of stories for juveniles, nine novels and romances, nineteen volumes of original short stories, and five volumes of selections from these. When to this list are added six books reissued with different titles in different countries, the grand total comprises seventy-one titles in all.

The sharply contrasting environments of Roberts' childhood and young manhood must have developed in him the duality that he states explicitly is part of his being in section one of "Two Rivers," one of his last poems. The rivers are, of course, the Tantramar and the Saint John, the one symbolizing freedom and restlessness, and the other, duty and roots.

First impressions normally make the strongest impact. It was by the Tantramar, not the Saint John, that Roberts spent his earliest days. Within a year of his birth, his father, the Reverend George Goodridge Roberts, became the Anglican rector of Westcock, a hamlet near Sackville, New Brunswick. In the absence of proper school facilities, Roberts' father himself taught his son. A kind man with great interest in painting, poetry, and music as well as the classics, George Goodridge Roberts knew how to make study interesting to a gifted lad who learned the more readily because he loved his father and desired his good opinion. Adjoining the rectory was a glebe, and as soon as he was large and strong enough, young Roberts was given the responsibilities for farm work and for the caring for the domestic animals. Since he was allowed to keep a share of the profits and was not interfered with, he developed an eagerness to work and a self-reliance that was to persist throughout his life.

As soon as Roberts was large enough, his father taught him the rudiments of woodcraft and marksmanship. But Roberts had no taste for killing; rather, he spent his time stalking animals and observing their ways with as great a zest as other boys displayed in hunting. From his observations, he learned the truth that later contact with the works of behaviourist science could not entirely obliterate, that animals are in fact individuals, that they learn from experience as well as instinct, and that they possess, in at least rudimentary form, a capacity for reason. Throughout all the chores and stalking, he must have soaked in, as well, the colour, the contour, the very spirit of the Tantramar country, for years later, and in far different locales, he was to catch both its aura and its authentic detail in many a poem and story.

In 1874 George Goodridge Roberts was made Rector of Fredericton and moved with his family to that city. At the time, young Charles, without having in the least suffered during the process, had already become well grounded in the masterpieces of English and classic literature, as well as in history; although only of medium size, he was physically strong and already knew more about woodcraft than most human beings would ever know. Kind and sensitive in his being, his freedom of will had never been tempted towards either hatred or destruction. He had exhausted what the Tantramar had to give him and was ready and eager to change it for the Saint John.

It was a move from a country of open spaces to what must have seemed a metropolis to a fourteen-year-old: from a one-to-one student-teacher relationship with his father or a tutor to a crowded classroom; from association with crops and animals on his own terms to constant association with members of his peer group. Such a change could have been disastrous, but circumstances were such that young Roberts adapted to it with ease.

The presence of his family remained a constant factor. In fact, it was more than a constant, for to the Reverend George Goodridge Roberts and his wife, the new charge meant a return home. Roberts found himself in the company of congenial friends and relatives, with one of whom, his young cousin, Bliss Carman, he had already been corresponding for several years. To the Robertses, family life in Fredericton was in no sense jarring. For the most part, their association was with well-established merchants and professional men and their families, who from positions of secure stability, often maintained over several generations, nourished their self-esteem during leisure hours by an interest in religion, outdoor recreation, and the arts. The Fredericton Collegiate School, in which Roberts was enrolled, was very much a preserve of the élite. Before its academic level had been reached, most of Fredericton's children had already joined the labour force. There remained only those to whom a classical education was a *sine qua non* to their future as professional men and community leaders. The twin roads to popularity in such an institution were academic excellence and athletic prowess, both of which Roberts possessed. He was, moreover, singularly fortunate in the young headmaster, George Parkin, newly returned from Oxford, who took him for long walks and introduced him to the new and heady poetry of Swinburne and Rossetti.

Roberts' education at the University of New Brunswick (1876–79) was a continuation of what he had received at Fredericton Collegiate, but with an increased emphasis on ideas.[2] It served to deepen his love for the British tradition, his respect for social institutions as a depository of human values, and his belief in the importance of the writer who perpetuates and improves these institutions and values by linking them to readers' observations and feelings. He prepared to take his place in the social establishment by a diligent attention to the writing of poetry and an equally diligent wooing of Mary Isobel Fenety, the daughter of the King's Printer, to whom he became engaged in December 1879.

Very soon after his graduation in 1879, Roberts became headmaster of the Grammar School in Chatham, New Brunswick. Within a year of this appointment, he married and, with his father-in-law's financial support, succeeded in having his first book, *Orion and Other Poems* (1880), published by the firm of Lippincott in Philadelphia. The acclaim he received for this publication made him a local celebrity at the age of twenty. In 1881 he received an M.A. from the University of New Brunswick, and in 1882 he returned to Fredericton as principal of the York Street School.

During these years, Roberts was contributing poems and reviews to various American and Canadian journals. Such activities attracted the attention of Goldwin Smith, a wealthy expatriate English intellectual then based in Toronto. Smith invited Roberts to become editor of his new periodical, *The Week*. In November 1883, Roberts moved to Toronto and remained in charge of *The Week* until its twelfth issue in February 1884. His energy, enthusiasm, judgement, and encouragement of young Canadian writers laid the foundation of that magazine's success, but he resigned from the editorial chair because he had quarrelled with Smith over what was to be *The Week*'s political policy. Roberts had become an ardent Canadian nationalist; Goldwin Smith believed that Canada's only viable future was to become annexed to the United States.

Roberts returned to the family home in Fredericton and — after failing to maintain himself as a freelance writer or to find employment in New York — was successful in 1885 in securing a post as professor at King's College, Windsor, Nova Scotia. There he remained with his family until 1895, at various times teaching such subjects as English literature, French, politics, and economics.

King's College and the town of Windsor possessed an ethos very similar to that of the University of New Brunswick and the city of Fredericton, but on a somewhat reduced scale. Here Roberts occupied a position among the social élite. He became president of the local Haliburton Society and was prominent in organizing the college's athletic events. In 1890 he was elected a Fellow of the Royal Society of Canada. The college authorities recognized the value of his writing; in consequence, his official duties were not onerous. Roberts was able to devote some time nearly every day, as well as entire college vacations, to writing.

In terms of quality and quantity of work, the ten years spent at Windsor were among the most fruitful of Roberts' life. After an idyllic beginning, however, tensions developed within the Roberts household and with respect to Roberts' position in the community. Most important of all, however, was the fact that these tensions were to affect radically the choice and treatment of the subject matter of his work. Metaphorically, the long submerged waters of the Tantramar rose to overwhelm the placid Saint John. The exact precipitating event is not known, but from his love poems and from his letters, it is clear that Roberts had become deeply involved with at least two women, one in Owen Sound, Ontario, and the other in his own neighbourhood. One or both involvements must have become discovered, for in 1895 Roberts suddenly resigned his position at King's College.

The Robertses moved to Fredericton. By this time, Roberts was able to support his family by his labours as a freelance writer; he was not, however, content to remain with them, and in 1897 he left for New York to become assistant editor of *The Illustrated American*. He did not take his family, and, apart from a few days spent together, usually at times of family crises, husband and wife remained separated until Mary Roberts' death in 1930.

The steady routine of an editor's life proved as distasteful to Roberts as the steady routine of domesticity, for in 1899 he resigned his post at *The Illustrated American*; from that date, except for a period of four years' war service, Roberts was to support his own and his wife's establishments by the proceeds of his literary labours. He soon discovered that he could write as well in one place as in another and, having no ties to keep him in one spot, indulged his curiosity by frequent trips to Britain, Europe, North Africa, and the West Indies. Without altering his mode of life appreciably, he transferred his base of operations from New York to London in 1912.

Spurred by his deeply engrained loyalty to Britain, Roberts' commitment to society reawoke at the outbreak of World War I. Early in that conflict, he volunteered for service as a trooper in the Legion of Frontiersmen. By December 1914, he was promoted to the rank of first lieutenant and for two years endured the monotony of instructing other ranks and officers at various barracks in Great Britain and Ireland. Wishing to be closer to combat action, he transferred in 1916 to the Canadian army and, with the rank of major, served on the European front as a special press correspondent.

Before the war had ended, his friendship and collaboration with Sir Max Aitken had resulted in *Canada in Flanders: The Story of the Canadian Expeditionary Force* (1918). After the war, Roberts remained in England and attempted to resume the career of freelance writer that he had abandoned at its beginning. After a promising start in which he published his romance of prehistory, *In the Morning of Time* (1919), Roberts soon found that the climate of opinion had altered and, with it, the market for such stories and poems as his beliefs permitted. He hung on, however, until the prospect of a lucrative reading tour lured him to Canada in 1925.

Back in Canada, Roberts discovered that, during his more than a quarter of a century of residence abroad, his work had become a legend in his own land, and he remained there. He led a busy life, writing, giving reading tours and lectures from coast to coast, serving on the editorial boards of the *Standard Dictionary of*

Canadian Biography (1934–38) and the *Canadian Who's Who*
(1936–39), and serving as president, first of the Toronto Branch of
the Canadian Authors Association, and later of the national body.
In 1926 he became the first recipient of the Lorne Pierce Gold
Medal of the Royal Society of Canada. In 1935 he received a
knighthood from King George V in the last honours list for which
Canadians were eligible. As early as 1906, he had received an
honorary LL.D. from his own alma mater; in 1942, he was
honoured by Mount Allison University of Sackville, New Bruns-
wick, with the degree of Doctor of Literature.

His remarkable wanderlust, vigour, and vitality remained with
him until the very end. In his eightieth year, he went on a cruise to
Venezuela, and in his eighty-third, a few months before his death,
he married Joan Montgomery.

NOTES

¹ I have drawn upon the yet unpublished complete poems arranged chrono-
logically and the yet unpublished letters, currently available to scholars at the
archives of the University of New Brunswick.

² For a more detailed discussion of this aspect of Roberts' background, the
reader is referred to the following articles: A.G. Bailey, "Creative Moments in
the Culture of the Maritime Provinces," *The Dalhousie Review*, 29 (Oct. 1949),
231–44; and Fred Cogswell, "Literary Traditions in New Brunswick," *Trans-
actions of the Royal Society of Canada*, 4th ser., 125 (1977), 287–99.

Bliss Carman (1861–1929)

TERRY WHALEN

WILLIAM BLISS CARMAN was born on 15 April 1861, in Fredericton, New Brunswick. Cousin to Charles G.D. Roberts, he was also a distant relative of Ralph Waldo Emerson on his mother's, Sophia Bliss's, side of the family. His background was a United Empire Loyalist one, and he was later to move to the New England ground of his ancestors and become one of the more popular American poets of his day. Lorne Pierce reports that when Carman's father, William Carman, heard that Bliss was contemplating a vocation as a poet, he remarked in a letter that "Bliss has decided to use his brain less and his literature more."[1] His father was a barrister. It was George Parkin, the inspired principal and teacher of the Collegiate School in Fredericton, who gave Carman his initial enthusiasm for poetry. Parkin taught both Carman and Roberts an appreciation for classical, Romantic, and Victorian poetry. He also accompanied the youths on a series of hiking and canoeing trips in the environs of the New Brunswick capital. Carman, therefore, grew up amidst the concerns of poetry and the beauty of the natural world. He was the graduate of a vitally fresh culture, one that Roberts has described as percolating with a "strange aesthetic ferment."[2]

Carman wrote a few poems while in high school and first published his efforts in the University of New Brunswick *Monthly* in 1879, while still an undergraduate. He graduated from the University of New Brunswick with honours in Greek and Latin in 1881, earning a gold medal in Latin despite rumours that he was a feckless scholar. For nearly a year after his graduation, he ambled about at home, reading, hiking, and writing, while he was preparing (ostensibly) for a difficult set of Gilchrist exams which held out the possibility of a scholarship at Oxford university. He did not win the scholarship but went to Oxford in 1882 anyway. Disappointed with the venture, depressed and feeling alienated, he spent the rest of the academic year at Edinburgh University, where he roomed with an old classmate from Fredericton. His sense of rudderlessness became so acute that he returned to Fredericton in 1883 in an attempt to find a settled career more immediately.

The next three years were punctuated with futile attempts at finding a satisfying profession. As one commentator quips: ". . . he nibbled at school-teaching, muddled in law, and dabbled in real estate."[3] Carman also tried surveying with an equal degree of commitment. But he did not simply stumble about during these years. While unhappily teaching during the 1883–84 academic year, he published "Ma Belle Canadienne" in *The Week* on 27 December 1883, and in the spring of that year he completed the long essay "English Literature from Chaucer to Elizabeth," which earned for him a Master of Arts from the University of New Brunswick in June of 1884. There was a logic to his efforts during these years, even if he was only partly conscious of it at the time.

Carman's father died in January 1885, leaving the family in a marginal financial state, and his mother died the following year in February 1886. He left Fredericton in the fall of 1886 and enrolled in English studies at Harvard University in the name of preparing for an academic career. His Harvard experience embodied everything that he had unsuccessfully sought after at Oxford: a stimulating intellectual context that would mature the enthusiasms instilled in him by Parkin, poetry, and nature. Typically, while he spent two years at Harvard, he did not sit for enough exams to earn a degree; in a sense, he was too busy learning and writing to bother with such mundane matters. He read and was instructed by Josiah Royce and George Santayana, whose idealistic philosophies fed his hunger for a monistic and optimistic view of Creation. Already a disciple of Tennyson's and Browning's hopeful visions, Carman's bias was primed towards the consciously antipessimistic perspectives of Royce and Santayana. They seemed to him to have a purchase on the Truth itself, and their insights were to animate a great deal of his poetry in the years that followed.

Professor Francis Child, an authority on the ballad form was also teaching at Harvard, and Carman's fascination with his work and his lectures was to stay with him throughout his writing career, aiding him in the mastery of one of his most characteristic traditional forms; but the figure who was to have the most profound effect on Carman's personal and professional life was Richard Hovey, who was also at Harvard at the time. Hovey was a poet in the latter-day transcendentalist tradition encouraged by Whitman, Thoreau, and Emerson. He was a Whitmanesque poet of the open road and the out-of-doors whose Thoreau-inspired disregard for the world of commercial business was happily in consonance with Carman's similar lack of concern for such matters. They became immediate lifelong friends, fellow travellers, and coauthors of a series of poetry volumes that celebrated the freedom of a mildly bohemian way of life. Decidedly, it was Hovey who convinced Carman that he should devote his full-time energies to the writing of poetry. The hidden logic of Carman's earlier career frustrations now made sense; he tossed aside all thoughts of a settled life of getting and spending and vocational boredom and committed himself to a career as a poet. He began publishing poems in *The Harvard Monthly*, and when *The Atlantic Monthly* accepted his "Carnations in Winter" in October of 1887, it must have proven to him the rightness of his friend's advice.

Carman left Harvard in 1888 and embarked on a life of travelling, visiting, writing, and editorial work. In the time between 1888 and the publication of his first and very successful volume, *Low Tide on Grand Pré: A Book of Lyrics* (1893), he moved continually between New York, Washington, Boston, Fredericton, and Windsor, Nova Scotia, where his cousin, Roberts, was teaching English at King's College. During these and later years, he scraped a very modest living out of his writing and out of a series of editorial tasks that he performed for such publications as *The Independent, Current Literature, Cosmopolitan, The Boston Transcript, The Atlantic Monthly*, and, more fulsomely, *The Chap Book*, which he established and edited with Hovey's support in 1894. His life became a mixture of short visits, brief editorial tasks, and much poetry writing. He remained a bachelor and was a gregarious one by most reports. During the late 1880s and the 1890s, he spent most of his winters with the Hovey family in Washington and many of his summers with the Roberts family in Windsor. Roberts reports that these latter visits were very productive ones, and his reminiscences of those days (when Carman would often visit him with other friends like Hovey in tow) provide a record of the imaginatively formative enthusiasm that Carman had for the Windsor and Annapolis Valley region.[4]

With the publication of *Low Tide on Grand Pré* in 1893, Carman achieved the twofold status of being a major Canadian poet and an interesting American one. His work was praised on both sides of the Atlantic, and he was encouraged to proceed with the publication of a virtual flood of volumes over approximately the next twenty-five years. A list of the more than thirty different titles he published between 1893 and 1929 demonstrates the pace of his writing, as well as the degree of his popularity. It also hints at why so many of Carman's critics have remarked that he is a thematically repetitious writer, careless with his craft and sometimes given to pot-boiling insincerity.

In 1896 Carman travelled to Europe and met Arthur Symons, Richard Le Galliene, and William Butler Yeats. From 1897 onwards, he spent more and more of his time visiting with Mary Perry King and her husband, Dr. King, and in 1908 he moved near their home in New Canaan, Connecticut, making the area his most usual place of residence for the rest of his life. But he would continue his wandering and visiting life-style, travelling to the Bahamas in 1898 and to California in 1905, where he would return for other visits later. Mary King was an advocate of the Delsarte system of self-expression, and Carman shared her tendentious enthusiasm for its high ideals, as did Hovey's wife, Henrietta.

Carman's relationship with Mary King developed into an intimate and somewhat dependent one, especially after Hovey's death in 1900 at the age of thirty-six. Commentators have noticed the trailing off of Carman's canon into a dogmatic and skeletal Delsartean recipe during the years 1899–1910 and often account for the fact with disparaging remarks about Mary King's effect on his career. Nonetheless, she greatly supported Carman after Hovey's death, amidst his failing health and spirits during the Great War period and during and after his sudden illness in 1920.

Carman's illness in 1920 provoked, in Canada, a newly enlivened interest in his work and his career. The upshot was that he began in 1921 to travel across Canada (and the United States) on a series of lecture tours. Despite one report that he was now simply a fatigued poet placed somewhat pathetically on show,[5] the tours were very successful and helped him in the 1920s to become recognized in Canada as a cultural hero, the embodiment of a bright hope for Canadian letters. This high stature was underlined in 1922 at the inaugural dinner of the Canadian Authors Association in Montreal, at which he was hailed as the unofficial poet laureate of the nation, and that honour was later made the more emphatic when he was awarded in 1928 the Lorne Pierce Medal for his contribution to Canadian writing. Distinctions abounded for Carman in the 1920s. He was elected a corresponding member of the Royal Society of Canada and was chosen to edit, in 1927, *The Oxford Book of American Verse*. By the time of his death of a brain haemorrhage on 8 June 1929 in New Canaan, he had received honorary degrees from the University of New Brunswick, McGill University, and Trinity College in Hartford, Connecticut, and his work had been casually praised by James Russell Lowell, Thomas Hardy, A.E. Housman, Walter de La Mare, and Rupert Brooke.

After a funeral service was held in New Canaan, his ashes were moved to a burial place in Fredericton. In keeping with his wishes, a maple tree was planted close by; it still weathers the turning seasons that Carman had so intimately known.

NOTES

[1] Lorne Pierce, *Three Fredericton Poets: Writers of the University of New Brunswick and the New Dominion* (Toronto: Ryerson, 1933), p. 21. The letter

is quoted by Pierce as "the last letter he was ever to write" (p. 21).

2 Charles G.D. Roberts, "Bliss Carman," *The Dalhousie Review*, 9 (Jan. 1930), 416. For additional items on the Fredericton cultural context, see Alfred G. Bailey, "Creative Moments in the Culture of the Maritime Provinces," *The Dalhousie Review*, 29 (Oct. 1949), 231–44; Wilfred Eggleston, *The Frontier and Canadian Letters* (Toronto: Ryerson, 1957), and "Bliss Carman and the Twenties," *Journal of Canadian Poetry*, 1, No. 2 (Autumn 1978), 59–68; and Malcolm M. Ross, "A Symbolic Approach to Carman," *The Canadian Bookman*, 14 (Dec. 1932), 140–44, "Carman by the Sea," *The Dalhousie Review*, 27 (Oct. 1947), 294–98, and " 'A Strange Aesthetic Ferment,' " *Canadian Literature*, Nos. 68–69 (Spring–Summer 1976), pp. 13–25.

3 W.P. Percival, *Leading Canadian Poets* (Toronto: Ryerson, 1948), p. 46.

4 See Charles G.D. Roberts, "More Reminiscences of Bliss Carman," *The Dalhousie Review*, 10 (April 1930), 1–9. For further commentary on Carman's visits to Windsor, see Lloyd Roberts, *The Book of Roberts* (Toronto: Ryerson, 1923), and "Bliss Carman: A Memory," *The Canadian Bookman*, 21 (April–May 1939), 42–46.

5 In *The Book of Roberts*, Lloyd Roberts conveys his discomfort at meeting Carman in a Montreal hotel. Carman was on tour. Roberts remembers Carman's vitality of the old Windsor days. He now sees Carman as pathetic: "Presently they had made a place for him at the high table, among the professional clowns, professorial jugglers and beardless lions and there, on his best behavior, elbows in, chin up, he was compelled to eat mortal food and look pleasant . . ." (p. 45).

Archibald Lampman (1861–99)

L.R. EARLY

ARCHIBALD LAMPMAN is the most intriguing and complex of our nineteenth-century poets. An atmosphere of mystery also surrounds Isabella Valancy Crawford, but in her case it arises from enforced obscurity rather than as an expression of character. Lampman was privately inclined by both temperament and circumstance, in contrast to his more publicly conspicuous friends Charles G.D. Roberts and D.C. Scott; at the same time, private demons shaped his poetry extensively. As a result, his outwardly unspectacular life has always been of interest, and Lampman criticism has been marked by disputes about his personality as well as about the character of his work. Ultimately, the two subjects are, in good nineteenth-century fashion, inseparable.

The outward facts are easily summarized.[1] Lampman was born of Loyalist ancestry on 17 November 1861 at Morpeth, Canada West. As a child, he lived at Perrytown, Rice Lake, and Cobourg and at one point suffered a severe rheumatic fever which probably damaged his heart and hastened his early death at the age of thirty-seven. In 1876 he entered Trinity College School, Port Hope, and passed in 1879 to Trinity College in Toronto. There his earliest published work appeared in *Rouge et Noir*, the college paper, and he won several scholarships before graduating in 1882 with a second in classics. In January 1883, after an unhappy term teaching at Orangeville High School, he accepted a clerkship in the Post Office Department at Ottawa, where he worked the rest of his life. After a courtship of three years, he married Maud Playter in 1887; they had three children, the elder son dying in infancy in 1894. Lampman enjoyed close friendships with a number of writers in Ottawa, Montreal, Boston, and elsewhere, notably with D.C. Scott and Edward William Thomson. With Scott and William Wilfred Campbell, he wrote a weekly column, "At the Mermaid Inn," for *The Globe* [Toronto] in 1892 and 1893. He belonged to the Ottawa Literary and Scientific Society, Social Science Club, and Fabian Society and in 1895 was made a Fellow of the Royal Society of Canada. From 1883, Lampman's poems appeared widely in Canadian and American periodicals, especially in *The Week*, *Scribner's*, and the *Youth's Companion* of Boston. His first volume, *Among the Millet and Other Poems*, was published in 1888, his second, *Lyrics of Earth*, appeared after some delay in 1896,[2] and a third, *Alcyone*, was in press when he died, after an attack of acute pneumonia, in the early hours of 10 February 1899.

The meaning of these facts is less easily established, though no doubt a childhood spent close to the countryside fostered Lampman's love of nature, just as a talented family and good schools nurtured his imagination. His sojourn at Rice Lake provides a footnote to the continuity of Canadian literature through his acquaintance there with Catharine Parr Traill and Susanna Moodie, then entering their seventies. There has been a theory, starting with the obituaries of 1899, that Lampman's situation in Ottawa stifled his creative potential, but most informed comment has emphasized the advantages: considerable leisure, interested companions, and ready access to both the cultivated countryside and the wilderness beyond.[3] Recent biographical attention has focused on the vicissitudes of Lampman's marriage and on his friendship with a woman named Katherine Waddell during the

1890s.[4] Conjectures about his relationship with "Kate," especially about the extent of their intimacy and its duration, should be treated cautiously. The evidence does suggest that for two years, at least, culminating in a crisis during the winter of 1895–96, Lampman was passionately attracted to her, and that consequently his writing suffered.

Lampman's character and work present a field of shifting contrasts. There was, for instance, the relish for strenuous exercise with which he defied his chronically fickle health. And his popularity with friends, writing for *The Globe* [Toronto], and activity in various associations contrast with the regard for privacy and predilection for dreams expressed in his correspondence and poetry. His letters to his wife are notable for their affection and lack of all but the most superficial literary interest. Those to his friends reveal other qualities: intelligence and sensitivity, with a certain diffidence and a tendency towards moodiness. His critical essays and lectures are perceptive, if somewhat conventional. His poems reflect some, but by no means all, of these qualities and present a number of further contradictions in themselves. Lampman's life and work richly illuminate one another, but the incongruities are as significant as the connections. To point to a final example: his letters convey, and several of his acquaintances confirm, Lampman's personal geniality and humour, qualities that he also valued highly in literature. That they are negligible features of his own poetry suggests something about the motives and priorities of his imagination.

NOTES

Courtesy of Twayne Publishers, Inc. Parts of this discussion are included in my *Archibald Lampman*, Twayne's World Authors Series, No. 770, Canadian Literature (Boston: Twayne, 1986).

[1] The principal biographical sources are the following: D.C. Scott, "Memoir," in his *The Poems of Archibald Lampman* (Toronto: Morang, 1900), pp. xi–xxv; D.C. Scott, Introd., in his *Lyrics of Earth: Sonnets and Ballads* (Toronto: Musson, 1925), pp. 3–47; Ernest Voorhis, "The Ancestry of Archibald Lampman, Poet," *Royal Society of Canada Proceedings and Transactions*, 3rd ser., 15, Sec. 2 (1921), 103–21; Carl Y. Connor, *Archibald Lampman:*

Canadian Poet of Nature (1929; rpt. Ottawa: Borealis, 1977); Margaret Coulby Whitridge, Introd., *The Poems of Archibald Lampman (Including At the Long Sault)* (Toronto: Univ. of Toronto Press, 1974), pp. vii–xxix; Arthur S. Bourinot, ed., *Archibald Lampman's Letters to Edward William Thomson (1890–1898)* (Ottawa: Bourinot, 1956); and unpublished correspondence in the Lampman Collection at Simon Fraser University, Burnaby, B.C., and in the Public Archives of Canada, Ottawa. Bourinot's selection of the Lampman-Thomson correspondence, cited here, is now superseded by an admirable scholarly collection: *An Annotated Edition of the Correspondence between Archibald Lampman and Edward William Thomson (1890–1898)*, ed. Helen Lynn (Ottawa: Tecumseh, 1980).

[2] Though the title page of *Lyrics of Earth* bears the date 1895, this volume was not actually published until the spring of 1896. See D.M.R. Bentley, Introd., *Lyrics of Earth (1895)* (Ottawa: Tecumseh, 1978), pp. 2, 11–13.

[3] [P.D. Ross], "Archibald Lampman," *Ottawa Journal*, 11 Feb. 1899, p. 4; Scott, "Memoir," p. xvii; Connor, pp. 78–79, 131–32; W.E. Collin, *The White Savannahs* (1936; rpt. Toronto: Univ. of Toronto Press, 1975), p. 25; Ralph Gustafson, "Among the Millet," *Northern Review*, 1, No. 5 (Feb.–March 1947), 26–34; rpt. in Michael Gnarowski, ed., *Archibald Lampman* (Toronto: Ryerson, 1970), pp. 142–53; D.C. Scott, "Copy of a Letter . . . to Ralph Gustafson, 17 July 1945," *The Fiddlehead*, No. 41 (Summer 1959), pp. 12–14; rpt. in *Archibald Lampman*, ed. Gnarowski, pp. 154–58; Munro Beattie, "Archibald Lampman," in *Our Living Tradition*, 1st ser., ed. Claude T. Bissell (Toronto: Univ. of Toronto Press, 1957), pp. 63–88.

[4] See: Bruce Nesbitt, "A Gift of Love: Lampman and Life," *Canadian Literature*, No. 50 (Autumn 1971), pp. 35–40, and his "The New Lampman," in *The Lampman Symposium*, ed. Lorraine McMullen (Ottawa: Univ. of Ottawa Press, 1976), pp. 99–110; Margaret Coulby Whitridge, Introd., *Lampman's Kate: Late Love Poems of Archibald Lampman 1887–1897* (Ottawa: Borealis, 1975), pp. 11–23, and her "Love and Hate in Lampman's Poetry," in *Lampman*, ed. McMullen, pp. 9–17.

Duncan Campbell Scott (1862–1947)

GORDON JOHNSTON

THE PUBLIC LIFE of Duncan Campbell Scott, because of his service in the federal Department of Indian Affairs, was more prominent than those of many writers. He entered the department as a clerk at the age of seventeen and was Deputy Superintendent General from 1913 until he retired in 1932. In that position, he was responsible for implementing and helping to shape government policy concerning the Native peoples. His professional experiences, especially travelling as an inspector and a commissioner, had an important influence on his writing. And yet, his job does not seem to have been the centre of his life; after he retired, he never spoke of the department.

As is the case with most writers, the important dimension of his life is the private one. His relation with family and friends, his travels, his interest in the arts (music and painting as well as poetry and fiction), his perceptions of places and human relationships, form the origin and substance of his imaginative life.

Scott was born in Ottawa on 2 August 1862 and lived for seventy of his eighty-five years in that city, though he spent much of his youth in small towns of Quebec and eastern Ontario.[1] His father, William Scott, was a Methodist minister who had worked with Natives at the Saint Clair Mission earlier in his career. He was almost fifty years old when Duncan, the second of three children, was born. Duncan's mother, Isabella Campbell MacCallum, was his father's second wife and was the cause of Duncan's interest in music and training in the piano. The family was living in Iroquois Falls at the time of Confederation, and later, only half facetiously, he told his friend Leonard Brockington that he attributed his lifelong hatred of noise to the celebrations of that July 1.[2] In his father's library, he read the classics and "modern" essays, especially those of Carlyle and Emerson. He was very taken with the woodcuts by Millais, Holman Hunt, and Rossetti, which he saw in the periodicals *Good Words* and *Good Words for the Young*. When he was thirteen at high school in Smiths Falls, he was deeply touched by Tennyson's description of Cleopatra in "A Dream of Fair Women."

So, early in his life, he was introduced to three modes of artistic expression, but he certainly did not plan a career in the arts. After attending the Wesleyan college in Stanstead, Quebec, he had to abandon plans to study medicine because of a lack of funds. His father, through an interview with the Prime Minister, Sir John A. Macdonald, secured a clerkship for him in the civil service in 1879.

After the itinerancy of his youth, Scott established himself firmly in Ottawa and seems to have detached himself from his family. His father died in 1891, and, after his marriage to Belle Warner Botsford in 1894, he was estranged from his mother and two sisters. Belle was an American violinist whom he had accompanied on the piano at her Ottawa recital. Much of the rest of his life was spent in the house he had built at 108 Lisgar Street in Ottawa, in its garden and the music room, or in his office at Indian Affairs, where he kept a silent piano for practising, or in walking between the two places. His only child, Elizabeth Duncan, was born in 1895. He collected paintings by Clarence Gagnon, Horatio Walker, Emily Carr, and his friends Lawren Harris and Edmund Morris, among others; he arranged private concerts; he enjoyed the visits of literary, musical, artistic, and academic friends.

His greatest friend was the poet Archibald Lampman, whom he met some time after Lampman arrived in Ottawa to take up a position in the Post Office (1883). Later he told his friend E.K. Brown that it never occurred to him to write a line of prose or verse until he was about twenty-five and after he had met Lampman.[3] He began to be published soon afterwards. *Scribner's Magazine*, the popular American literary periodical, accepted a short story, "The Ducharmes of the Baskatonge," in 1887 and published the second poem he wrote, "The Hill Path," in May 1888. His first poem, "Ottawa — Before Dawn," was included by W.D. Lighthall in *Songs of the Great Dominion* in 1889.

From his permanent base in Ottawa, Scott travelled a great deal, partly in connection with his work on tours of inspection and treaty negotiation, but more often as a tourist, to the eastern seaboard, to the Canadian and American West, and to Europe. On one of those trips, in 1907, he and his wife left their daughter at a convent school in Paris and a few days later in Madrid received word that she had died. Her death and that of Lampman in 1899 were the greatest sorrows Scott suffered. Long after his daughter's death, he wore a wide black band on his hat and sleeve and kept toys on the hearth. His travels, the sights he saw and the stories he heard, provoked important poems throughout his career. The range of his travelling is suggested by the titles of two of his books, *Via Borealis* (1906), out of northern Ontario, and *The Green Cloister* (1935), out of Italy. Perhaps the centrality of Ottawa is suggested by the title of his last book, *The Circle of Affection* (1947). One such circle closed when his wife died in 1929; another opened when he married Elise Aylen of Ottawa, herself a writer, two years later.

The public events of his life consist of his promotions through the ranks of the Department of Indian Affairs: to first-class clerk in 1889, to Secretary in 1896, as a commissioner for Treaty 9 in 1905 and 1906, and to Deputy Superintendent General in 1913. In 1931 he was invited to give a paper on Indian affairs for the Fourth Biannual Conference of the Institute of Pacific Relations, and in 1932 he retired. His public literary life consists of his publications as author and editor. For slightly more than a year, he contributed to the weekly column "At the Mermaid Inn" for *The Globe* [Toronto], written in conjunction with Lampman and William Wilfred Campbell. It was short-lived because Campbell's volatile, iconoclastic, not to say aggressive stance did not match Scott's more genteel interests and methods and finally was too much even for Lampman. Scott's first published book, *The Magic House and Other Poems*, was published by Methuen in London in 1893. If much of it sounds like the ventriloquism of an apprentice writer, there is evidence of a remarkable gift and already versions of the themes and points of view that characterized all his writing. His first collection of stories, *In the Village of Viger*, appeared in 1896 and draws successfully on his experience of small Quebec towns. The stories are polished in method and assured in tone. *Labour and the Angel* (1898), his second book of poems, includes two poems about Native women, the beginning of a rich strain in his writing, and also "The Piper of Arll," perhaps his most famous poem. In 1900 he published a memorial edition of Lampman's poems with a memoir, the beginning of his long, devoted, and worthy stewardship of Lampman's career; he went on to publish three more selections of Lampman's published and unpublished verse. For the next few years, he worked with his friend Pelham Edgar as coeditor of the Makers of Canada series of biographies. The work was complicated and not very gratifying, and the results are not very distinguished; his own contribution was a life of John Graves Simcoe in 1905. In the same year, the first poetic fruits of his work as a commissioner for Treaty 9 appeared in *New World Lyrics and Ballads*; this was followed by a slim volume of northern poems the next year, *Via Borealis*. These poems were included along with his elegy to his friend the painter Edmund Morris in *Lundy's Lane and Other Poems*, published in 1916 after the only hiatus in his writing career. *Beauty and Life* (1921) was his favourite among his own books at the end of his life; it is a coherent, elegiac book, perhaps thinner in its substance than others. His second collection of stories, *The Witching of Elspie* (1923), draws in large part on his knowledge of the North and the interaction of white and Native cultures. In that year, he helped found the Ottawa Little Theatre and saw his one-act play, *Pierre*, performed on the opening night. His poems were collected in a volume in 1926. The poems in *The Green Cloister* (1935) are mostly mature, reflective, cosmopolitan poems from his European travels, with, in addition, a few powerful narratives and scenes from northern Canada. His last book, *The Circle of Affection*, published the year of his death (on 19 December 1947), combines earlier unpublished stories, essays, and poems with some new pieces.

In 1899 he had been elected to replace Lampman as a Fellow of the Royal Society of Canada. He was Honorary Secretary from 1911 to 1921, and then President for 1921–22. He received the Lorne Pierce Medal in 1927, an honorary Doctorate of Literature from the University of Toronto in 1922, the C.M.G. in 1934, and in 1939 an LL.D. from Queen's University. He had served on the executive of the Canadian Authors Association and on the Board of Governors of the Canadian Writers Foundation. By the end of his life, he and Charles G.D. Roberts had become the grand old men of Canadian poetry, and, although he never received the attention given to Roberts, Carman, and Lampman, he did achieve a kind of eminence. Indeed, he is most widely thought of as a distinguished, cultured, elderly man.

The private events, the significant ones in his life, are the ones we would need to consider or imagine in order to know him: playing the piano for Belle Botsford at her recital; his long canoe trip with Lampman to Lake Achigan in 1897 (the lake is a central place in his imagination, appearing in his novel and a number of poems and stories); "poor Archie's" death in 1899; his trips with Pelham Edgar and Edmund Morris in 1906, with Edgar reading poetry to him as they paddled; the moment he received the brutally short telegram at the hotel in Madrid, "Elizabeth morte"; the visit from Rupert Brooke in 1913, when Brooke lay on the rug in the library and played with the kitten Skookum ("Now I shall have to talk down to you," Scott said); sitting in his library with E.K. Brown in the summer of 1942, reading poetry to him, thinking about Lampman; and then, any of those walks he took when he saw or heard something that fed his imagination.

NOTES

[1] E.K. Brown, "Memoir," in *The Selected Poems of Duncan Campbell Scott* (Toronto: Ryerson, 1951), pp. xi–xlii; rpt. in *Responses and Evaluations: Essays on Canada*, ed. David Staines, New Canadian Library, No. 137 (Toronto: McClelland and Stewart, 1977), pp. 112–44. This is at present the richest source of biographical details.

[2] Leonard W. Brockington, "Duncan Campbell Scott's 80th Birthday," *Saturday Night*, 1 Aug. 1942, p. 25.

[3] Brown, p. 115.

E.J. Pratt (1882–1964)

PETER BUITENHUIS

EDWIN JOHN PRATT was born in Western Bay, Newfoundland, on 4 February 1882. He was the son of the Yorkshire-born Reverend John Pratt and Fanny Knight, the daughter of a Newfoundland sea captain.[1]

He spent his early years in various outport parishes, where his father's duties took the family, and was educated in local schools and at St. John's Methodist College. Before entering college, he worked as a draper's apprentice between 1897 and 1901.

After leaving St. John's in 1902, he became a teacher at Moreton's Harbour, a whaling village in Notre Dame Bay in Newfoundland. In 1904 he became a preacher-probationer in the Methodist ministry and served in parishes at Clarke's Beach, Bell Island, and Portugal Cove. All these early experiences gave him a profound knowledge of the ways of the sea and of fishers, and brought him into direct contact with the harsh elemental lives of the outport peoples.

In 1907 Pratt entered Victoria College in the University of Toronto and became a student of philosophy. He graduated in 1911 and then took graduate work, receiving a master's degree in 1912 with a thesis on demonology. The next year he took his Bachelor of Divinity degree and was ordained into the Methodist ministry. He then combined his calling to the church with further studies at the University of Toronto. He became a demonstrator in psychology and also an itinerant preacher, like his father. Psychology and religion combined in his Ph.D. thesis, *Studies in Pauline Eschatology, and Its Background*, and he received his last degree in 1917.

In the meantime, he had discovered his poetic vocation. Naturally, much of his early work dealt with his Newfoundland experience, and his first published work, *Rachel: A Sea Story of Newfoundland in Verse* (privately printed, 1917), derivative as it was, still carries the force and feeling of his early years on the island.

In 1918 Pratt married Viola Whitney and settled down in Toronto, which was to remain his home for the rest of his life. In 1921 his only child, Mildred Claire, was born. In the year previous, he had been invited by Pelham Edgar, who had encouraged and criticized his early poetry, to join the Department of English at Victoria College, where he was to remain until his retirement thirty-three years later. Generations of students were entertained and instructed by his lectures in Shakespeare, Romantic and nineteenth-century poetry, and modern drama. He built up a stock of admiration and affection in students and colleagues still cherished in those who knew him.

In the 1920s Pratt became a regular contributor to *The Canadian Forum*, where A.J.M. Smith and F.R. Scott also published their early work. He encouraged many younger poets and became a moving force in the development of Canadian poetry over the next thirty years, particularly as editor of *Canadian Poetry Magazine* from 1936 to 1942. His first collection, *Newfoundland Verse*, was published by Ryerson in Toronto in 1923. The decorations for the edition were by Frederick H. Varley, an indication of Pratt's close association with members of the Group of Seven, who were changing the face of Canadian painting, just as Pratt was changing the face of Canadian poetry.

With the publication of *The Witches' Brew* in 1925, his work took a new turn. This rollicking comic epic was, he later claimed, a psychological reaction to his doctoral work on Saint Paul, in which he got the hell out of his system. The comic binge of the poem shows the consequences of a release of demonic power. In his next publication, *Titans* (1926), Pratt once again showed his fascination with power in the battle between whale and kraken in "The Cachalot" and the struggle between land and sea creatures in the Pleiocene age in "The Great Feud." A marked change of mood is seen in *The Iron Door*, an ode written to commemorate the death of the poet's mother, published in 1927, in which he explores the enigma of death and the challenge it proposes to faith.

With *The Roosevelt and the Antinoe* (1930), Pratt first showed his pace as an epic poet. This story of a sea rescue under appalling conditions also involves sacrifice of some of the rescuers — a theme always appealing to Pratt. This theme is also present in *The Titanic* (1935), perhaps Pratt's most popular poem, although more insistent is the irony central to the loss of this supposedly unsinkable liner. His most successful epic poem, *Brébeuf and His Brethren* (1940), was based on the account in the *Jesuit Relations* of the martyrdom of Brébeuf and his fellow missionaries by the Iroquois in New France in the first half of the seventeenth century.

The 1939–45 war against fascist tyranny and militarism gave Pratt several opportunities to exercise his talent for epic. In *Dunkirk* (1941), he celebrated the escape of the British army from the German invaders of France; in *They Are Returning* (1945), he celebrated the end of the war and the return of the soldiers; and in *Behind the Log* (1947), he portrayed the sufferings and triumph of an allied convoy under attack from a wolf pack of German submarines.

Pratt's last epic poem was *Towards the Last Spike* (1952), in which he chronicled the building of the Canadian Pacific Railway to the west coast of Canada. In 1958 Northrop Frye brought out his edition of *The Collected Poems of E.J. Pratt*, which has so far served as the basic text of his works.

Many honours came to Pratt. He was elected to the Royal Society of Canada in 1930, and he won the Governor General's Award for Poetry in English for *The Fable of the Goats and Other Poems* in 1937, for *Brébeuf and His Brethren* in 1940, and for *Towards the Last Spike* in 1952. He was awarded the Lorne Pierce Medal for distinguished services to Canadian literature in 1940 and the

Canada Council Medal for distinction in literature in 1961. He was given honorary degrees by nine Canadian universities, and he was made a Companion of the Order of St. Michael and St. George by King George VI in 1946.

Up to the end of his life, Ned Pratt was noted for his generosity and bonhomie. His York Club dinners to his friends are legendary, and his skill as a raconteur was unequalled. He died in Toronto, on 26 April 1964.

NOTE

[1] Much of the material for this biographical sketch was gained from Mrs. Viola Pratt for my edition of *Selected Poems of E.J. Pratt* (Toronto: Macmillan, 1968).

W.W.E. Ross (1894–1966)

DON PRECOSKY

WILLIAM WRIGHTSON EUSTACE ROSS was born on 14 June 1894 in Peterborough, Ontario, but was raised in the more northerly community of Pembroke, Ontario. He attended Pembroke High School and then the University of Toronto, from which he graduated in 1914 with a science degree. While a university student, he worked in northern Ontario for two summers (1912 and 1913) as a chainperson on a surveying crew. During World War I he enlisted in the army and was stationed in England. By 1924 Ross had begun his career as a geophysicist at the Dominion Magnetic Observatory in Agincourt, Ontario, where he worked until his retirement in the early 1960s. He began writing around 1923 but did not have his first poems published until April 1928 in *The Dial*. This five-year lag is but one sign of his reserve in putting his work before the public.

Four collections of Ross's poems have been published in book form: *Laconics* (1930) and *Sonnets* (1932) were published privately by Ross himself; *Experiment 1923–29: Poems by W.W.E. Ross* (1956) is a selection from Ross's early work made by Raymond Souster and published by the latter's Contact Press as a mimeographed booklet; and *Shapes and Sounds: Poems of W.W.E. Ross* (1968), the only commercial edition of Ross's work, is a posthumous selection of 122 poems made by Souster and John Robert Colombo, who chose mainly from the final versions of poems transcribed by Ross into his journals.[1] The dates of the books reflect the ups and downs of his career. Ross did his best writing in the 1920s and 1930s, for which he received only small recognition. He then dropped out of sight, except for poems published in magazines at widely spaced intervals, to be rediscovered by younger poets, most notably Raymond Souster, who admired his blending of Imagism with Canadian subjects. A selected poems had been proposed by A.J.M. Smith, but Ross did not encourage the project. In a letter to Smith, dated 29 October 1962, he tried to explain his attitude towards this book and his near silence after the 1930s:

> I have to say I feel embarrassed about my failure to take up your kind offer last year to write an introduction to my "selected poems" (Ryerson Press) and help choose them. I really can't excuse myself. For some weird reason I haven't made any reply at all about this matter of the "selected poems" offer, but have been putting it off from day to day ever since! The reason has been a lapse, or considerable diminution, some years ago in my poetic "drive," judgment etc. I have been constantly hoping for a revival, but meanwhile I have felt unable to do anything about my pieces — such as finishing some incompleted ones — and very hesitant, for that reason, about having anything done with them. This "lapse" is probably connected with my retirement from the observatory work, and perhaps with my father's death, since his literary interest was very great.[2]

This is one of the few clues Ross has left about his private self. Once again, his reticence is apparent. He seems to have suffered from a monumental writer's block that kept him from writing, publishing, or even selecting old poems for an edition.

If we look for evidence of the man in his poems, we shall be disappointed. They only lead us to some obvious generalities: he loved nature, camping, canoeing, and fishing; he disliked the city and industry; he was well-read in the classics. One poem mentions his mother ("As I Left" [SS, p. 42]), another his father ("Over the Water" [SS, p. 39]). A third shows scientists, and among them possibly himself, at work:

In the bright-lit
laboratory
the coloured liquids
glow in the light;
liquids in bottles,
or test-tubes or beakers,
of many colours,
or water-clear. —

("Laboratory," in SS, p. 76)

We have three sources that give us glimpses of what Ross the man was like: his letters to A.J.M. Smith, the correspondence between Ross and Ralph Gustafson,[3] and Barry Callaghan's "Memoir" in *Shapes and Sounds*. The letters reveal him to have been a crusty humorist who enjoyed parodying other writers and gossiping about the politics of Canadian literature. They also reveal a man who took his own writing very seriously and who was apprehensive about putting his work before the public. Ultimately, they show a man whose inspiration dried up one day, leaving him puzzled and defensive.

According to Callaghan, Ross lived in a "narrow, red-brick corner house on Delaware Avenue" in Toronto (SS, p. 1), with his wife Mary and his daughters Mary and Nancy. He wrote in an attic room. Callaghan's first impression upon meeting him is the same one the reader receives from Dennis Burton's portrait of Ross on the cover of *Shapes and Sounds*: "square-jawed . . . his face creviced and grey" (SS, p. 1).

Callaghan's depiction of Ross adds to his image as a crusty humorist, "witty and cutting" (SS, p. 1):

When a political or social issue blew up, Eustace wrote preposterous letters to the newspaper editors. They were letters in support of the Anglophile cause, but ridiculous and full of diatribe and ignorance. He signed them "Old Flag," knowing the editors would print such nonsense. No one, of course, knew who "Old Flag" was. (*SS*, pp. 2–3)

Why didn't Ross make it? Callaghan takes a stab at an answer:

. . . Eustace was incapable of hustling editors and critics; his work was never published by a commercial house, and in the fifties many editors forgot about him — some encouraged to do so by the chief academic critic in the country who had dismissed Ross's poems. (*SS*, p. 3)

He's half right. Ross was incapable of action, of pushing himself forward. As for the evil opposition of "the chief academic critic," who can only have been Smith, Callaghan is mistaken. Smith was supportive and wanted to reintroduce Ross to the public. It all returns to Ross's shyness, even fear. There is a sad irony in the title of his first work. Laconism, at first a feature of his style, became an overwhelming force that drove him into silence.

NOTES

[1] See Raymond Souster and John Robert Colombo, "Editorial Note," in *Shapes and Sounds: Poems of W.W.E. Ross*, ed. Raymond Souster and John Robert Colombo (Don Mills, Ont.: Longmans, 1968), p. 8. Further references to this work (*SS*) appear in the text.

[2] Michael E. Darling, ed., "On Poetry and Poets: The Letters of W.W.E. Ross to A.J.M. Smith," *Essays on Canadian Writing*, No. 16 (Fall–Winter 1979–80), p. 122.

[3] See Bruce Whiteman, ed. and introd., *A Literary Friendship: The Correspondence of Ralph Gustafson and W.W.E. Ross* (Toronto: ECW, 1984).

Raymond Knister (1899–1932)

JOY KUROPATWA

JOHN RAYMOND KNISTER was born in Ruscom,[1] near Stoney Point on Lake St. Clair, in Essex County, Ontario, on 27 May 1899. His mother was a teacher, his father a farmer "extremely active in the social and political life of Ontario farmers."[2] What is probably a fictionalized account of this activity is found in Knister's still unpublished novel "Turning Loam." Reading and writing appealed to Knister from the first; he kept a record of his reading between late 1914 and mid-1924 in which over a thousand works are listed,[3] and he started writing as a teenager. There is evidence that much of his poetry was written in the early 1920s,[4] and his first published story, "The One Thing," appeared in the January 1922 issue of the American publication *The Midland*,[5] a magazine that H.L. Mencken described as "perhaps the most important magazine ever founded in America."[6]

In 1919 Knister attended the University of Toronto, until he was hospitalized for pneumonia (Waddington, p. 176). While at the university, he contributed to his college's publication *Acta Victoriana*[7] and was the student of Pelham Edgar, author of *Henry James, Man and Author* (1927).

From 1920 to 1923 he wrote while working on his father's farm near Blenheim, Ontario. It was during this time that "Mist-Green Oats," probably his best-known short story, appeared.[8] By the autumn of 1922, Knister turned his attention to novel writing; he also began reviewing books for a Windsor newspaper, *The Border Cities Star*, and "within a year earned for the *Star* the reputation of printing one of Canada's outstanding Literary Pages" (Waddington, p. 179).

In the autumn of 1923 Knister moved to Iowa City:

> Knister began his work with *The Midland* in October, 1923 as the Associate Editor. This was a special new position representing a kind of scholarship Frederick [the editor] had created for young writers of exceptional promise. Ruth Suckow had been the first appointed to the position a year before. Knister's duties ranged through almost every aspect of *Midland* work, and included reading and judging manuscripts, proofreading them and participating in editorial decisions. He was entitled to choose his own hours, perhaps two or three a day, so as to have substantial leisure for his own creative work. (Waddington, p. 179)

Knister attended courses at Iowa University and completed two still-unpublished novels, "Group Portrait" and "Turning Loam," while working on *The Midland*.[9] After his term as associate editor ended in June 1924, he went to Chicago, where he wrote during the day and drove taxi by night. Chicago would become the setting for more than one work: the short story "Hackman's Night," the published novella "Innocent Man," and the unpublished novella "Cab Driver" (which surfaced only in January 1984). In October 1924 Knister left Chicago to return to Canada; this homecoming is considered to be the background to the poem "After Exile" (Waddington, p. 181).

By 1925 his work appeared in *This Quarter*, an American expatriate magazine published in Paris, in which the work of Djuna Barnes, e.e. cummings, Ernest Hemingway, James Joyce, and Carl

Sandburg also appeared (Waddington, p. 182). In a letter from Ernest Walsh, editor of *This Quarter*, Knister was told, "Your stuff is real."[10]

Knister wrote many reviews, articles, and sketches for popular magazines and newspapers, but a 1925 letter suggests that he tolerated rather than rejoiced in bread-and-butter composition:

> You will be interested to know that I have taken on the job of turning out a story a week . . . . a series of rural character sketches — *Toronto Star Weekly's* request . . . . Loth to have anything to do with Can. (or any other kind of) journalism, I says, How much? 2 c. per word, quoth 'e. Aweel, says I, you've brought it on yourself.[11]

In 1926 Knister moved to Toronto, where he wrote full-time. It was during his years in Toronto that he met Morley Callaghan, Dorothy Livesay, Wilson MacDonald, Charles G.D. Roberts, Mazo de la Roche, and Duncan Campbell Scott. It was also during the Toronto years that Knister became the mentor of Thomas Murtha, whose short stories were not published in book form until 1980.[12]

Knister married Myrtle Gamble in 1927, and the couple spent the summer at the "Poplars," a cottage at Hanlan's Point, Toronto Island. Here Knister completed the final draft of *White Narcissus*, his only novel to be published during his lifetime. In September 1927, Macmillan accepted the novel for publication and in October commissioned him to edit an anthology of Canadian short stories (Waddington, p. 186). *Canadian Short Stories*, dedicated to Duncan Campbell Scott, was published in 1928 and is thought to be the first anthology of its kind. Knister's Introduction to the collection is still considered a helpful discussion of the Canadian short story. In 1929 *White Narcissus* was published in Canada, England, and the United States.

In the spring of 1929 Knister and his wife moved to a farmhouse on the lake road near Port Dover, Ontario; here he wrote *My Star Predominant*, a well-researched novel based on the life of John Keats. A daughter, Imogen, was born in Port Dover in 1930. *Show Me Death*, a World War I novel, appeared in 1930 under the name of W. Redvers Dent, but was actually, to a currently unknown extent, ghost-written by Knister. Frederick Philip Grove encouraged

Knister to submit *My Star Predominant* to the Graphic Publishers' Canadian Novel Contest; Grove was chairman of the committee adjudicating the award, the other committee members being W.T. Allison, who taught English at the University of Manitoba, and Barker Fairley, who taught German at the University of Toronto.[13] The novel won the $2,500 first prize in 1931, but Graphic went bankrupt and the novel did not appear until 1934, when it was published in Canada and England. Knister had written *My Star Predominant* between 1929 and 1931; the dates of composition of other works overlap with the time of writing the novel: "Innocent Man" was written between 1927 and 1931, while "Cab Driver" was written between 1927 and 1930.[14] The novella, "There Was a Mr. Cristi," became available in February 1986; the typescript ends with the notation, "May–June, 1928, Toronto — December, 1930, Port Dover."[15]

In 1931 and 1932 Knister lived in Quebec, first in Montreal and then in Ste. Anne de Bellevue; it was while in Quebec that his friendship with Leo Kennedy was established.[16] Knister's last novel, "Soil in Smoke," was written between 1931 and 1932; it is a revised version of his first novel, "Group Portrait."[17] Both remain unpublished. During the same period, Knister wrote a number of short stories and the novella "Peaches, Peaches" (O'Halloran, p. 198). He returned to Ontario in 1932 and was offered a job on the editorial staff of Ryerson Press that would allow him time for his own writing.

Raymond Knister drowned while swimming off Stoney Point, Lake St. Clair, on 29 August 1932. An account of this last day has been published.[18] He was thirty-three at the time of his death.

Knister was a writer of short stories, poems, novels, and novellas, and a playwright, as well as being a critic and editor. Much of his writing remains unpublished, and therefore unknown. Moreover, during the 1970s some works were published for the first time, and some reprinted, and with this revival of interest emerged a reevaluation of his role in Canadian letters as being that of an interesting but minor author. An important contribution to this reevaluation is the Knister issue of the *Journal of Canadian Fiction* (1975), also published in book form as *Raymond Knister: Poems, Stories and Essays*, edited and introduced by David Arnason, in which work by and about Knister appears.

A selection of Knister's poetry, edited by Dorothy Livesay, was published as *Collected Poems of Raymond Knister* (1949). Further poems, many previously unpublished, appear in *Raymond Knister: Poems, Stories and Essays* and *Windfalls for Cider: The Poems of Raymond Knister* (1983). There is no collected edition of Knister's short stories, but a few appear in *Selected Stories of Raymond Knister* (1972), and many can be found in *Raymond Knister: Poems, Stories and Essays* and *The First Day of Spring: Stories and Other Prose* (1976). Of Knister's nine currently known works of longer prose fiction, five remain unpublished. A 1990 reprint of *White Narcissus* includes an Afterword by Morley Callaghan (in McClelland and Stewart's New Canadian Library series).

NOTES

[1] For this and subsequent information, I am indebted to Imogen Knister Givens.

[2] Marcus Waddington, "Raymond Knister: A Biographical Note," *Journal of Canadian Fiction*, No. 14 (1975) [Raymond Knister issue], p. 175. Further references to this work appear in the text.

[3] Imogen Givens courteously provided a copy of this list.

[4] "Raymond Knister," an unpublished essay, kindly made available by Imogen Givens. It may have been written by Knister and seems to form the basis for Leo Kennedy's "Raymond Knister," *The Canadian Forum*, Sept. 1932, pp. 459–61.

[5] Anne Burke, "Raymond Knister: An Annotated Bibliography," in *The Annotated Bibliography of Canada's Major Authors*, ed. Robert Lecker and Jack David, III (Downsview, Ont.: ECW, 1981), 292.

[6] David Arnason, "Canadian Poetry: The Interregnum," *CV/II*, 1, No. 1 (Spring 1975), 31.

[7] Bonita O'Halloran, "Chronological History of Raymond Knister," *Journal of Canadian Fiction*, No. 14 (1975) [Raymond Knister issue], p. 194.

[8] O'Halloran, p. 195.

[9] Raymond Knister, letter to Elizabeth Frankfurth [copy], 11 April 1924, Raymond Knister Papers, Queen's Univ. Archives, Kingston, Ont.

[10] Ernest Walsh, letter to Raymond Knister, 23 April 1925, Raymond Knister Papers, Queen's Univ. Archives, Kingston, Ont.

[11] Raymond Knister, letter to Elizabeth Frankfurth [copy], 19 Nov. 1925, Raymond Knister Papers, Queen's Univ. Archives, Kingston, Ont.

[12] William Murtha, ed. and introd., *Short Stories of Thomas Murtha* (Ottawa: Univ. of Ottawa Press, 1980). The Introduction discusses the friendship of Murtha and Knister.

[13] Desmond Pacey, ed. and introd., *The Letters of Frederick Philip Grove* (Toronto: Univ. of Toronto Press, 1976), pp. 283–84.

[14] Joy Kuropatwa, "A Handbook to Raymond Knister's Longer Prose Fiction," Diss. Western Ontario 1985, pp. 135, 162.

[15] Raymond Knister, "There Was a Mr. Cristi," p. 129. Knister Family Papers. Imogen Knister Givens kindly provided a copy of the typescript, and permitted quotation from the work in this essay.

[16] Leo Kennedy, "A Poet's Memoirs," rev. of *Journal of Canadian Fiction*, No. 14 (1975) [Raymond Knister issue], *CV/II*, 2, No. 2 (May 1976), 23–24.

[17] Marcus Waddington, "Raymond Knister and the Canadian Short Story," M.A. Thesis Carleton 1977, p. 223.

[18] Imogen Givens, "Raymond Knister — Man or Myth?" *Essays on Canadian Writing*, No. 16 (Fall–Winter 1979–80), pp. 5–19.

F.R. Scott (1899–1985)

SANDRA DJWA

FRANCIS REGINALD SCOTT was born in Quebec City on 1 August 1899, the son of Canon Frederick George Scott, an Anglican priest and poet.[1] The elder Scott, popularly known as "The Poet of the Laurentians," gained distinction as the "beloved padre" of the First Canadian Division during the First World War. From his father, F.R. Scott absorbed the religious and poetic impulses, a sense of duty to society, and a love for the Canadian northland. On family camping trips, Canon Scott would often comment on the great expanse of the Laurentian rock, "Frank, . . . look . . . . There's nothing between you and the North Pole."[2] A keen astronomer, he taught his son to chart the stars in the northern sky. In 1916 F.R. Scott left Quebec City to attend Bishop's College at Lennoxville near Montreal. In 1919 he received his B.A. and was awarded a Rhodes Scholarship to Oxford.

At Magdalen College, Oxford, Scott studied history. In his spare time he rowed for his college, wrote verse, and read widely, especially the scientific writings of Henri Bergson, Sir Arthur S. Eddington, and Albert Einstein. It was also at Oxford that Scott first became interested in socialism through study sessions sponsored by the Student Christian Movement, including one on R.H. Tawney's *The Acquisitive Society* (1920). He received an Oxford B.A. in 1922 and a B.Litt. in 1923 for a thesis on "The Annexation of Savoy and Nice by Napoleon III, 1860."

In November 1923 Scott returned to Canada and a brief post as a teacher at Lower Canada College in Montreal. In 1924 he entered the Faculty of Law at McGill University and in 1927 apprenticed with the Montreal firm of Lafleur, MacDougall, Macfarlane and Barclay. More informal training came through a series of "groups" and magazines that afforded freewheeling discussion and the opportunity to find self-expression. The first, simply named "The Group" (1924–29), was a small gathering of friends who met regularly to discuss topics of cultural and national concern. The second was *The McGill Fortnightly Review* (1925–27), an undergraduate little magazine associated with the beginnings of Canadian modernism. In 1928 Scott was invited to teach constitutional and federal law at McGill, a post in which he continued until retirement as dean of the Faculty of Law in 1964. In 1928 he also married Marian Dale, a young Montreal artist; their only child, Peter, now a professor of English at Berkeley, was born in 1929.

Scott's active political life began with the Depression. In 1932, with Frank Underhill, he became a founding member of the League for Social Reconstruction. A year later he was a contributor to the Regina Manifesto, which resulted in the consolidation of the Co-operative Commonwealth Federation under J.S. Woodsworth. In the 1940s he helped found the little magazine *Preview*, which helped initiate a second wave of modernism in Canadian poetry. He was a member of the Canadian Institute for International Affairs from 1935 to 1957, national chair of the CCF from 1942 to 1950, United Nations technical-assistance resident representative to Burma in 1952, and chair of the Canadian Writers Conference in 1955. In the late 1950s he successfully pleaded the celebrated Roncarelli case and the Switzman vs. Elbling case, overturning in the latter the repressive legislation of Premier Duplessis' Padlock Act, which had been used to control religious minorities and political groups that opposed the government. In the 1960s he defended D.H. Lawrence's novel *Lady Chatterley's Lover* against charges of obscenity in the Quebec Court of Queen's Bench and the Supreme Court of Canada. He was a member of the Royal Commission on Bilingualism and Biculturalism from 1963 to 1971.

His works include *Overture: Poems* (1945); *Events and Signals* (1954); *The Eye of the Needle: Satires, Sorties, Sundries* (1957); *Signature* (1964); *Selected Poems* (1966); *Trouvailles; Poems from Prose* (1967); *The Dance Is One* (1973); and *The Collected Poems of F.R. Scott* (1981). With A.J.M. Smith he coedited *New Provinces: Poems of Several Authors* (1936) and *The Blasted Pine: An Anthology of Satire, Invective and Disrespectful Verse, Chiefly by Canadian Writers* (1957). Scott was an early translator of Quebec poetry whose publications include *St-Denys Garneau & Anne Hébert: Translations/Traductions* (1962); *Dialogue sur la traduction à propos du Tombeau des rois* (1970), with Anne Hébert; and *Poems of French Canada* (1977). Other publications include *Social Planning for Canada* (1935); *Canada Today: A Study of Her National Interests and National Policy* (1938); *Make This Your Canada: A Review of C.C.F. History and Policy* (1943), with David Lewis; *Quebec States Her Case: Speeches and Articles from Quebec in the Years of Unrest* (1964), coedited with Michael Oliver; and essay collections including *Essays on the Constitution: Aspects of Canadian Law and Politics* (1977), and *A New Endeavour: Selected Political Essays, Letters, and Addresses* (1986).

Scott received numerous honours throughout the years. He was a Guggenheim Fellow in 1940 and was elected to the Royal Society of Canada in 1947. In 1962 he was awarded the Lorne Pierce Medal for distinguished service to Canadian literature and in 1965 the Molson Prize given by the Canada Council for outstanding achievements in the arts and humanities and the social sciences. Scott was awarded the Canada Council's prize for translation in 1978 for *Poems of French Canada*. He received the Governor General's Award for Nonfiction in English in 1978 for his *Essays on the Constitution* and again for Poetry in English in 1982 for *The Collected Poems of F.R. Scott*. In the wider field of Canadian culture, Scott is a figure of extraordinary importance. He achieved distinction not only as a poet, but also as a political activist and a leading constitutional lawyer. These activities cannot be neatly divided, for all find expression in his poetry and all stem from the nationalist concerns of the 1920s.

NOTES

[1] For a full biography of F. R. Scott, see Sandra Djwa, *The Politics of the Imagination: A Life of F. R. Scott* (Toronto: McClelland and Stewart, 1987).

[2] Quoted in Vincent Tovell, "The World for a Country: An Edited Interview with Frank Scott," *Canadian Poetry: Studies, Documents, Reviews*, No. 2 (Spring–Summer 1978), p. 67.

Robert Finch (1900–)

SUSAN GINGELL

THE MODEST FIRST-PERSON persona of Robert Finch's "Manifesto" says of his verses,

> I complain in them, if I have cause to complain,
> I confide in them my secrets and my joy,
> They are the secretaries of my heart,
> Combing or curling them would make them vain,
> All I can call my lines, and not be coy,
> Is random note and comment without art.[1]

The artful play of image and sound in this poem should caution readers against too quick an identification of persona with poet: autobiographical is scarcely a term one would choose to describe Finch's poetry. Nonetheless, a knowledge of his life, and particularly of the cultivated atmosphere and material privilege of his

earliest and his adult years, explains a great deal about the parti-
cular nature of his verse.

Born 14 May 1900, in Freeport, Long Island, U.S.A., Robert
Duer Claydon Finch spent most of his early years on his family's
Morris Park estate on Long Island. There his parents enjoyed
horseback riding and entertaining the numerous guests who came
down from New York to play tennis and spend the weekend. With
the help of a gardener, his father raised prize-winning roses and
strawberries, amid three acres of gardens. Something of this pas-
sion was passed on to his son, who lists gardens among his many
interests and reflects his aesthetic delight in flowers and shrubs,
particularly the exquisite beauty of the rose, in many of his poems.
His first summers were spent on the beaches and dunes of Fire
Island and experiences of this landscape are captured in poems like
"Bees, Thistles and Sea" from *Poems* and Part 1 of "Variations"
in *Variations & Theme*.

Finch's parents were, in his words, "inveterate readers"[2] and
possessed an extensive library from which he was daily read
selections from English poets. Also on a daily basis he was required
to memorize a passage from Scripture, yet living in "an atmosphere
of animated conversation" in which his parents and their guests
"often discussed points of language," he nonetheless let no one
"either at home or outside, know of [his] own attempts at verse."

Finch's aesthetic tastes were further fostered by regular weekend
visits with his godfather John King Duer of the wealthy Duer Du
Pont Breck family. During these visits Duer taught his godson to
admire the antique Japanese miniature gardens that he sold from
his Madison Avenue shop and explained the history of pictures and
objects d'art in the Breck collection.

At home, Finch learned to read English at three and French at
four (his maternal ancestry is partly French), but the Dickinson
School for Small Boys gave him his first two years of formal
schooling and strengthened the foundations of his interest in
language and poetry because of the constant attention paid to "the
correctness of our pronunciations, the clarity of our enunciation
and the way we chose words and put them together," and because
students were required to memorize a poem a day as homework.

After Finch had had two brief exposures to the American public
school system, his family moved in 1906 to a ranch his father had

bought in the foothills of the Rockies where there were no schools. His mother took over the task of educating her children, and Finch continued to read voraciously, making use of the "several barrels of the complete works of well-known Victorian writers" left behind by two remittance men. He would go on to attend University College, University of Toronto, where he won the Jardine Memorial Prize for a still-unpublished poem, "Rain," graduating in 1925 (Honour Moderns in French and German) and winning the Governor General's Proficiency Medal.

His undergraduate studies had been interrupted by a two-year stint of teaching at Ridley College in St. Catharines, where the Headmaster of the Lower School, H.G. Williams, nurtured Finch's poetic leanings in a variety of ways. He gave the young poet "the regular benefit of . . . searching criticism," allowing him "the run of his private library, with its vast collection of poetry" and introducing him to a number of poets in person, among them Amy Lowell, Alfred Noyes, and the Canadian Ethelwyn Wetherald. These encounters had, according to Finch, a single importance: "They revealed, once and for all, that making the acquaintance of a poet has nothing to do with making the acquaintance of his poems, knowledge which thenceforth was to save me time, energy and speculation."

In 1926, on a Bourse d'études du gouvernement français, he began postgraduate studies at the Sorbonne on the subject of *Alfred de Vigny et l'Angleterre.*[3] Then in 1928 he took up a post as lecturer in French at University College, University of Toronto, where he was to spend the rest of his academic career. Finch was made a full professor in 1952 and a decade later was invited by his long-time admirer, Robertson Davies, to join Massey College, the university's élite graduate college, when Davies became Massey's first master. Finch is now professor emeritus at Massey College.

In 1953 Finch's masque celebrating the one-hundredth anniversary of the founding of the university, *A Century Has Roots*, was produced at the Hart House Theatre, University of Toronto, and published by the University of Toronto Press. His most important critical work, *The Sixth Sense: Individualism in French Poetry, 1686–1760*, was followed by a companion anthology, *French Individualist Poetry, 1686–1760*, compiled together with his close friend and colleague Eugène Joliat.

Finch's academic career facilitated his extensive travels in Europe (he returns regularly to France) and North America, as well as the pursuit of his lively interests in painting, music, and theatre. His paintings have been exhibited in Toronto, Paris, and New York, and are held in private and public collections in five countries, including the collections of several provincial museums and the National Gallery in Ottawa. Formal music study began for Finch at an early age and continued in both Canada and France until 1935. He has a special fondness for the harpsichord and the clavichord, has given piano recitals, lecture recitals, and illustrated lectures (the latter two on medieval, seventeenth- and eighteenth-century, and modern music), participated in a variety of choral groups, been a long-standing member of a chamber-music ensemble, and composed a number of pieces, including the incidental music for a Hart House production of Sophocles' *Antigone*. His theatre experience as actor, director, and producer has embraced works in both English and French.

Not surprisingly, then, Finch has been repeatedly honoured for his contributions to the cultural and intellectual life of Canada. He was elected a Fellow of the Royal Society of Canada in 1963, won the Lorne Pierce Gold Medal in 1968, and was granted honorary degrees by the University of Toronto in 1973 and York University in 1976. Although the many activities detailed above are by no means to be discounted, his primary achievements have been poetic.

The first significant sample of his work appeared in 1936 in the landmark anthology *New Provinces: Poems of Several Authors*, along with contributions by his friend and University of Toronto colleague E.J. Pratt, and the four Montreal poets Leo Kennedy, A.M. Klein, F.R. Scott, and A.J.M. Smith. The controversial 1946 Governor General's Award-winning volume *Poems* was followed in 1948 by *The Strength of the Hills*. After a thirteen-year publishing hiatus, in 1961 Finch again won the Governor General's Award for Poetry in English for *Acis in Oxford and Other Poems*. Two more volumes, *Dover Beach Revisited and Other Poems* and *Silverthorn Bush and Other Poems* preceded a fourteen-year silence that was finally broken in 1980 by the publication of *Variations & Theme*. Thereafter Finch has again published volumes of poems on a regular basis, with *Has and Is* appearing in 1981, *Twelve for Christmas* in

1982, *The Grand Duke of Moscow's Favourite Solo* in 1983, *Double Tuning* in 1984, *For the Back of a Likeness* in 1986, and *Sail-Boat and Lake* in 1988, and *Miracle at the Jetty* (1991).

NOTES

¹ Robert Finch, *Double Tuning* (Erin, Ont.: Porcupine's Quill, 1984), p. 29.

² Response by Robert Finch to a questionnaire on details of his life and poetic practice. All quoted material and much of the information relating to Finch's biography is from the responses elicited in this way unless otherwise stated. I am greatly indebted to Dr. Finch for his generous cooperation in providing this information and for his responses to my many inquiries.

³ This work was abandoned because of circumstances beyond Finch's control, but he did publish, many years later, an article connected with his study of de Vigny, "Ivory Tower," *University of Toronto Quarterly*, 25 (October 1955), 23–37.

A.J.M. Smith (1902–80)

MICHAEL DARLING

ARTHUR JAMES MARSHALL SMITH was born on 8 November 1902 in Westmount, Quebec, the son of Alexandra Louise Whiting and Octavius Arthur Smith, both born in England. Octavius (an eighth son) was an accountant, interested in Esperanto and a universal keyboard for the piano.[1] The Smiths' home was not a typical Westmount mansion on the slopes of the mountain, but "a small middle class, shabby-genteel semi-detached house on Elm Avenue just below what was then Western."[2] Arthur attended Roslyn Avenue School and Westmount High School, where his education was interrupted during 1918–20 by a sojourn to England with his parents.

In 1921 he entered McGill University and soon began to contribute poems and reviews to "The Dilettante," a weekly literary page of *The McGill Daily*. Smith edited its successor, *The McGill Daily Literary Supplement*, in his graduating year of 1924–25, and, when the Students' Council refused to support the *Supplement* for a subsequent year, he and a group of associates, which included F.R. Scott and Leon Edel, founded an independent journal, *The McGill Fortnightly Review*. Its first issue appeared on 21 November 1925 and included two poems by Smith, one of which was attributed to Vincent Starr, one of the many pseudonyms he used in McGill publications.[3]

After completing his M.A. in 1926 with a thesis on W.B. Yeats, Smith secured a teaching position at Montreal High School, but the work was not congenial to him, and he was pleased to accept a teacher-exchange fellowship to study at the University of Edinburgh. Having folded the *Fortnightly* earlier in the year, he married Jeannie Dougall Robins, also a McGill graduate, and they left for Edinburgh in August 1927.

While lecturing in the Edinburgh Teaching Training Centre at Moray House,[4] Smith studied with Professor H.J.C. Grierson, the leading authority on the seventeenth-century metaphysical poets. He also wrote for a variety of magazines and succeeded in publishing a number of poems in *The Dial*, the most prestigious literary journal of its day. His commitment to the ideals of modernism embodied in the work of Yeats and Eliot led him to denounce the absence of innovation in his own country in "Wanted — Canadian Criticism," which sent shock waves through the Canadian Authors Association when it first appeared in *The Canadian Forum* in April 1928.[5]

Returning to Montreal in 1929 on the eve of the Depression, Smith found that academic jobs were scarce, and he was forced to return to high-school teaching for a year. During 1930–31 he was an assistant professor at Ball State Teachers College in Muncie, Indiana. While there, he completed revisions on his doctoral dissertation on the metaphysical poets and received his Ph.D. from Edinburgh. He then obtained a two-year replacement contract at Michigan State College in East Lansing, and, when that appointment terminated in 1933, he spent the next year unemployed, marking papers for twenty-five cents an hour. In the fall of 1934, he moved to Crete, Nebraska, where he was "head of the English Department, and half of the English Department"[6] at Doane College, earning a salary of $1,200. He taught for a year at the University of South Dakota and, in 1936, returned to Michigan

State, where he was to remain for thirty-six years as professor of English and eventually poet-in-residence.

In the same year, Macmillan of Canada published a small anthology entitled *New Provinces: Poems of Several Authors*, which introduced the work of some of the younger Canadian poets — A.J.M Smith, F.R. Scott, Leo Kennedy, A.M. Klein, and Robert Finch — as well as E.J. Pratt, who was already an established figure. By the time of its publication, however, Smith had lost interest in the project[7] and was actively seeking a publisher for his own first collection. A manuscript version of *News of the Phoenix and Other Poems* already existed as early as 1936[8] and had been refused by New Directions, Yale University Press, and the University of Chicago Press before Lorne Pierce of Ryerson agreed to co-publication with Coward-McCann in New York.[9] It was Smith's preparation of an anthology of Canadian poetry that brought him to Pierce's attention. Although the Guggenheim Fellowship that supported his research was originally awarded for "a critical and historical study of Canadian poetry,"[10] Smith soon realized that an historical anthology based on sound evaluative principles was a necessary prerequisite. Work on the anthology was exhausting, with no reliable precedents to guide him, but Smith found the challenge stimulating, and he enjoyed the opportunity to travel in Canada and meet many of the poets whose work he admired, including Ralph Gustafson, Earle Birney, Margaret Avison, P.K. Page, and E.J. Pratt, who was instrumental in securing publication of the anthology. *The Book of Canadian Poetry: A Critical and Historical Anthology* appeared in September 1943, followed closely by publication of *News of the Phoenix and Other Poems*. Smith received the Governor General's Award for Poetry in English, and, although his anthology was criticized by some reviewers for its modernist bias,[11] it was quickly recognized by others, including Northrop Frye,[12] as a landmark of Canadian literary scholarship, making possible the teaching of Canadian poetry at the university level.

In the late 1940s and 1950s, Smith's interests turned increasingly from writing poetry to writing about it, as he began to review books for *The Canadian Forum* and other journals and to enter into the literary controversies that these reviews provoked.[13] He also returned to Canada more frequently, not only to relax at his summer home on Lake Memphremagog, Quebec, but also to teach summer school at Queen's University and the University of British Columbia. By the time his *Collected Poems* was published in 1962, Smith was widely regarded as the most influential English-Canadian poet of his generation,[14] and in addition to honorary degrees from McGill, Queen's, Bishop's, and Dalhousie universities, he was awarded the Lorne Pierce Medal of the Royal Society of Canada and the Canada Council Medal. He retired from Michigan State University in 1972. After his wife Jeannie died in 1977, Smith's health declined rapidly, and cataracts made reading and writing extremely difficult. After a long illness, he died on 21 November 1980 in East Lansing.

The image of Smith the man as an ascetic, death-obsessed intellectual is a myth perpetuated by critics who have confused the author with the persona of some of his early poems.[15] In rejecting the idea that the "I" of the poem should be identified with the poet himself, Smith was fond of quoting a line from Rimbaud: "Je est un autre."[16] Nevertheless, it is often possible to discover the real Smith beneath the poetic masks — an unassuming man, given to self-deprecation, but also a man who took the greatest pleasure in what life had to offer.[17]

NOTES

[1] Information supplied by A.J.M Smith's son, Peter Smith, letter to Michael Darling, 28 March 1982.

[2] A.J.M. Smith, letter to Germaine Warkentin, 18 Feb. 1975, A.J.M Smith Papers, Trent Univ. Archives, Peterborough, Ont. 81–019/1(14). Quoted by permission of Professor Warkentin, Trent University, and the estate of A.J.M. Smith. The Trent copy is undated, and Professor Warkentin has kindly supplied the date from the original in her possession.

[3] Some others include Michael Gard, Simeon Lamb, Corydon, Tomfool, and Max.

[4] Incorrectly transcribed as Murray House in Michael Darling, "An Interview with A.J.M. Smith," *Essays on Canadian Writing*, No. 9 (Winter 1977–78), p. 56.

[5] See A.J.M. Smith, "Wanted — Canadian Criticism," *The Canadian Forum*, April 1928, pp. 600–01; rpt. in his *Towards a View of Canadian Letters: Selected Critical Essays 1928–1971* (Vancouver: Univ. of British Columbia Press, 1973), pp. 167–69.

6 Darling, "An Interview with A.J.M. Smith," p. 57.

7 See Michael Gnarowski, Introd., *New Provinces: Poems of Several Authors*, ed. F.R. Scott et al., Literature of Canada: Poetry and Prose in Reprint, No. 20 (1936; rpt. Toronto: Univ. of Toronto Press, 1976), p. xx.

8 A typescript copy of this early version of *News of the Phoenix and Other Poems* is in the A.J.M Smith Papers, TUA 78–007/5(1). The dating is mine. Another typescript, dated 1936 and once owned by Theodore Roethke, was offered for sale by William Hoffer in October 1982. For a description, see Hoffer's *Canadian Literature List No. 53* (Vancouver: William Hoffer Bookseller, n.d.), item 127.

9 A more detailed account of the circumstances surrounding publication of *News of the Phoenix and Other Poems* may be found in Michael E. Darling, *A.J.M. Smith: An Annotated Bibliography* (Montreal: Véhicule, 1981), pp. 15–18.

10 Henry Allen Moe [secretary, Guggenheim Memorial Foundation], letter to A.J.M. Smith, 12 March 1941, TUA 78–007/1(2).

11 See [William Arthur Deacon], "A.J.M. Smith's Canadian Anthology Is Both Antiquarian and Modernistic," rev. of *The Book of Canadian Poetry: A Critical and Historical Anthology*, ed. A.J.M. Smith, *The Globe and Mail* [Toronto], 30 Oct. 1943, p. 20; and P.D.R[oss]., "Canadian Poetry, Old and New — The New Free Verse and Versifiers," rev. of *The Book of Canadian Poetry: A Critical and Historical Anthology*, ed. A.J.M. Smith, *The Ottawa Journal*, 30 Oct. 1943, p. 17.

12 See Northrop Frye, "Canada and Its Poetry," rev. of *The Book of Canadian Poetry: A Critical and Historical Anthology*, ed. A.J.M. Smith, *The Canadian Forum*, Dec. 1943, pp. 207–10; rpt. in his *The Bush Garden: Essays on the Canadian Imagination* (Toronto: House of Anansi, 1971), pp. 129–43.

13 One such "controversy" was carried on in letters from Smith and Irving Layton to the editor of *The Canadian Forum*, from October 1956 through March 1957, and was followed up by Smith's poem "On Reading Certain Poems and Epistles of Irving Layton and Louis Dudek," *The Canadian Forum*, May 1957, pp. 41–42. Smith did not take these exchanges quite as seriously as have some literary historians. In an unpublished comment, he states, "Layton, like myself . . . entered into these controversies with a certain high-spirited humour that enabled each of us to enjoy the other's verses" (TUA 78–007/2[4]). Quoted by permission of Trent University and the estate of A.J.M. Smith.

14 See Desmond Pacey, "A.J.M. Smith," in his *Ten Canadian Poets: A Group of Biographical and Critical Essays* (Toronto: Ryerson, 1958), p. 194.

15 See especially W.E. Collin, "Difficult, Lonely Music," in his *The White*

Savannahs (Toronto: Macmillan, 1936), pp. 235–63.

[16] A.J.M. Smith, "A Self-Review," *Canadian Literature*, No. 15 (Winter 1963), pp. 20–26; rpt. in his *Towards a View of Canadian Letters*, p. 213.

[17] The biographical information I have used in the preparation of this essay is largely drawn from the A.J.M. Smith Papers in the Trent University Archives, especially his own *curriculum vitae*, TUA 78–007/5(27). Useful published sources include the following: A.J.M. Smith, "The Confessions of a Compulsive Anthologist," *Journal of Canadian Studies*, 11, No. 2 (May 1976), 4–14 (rpt. [revised] in his *On Poetry and Poets: Selected Essays of A.J.M. Smith*, New Canadian Library, No. 143 [Toronto: McClelland and Stewart, 1977], pp. 106–22); Darling, "An Interview with A.J.M. Smith"; John Ferns, *A.J.M. Smith*, Twayne's World Authors Series, No. 535 (Boston: Twayne, 1979), pp. 11–29; Gordon Johnston, "A.J.M. Smith," in *Profiles in Canadian Literature*, ed. Jeffrey M. Heath, 1 (Toronto and Charlottetown: Dundurn, 1980), pp. 78–79; and Leon Edel, "The 'I' in A.J.M. Smith," *Canadian Poetry: Studies, Documents, Reviews*, No. 11 (Fall–Winter 1982), pp. 86–92.

Earle Birney (1904–)

PETER AICHINGER

EARLE BIRNEY was born on 13 May 1904 in Calgary at a time when Alberta was still part of the Northwest Territories. Both parents were immigrants; his mother came of Shetland fisher folk and his father was English. Although neither of them had much formal education, they were intensely aware of its benefits and were determined that their only son should become an educated man. The first few years of young Birney's life were spent on a farm near Lacombe, Alberta, but his family eventually settled in Banff, where he could have access to the village school. Similarly, in 1922 when Birney was ready to enrol in the University of British Columbia, the family moved to Vancouver. Prior to this move, Birney had to spend two years working as a labourer in order to save up enough money to enter the university.

Although Birney initially enrolled in engineering, his love of reading and the influence of Professor Garnett Sedgewick caused

99

him to switch to honours English in his third year and to become editor-in-chief of *The Ubyssey*. His fourth-year honours thesis was on Chaucer's irony, a subject he was to pursue in both his master's studies at the University of Toronto and his later doctoral studies at Berkeley and Toronto. While working towards his doctorate, he supplemented his graduate fellowships by working as a teaching assistant during the summers. These labours, among other factors, kept him from serious literary production, although he had been trying his hand at poetry ever since he was in his teens.

During 1934–35 Birney studied at the University of London on a Royal Society of Canada Fellowship. While in London, he met Esther Bull, who returned to Canada with him and married him. He received his doctorate from the University of Toronto in 1936 and was appointed lecturer in English at University College. He also became literary editor of *The Canadian Forum*, a post that he retained until 1940.

When Germany invaded Russia in 1941, Birney joined the Canadian army. He was prevented by a medical category from going into a fighting arm and thus became a Selection of Personnel Officer. Now, in his mid-thirties, he realized that the time had come to write those poems which had so far lain dormant in his mind. In a relatively short time, he wrote "David," "Dusk on English Bay," "Vancouver Lights," and others. Finding a publisher was not easy, but after "David" had appeared in *The Canadian Forum*, Ryerson agreed to bring out *David and Other Poems*. Birney had the satisfaction of receiving critical acclaim before he went off to war: *David and Other Poems* was widely praised and won the Governor General's Award for Poetry in English in 1942.

Birney's time in the army turned out to be a richer experience than he had anticipated. He met people from every walk of life and every region of Canada; he visited a good part of England and Europe, saw the war bring out the best and worst in the people around him, and had, for the first time in his life, plenty of time to write and think. Thus, when he was invalided home in 1945, he had the material for another volume of poetry, *Now Is Time*, which also won the Governor General's Award for Poetry in English.

After leaving the army, Birney worked for a year for the International Service of the Canadian Broadcasting Corporation before going to teach at the University of British Columbia. In 1948 he published *The Strait of Anian*, which contained twenty-two new poems in addition to others reprinted from his first two book. During the summers, he worked on *Turvey*, his comic novel about the Canadian army, which appeared in 1949 and which had the distinction of being banned in various Ontario libraries despite the fact that it had been savagely bowdlerized. It also was pirated by a British publishing company in 1960 under the title of *The Kootenay Highlander*. The unexpurgated Canadian version only appeared in 1976.

In 1952 Birney published a radio play and some poems, *Trial of a City and Other Verse*. The play, *Trial of a City*, is an examination of Vancouver since the arrival of white colonists, while the poems tend to reflect Birney's growing uneasiness about the Cold War. In this year he was also awarded the Lorne Pierce Medal of the Royal Society of Canada, traditionally won by the Canadian author "whose critical or creative writing notably succeeds in interpreting Canadian life to the Canadian people,"[1] and left to spend a year in France writing another novel, *Down the Long Table*, which was published in 1955.

Birney's next book, a collection of poetry entitled *Ice Cod Bell or Stone*, did not appear until 1962. He had spent a year of the interim in England doing research for a book on Chaucer, but other factors, including political disillusionment, depression over the dangers facing the world, and physical illness, seem to have underlain this period of relative silence. In any case, *Ice Cod Bell or Stone* is probably Birney's best single volume of poetry, vigorous, wide-ranging in its themes, polished, and self-assured, taking the whole world rather than just Canada as its theatre. It was followed in 1964 by *Near False Creek Mouth*, a collection of poems arising from Birney's increasingly frequent travels in the Caribbean and South America.

Birney retired from teaching in 1965. Although for the next three years he accepted posts as writer-in-residence at Canadian and American universities, he eventually gave up teaching completely and devoted himself to writing and travelling. As a result, he was able to collect and revise the poems that appeared in *Selected Poems: 1940–1966*, many of which had been out of print for several years, and *The Poems of Earle Birney* (1969). He also edited the poems of Malcolm Lowry, whom he had known well in British

Columbia and, under the influence of such younger poets as bpNichol and Andy Suknaski, began a series of experiments into the realm of concrete poetry, found poems, and computer poems. Out of this period of ferment came *pnomes jukollages & other stunzas* (1969), an envelope full of loose pages and folders containing the results of his experiments. This was really only a dalliance with some aspects of the avant-garde; *Rag & Bone Shop* (1971), while retaining some concrete and found poems, marks a new departure in Birney's life and work. While regretting the approach of old age, Birney still manages to celebrate the fact of romantic love in a manner more open and candid than he had ever done before.

The poems in *what's so big about* GREEN? (1973) tend to form a harsh and at times despairing denunciation of human folly, especially in regard to the destruction of the environment, the continuing threat of nuclear war, and the lack of trust and sympathy among people. In the same year, *The Bear on the Delhi Road*, a selection of his previous work, appeared in the United Kingdom. His *Collected Poems* was published in 1975, followed by *The Rugging and the Moving Times* and *Alphabeings & Other Seasyours* in 1976, *Ghost in the Wheels* in 1977, and *Fall by Fury & Other Makings* and a collection of short stories, *Big Bird in the Bush*, in 1978. These books have been followed more recently by a book of essays and memories, *Spreading Time: Book 1 1904–49* (1980), two collections of selected and new poems, *The Mammoth Corridor* (1980) and *One Muddy Hand* (1991), a book of new poems, *Copernican Fix* (1985), a selection of radio plays, *Words on Waves* (1985), and a book of *Essays on Chaucerian Irony* (1985). Birney has also recorded a three-album recording of *Music & Poetry: Earle Birney & Nexus* (1982). He was admitted to the Order of Canada in 1970.

NOTE

[1] Roy Daniells, "Lorne Pierce Medal," *Proceedings and Transactions of the Royal Society of Canada*, 3rd ser., 47 (1953), 37–38.

Leo Kennedy (1907–)

FRANCIS ZICHY

LEO KENNEDY was born in 1907, in Liverpool, England, where, as he has revealed, his family had been involved in shipping and dockworking for several generations.[1] In 1912 Kennedy's family immigrated to Montreal, where Kennedy grew up in the Catholic Irish community known as Griffintown, which he later evoked in the story "We All Got to Die." Kennedy's father was a ship's chandler; Kennedy himself worked on the Montreal docks for a time, and W.E. Collin, the first critic to notice his work, has reported that as "a youngster he ran off to sea and spent four months peeling potatoes and washing dishes on a C.P.R. tramp among West Indian ports."[2]

W.E. Collin has also remarked that Kennedy's family was "not literary." Kennedy himself has stressed that after graduating from secondary school he went to the Université de Montréal, and not to McGill, with which he has often been associated because of his connection with A.J.M. Smith, F.R. Scott, A.M. Klein, Leon Edel, and others involved in producing *The McGill Fortnightly Review* (1926–27).[3] Leon Edel has revealed that Kennedy's first published literary efforts consisted of "soulful letters and mocking verses under a feminine *nom de plume* in the lonelyhearts column of the Montreal *Star*."[4] According to Edel, it was the pungency of these youthful productions that first attracted the attention of the young writers at McGill.

For *The McGill Fortnightly Review* Kennedy wrote poetry, reviews, and other fiction. His literary ideas and poetic practice were influenced by his association with Smith and Scott; he was a friend of A.M. Klein, and later wrote a sympathetic survey of Klein's work for *The Jewish Standard*. After the demise of the *Fortnightly* in 1927, Kennedy became a founding member of the editorial board of *The Canadian Mercury* (1928–29); the name of this magazine suggests the iconoclastic model of H.L. Mencken's *American Mercury*. It was then with the *Mercury* that Kennedy got his start as an editor and literary journalist, an aspect of his career that was perhaps as important in the long run as his poetry and fiction. Kennedy gave every sign of thriving on literary polemics, as in his well-known article "The Future of Canadian Literature," a blunt attack on the Canadian literary establishment of the day, personified for Kennedy by the members of the Canadian Authors Association and their publication, *The Canadian Author and Bookman*. In these articles, and in his reviews of the work of Archibald Lampman and Raymond Knister in *The Canadian Forum*, Kennedy was writing as one speaker for a larger movement to update Canadian awareness of modern developments in literature and ideas.

In 1929 Kennedy married Miriam Carpin of Montreal; about the same time he began to support his family by working as a writer of advertising copy. At this time, Kennedy and his wife spent a year in New York City, where he wrote reviews for the *Commonweal* and *Bookman* and continued writing advertising copy.[5] In 1930 Kennedy was back in Montreal, doing odd jobs such as driving a wagon for a bakery and serving as a "space writer" for the *Montreal Herald*: "that is to say, I was unemployed, but hung around the office expectantly."[6] It was at this time that Kennedy met Raymond Knister, whose independent activities as a forerunner of the modern literary movement in Canada went back even before those of the *Fortnightly* group. When Knister drowned in 1932, Kennedy "did the last thing I knew how to do for him. I dedicated *The Shrouding* to Knister's memory."[7]

After the early *Fortnightly* days, in the period between 1928 and 1933, Kennedy was publishing poems, reviews, and short stories in several magazines, both Canadian and American (*Queen's Quarterly*, *The Dial*, *Commonweal*, *The McGilliad* [another venture of the *Fortnightly* group], *The Canadian Mercury*, and *The Canadian Forum*). It was in the *Forum* that most of Kennedy's poems and stories first saw print. *The Shrouding*, a volume containing thirty-nine poems, was published in 1933 by Macmillan, who were E.J. Pratt's publishers and were also to be the publishers of *New Provinces* (1936), a volume of poems by several writers of the modern movement in Canada, edited by Scott and Smith.[8] Published at a time when the Depression was taking a heavy toll on Canadian life, *The Shrouding* was really a retrospective volume containing poems written up to five years earlier. Under the pressure of the events of the day, "In this time of impending war and incipient fascism,"[9] Kennedy himself repudiated his *Shrouding* verse in favour of poetry that would be directly concerned with what he called the "immediates" of contemporary life. Kennedy's creative energies during the latter part of the 1930s (he continued to work as an advertising copywriter to make a living) went into his duties as an editor of the left-wing magazine *New Frontier* and into writing articles and poems on political and social subjects such as the injustices of the Depression and the iniquity of the war in Spain. It is worth noting that many of these pieces, both in prose and verse, were published pseudonymously, under the names Arthur Beaton and Leonard Bullen (Bullen was Kennedy's mother's birth name).[10] This suggests that Kennedy himself was aware of the possible ephemerality of these pieces. Even more likely is the possibility that Kennedy was protecting himself from recriminations at a time when he was working as an advertising copywriter. At any rate, between February 1936 and November 1937, even while he was writing political poetry for *New Frontier*, Kennedy published in *Saturday Night*, under his own name, a group of very different poems, traditional lyrics written in sonnets and other regular rhyming forms, centred on the conventional poetic subjects of love and the effects of time. At this time Kennedy was leading a kind of double life as a poet, devoting himself both to social polemics and to personal, lyrical writing.

In 1936 several poems by Kennedy appeared in *New Provinces*, but only two of these, the autobiographical "Testament" and "A Bright Swan for My Daughter," were newly published work. In the next few years several poems appeared in various magazines, and some poems were reprinted in anthologies,[11] but this output was meagre and uneven in quality. Many of Kennedy's last poems were satiric and marred by a bitter facetiousness in tone. In the late 1930s Kennedy emigrated to the United States to work as a writer of advertising copy, first in Detroit, then in Chicago, and then in the Minneapolis area. In the early 1960s he took a job as editor for the *Reader's Digest* and lived for the next few years in Norwalk, Connecticut. He returned to Montreal after retiring in the late 1970s. He lives there still and is working at present on a volume of memoirs of the 1930s.[12]

NOTES

[1] See Kennedy's poem "Testament," in Robert Finch, Leo Kennedy, A.M. Klein, E.J. Pratt, F.R. Scott, and A.J.M. Smith, *New Provinces: Poems of Several Authors*, Literature of Canada: Poetry and Prose in Reprint, introd. Michael Gnarowski (Toronto: Univ. of Toronto Press, 1976), pp. 24–25.

[2] W.E. Collin, *The White Savannahs*, Literature of Canada: Poetry and Prose in Reprint, introd. Germaine Warkentin (Toronto: Univ. of Toronto Press, 1975), p. 267.

[3] "I've just read again that I attended McGill. Wrong. I attended the U of Montreal." Cited by Michael Gnarowski, Introd., *New Provinces*, p. viii.

[4] Leon Edel, Introd., *The Shrouding*, by Leo Kennedy (Ottawa: Golden Dog, 1975), n. pag.

[5] Collin, *The White Savannahs*, p. 267. See also *Encyclopedia Canadiana* (Toronto: Grolier, 1957), p. 395; and W.E. Collin, "Leo Kennedy and the Resurrection of Canadian Poetry," *The Canadian Forum*, Oct. 1933, pp. 24–27.

[6] Leo Kennedy, "A Poet's Memoirs," *CV/II*, 2, No. 2 (May 1976), 23.

[7] Kennedy, "A Poet's Memoirs," p. 23.

[8] See Gnarowski, pp. vii–xxiii.

[9] Leo Kennedy, "Direction for Canadian Poets," *New Frontier*, June 1936, pp. 21–24; rpt. in Peter Stevens, ed., *The McGill Movement: A.J.M. Smith, F.R. Scott and Leo Kennedy* (Toronto: Ryerson, 1969), p. 12.

[10] See Peter Stevens, "Leo Kennedy's Poetry," in *The McGill Movement*, p. 43, and the entry under Kennedy's name in *Encyclopedia Canadiana*, 1957 ed.

[11] Among the magazines were *Canadian Poetry Magazine*, *Canadian Bookman*, *Contemporary Verse*, and *The Canadian Forum*. Poems by Kennedy were anthologized in Ethel Hume Bennett, ed., *New Harvesting* (Toronto: Macmillan, 1938); Ralph Gustafson, ed., *Anthology of Canadian Poetry* (Middlesex, England: Penguin, 1942); and A.J.M. Smith, ed., *The Book of Canadian Poetry: A Critical and Historical Anthology* (Chicago: Univ. of Chicago Press, 1943).

[12] See Kennedy, "A Poet's Memoirs," p. 23.

Ralph Gustafson (1909–)

DERMOT MCCARTHY

A MUCH-TRAVELLED POET, and one who has made much poetry out of his travels, Ralph Gustafson is also a poet of local realities and backyard particulars. His earliest and his most recent poems are rooted in his place of origin, the Eastern Townships of Quebec. Gustafson has always known that to deny one's origins is to tamper dangerously with the deepest sources of creative power: ". . . the village pump, one's own backyard is the place of poetry. The rag-and-bone shop of the human heart. Move that into myth, into universality if you will, but start elsewhere at grave poetic peril."[1]

Gustafson came by his desire to travel naturally. His father, Carl Otto Gustafson (1871–1934), left his native Sweden for America in the late 1880s, going first to New York and then to Illinois. From there he moved north to Quebec and the small mining village of Lime Ridge. Carl had been preceded there by his older brother, John Gustafson, who was a dynamiter for the Dominion Lime Company.[2] The poet's mother, Gertrude Ella Barker (1874–1934), was the daughter of the superintendent of Dominion Lime. The Barkers descended from United Empire Loyalists. She was a major influence on her son's interest in music, particularly the piano, and in the arts generally. Her first child was a daughter, Pauline; her second, Ralph Barker Gustafson, was born in Lime Ridge on 16 August 1909.

Gustafson's childhood and adolescence were spent in nearby Sherbrooke, where his father had set up as a photographer. He attended Sherbrooke High School, graduating in 1926, and remained in the Townships to attend Bishop's University at Lennoxville. He graduated with an honours B.A. in English and history in 1929. A very successful student, he placed first in his graduating class and won the Governor General's Medal. He also received prizes for a poem on music and an essay on Canadian literature; the prizes are indicative of Gustafson's early promise and of the three interests that have guyed his creative life from the beginning: poetry, music, and Canadian literature.[3] His literary tastes at this time were formed largely by the curriculum at Bishop's and by two poets on faculty there, Frank Oliver Call and Canon Frederick George Scott. Gustafson's graduating year also marked the appearance of his first publications: a short story, "The Last Experiment of Dr. Brugge," in the Bishop's literary magazine, *The Mitre*, and poems in *Willison's Monthly* and the Canadian Authors Association's *Poetry Year Book: 1928–29*.

During 1929–30 Gustafson worked as a music master at Bishop's College School and studied for his M.A. in English from Bishop's University. His thesis, "The Sensuous Imagery of Shelley and Keats," grew out of his undergraduate admiration for those poets. After receiving the M.A., Gustafson decided to continue with academic studies and, with an IODE scholarship, left Canada for Oxford in 1930. This was the beginning of a long sojourn abroad, first in England during the 1930s and then in New York during the war years and after.

Oxford required Gustafson to enter their B.A. program, and so he spent the next three years in Keble College reading for the degree. During this time, he appeared twice in the university's annual, *Oxford Poetry*, and, in his first year there, he finished his first book of poems, *The Golden Chalice* (published in 1935). It was at Oxford that Gustafson began reading his British and American contem-

poraries with an earnest, crafter's eye and revising his under-
graduate romantic attitudes to poetic style and language.

After graduating with his second B.A. in 1933, Gustafson came
back to Canada for a year and taught at St. Alban's School for Boys
in Brockville, Ontario. The following year, he returned to England
and settled in London. Private tutoring and freelance journalism
provided him with an income. In 1935 *The Golden Chalice* won
the Prix David, an award from the Quebec government. His second
book was a verse-drama, *Alfred the Great* (1937). It was also
during these years that Gustafson began his long association with
the Canadian pianist Ellen Ballon. In her company, he moved
among the élite of British society. Gustafson left England in the
summer of 1938 and, after a short stay in Sherbrooke, moved on
to New York and his second expatriate residence.

In New York, Gustafson did valuable war work for British
Information Services. As well, he began an editing venture that was
to become most important for modern Canadian literature. Allan
Lane of Penguin Books commissioned Gustafson to put together
an inexpensive, pocket-sized anthology of Canadian poetry for
Canadian soldiers abroad; this was to be the first of a series of
Penguin anthologies that Gustafson would edit. The task forced
him to gather his thoughts about the history of Canadian literature
and, more importantly for his own poetry, to orient himself
towards particular modern and contemporary developments. The
Anthology of Canadian Poetry (English) appeared in 1942, and it
is, as Wendy Keitner has noted, Gustafson's "single most important
critical contribution to the development of Canadian literature."[4]

There were other literary projects during the early 1940s. With
A.J.M. Smith, Gustafson worked on another, unpublished anthol-
ogy, titled "Canadian Poetry Today."[5] In 1943 he edited a Cana-
dian issue of *Voices* and put together a collection of Canadian
poetry for New Directions, *A Little Anthology of Canadian Poetry*.
Capitalizing on the success of the first Penguin anthology, he edited
a new collection devoted solely to contemporary Canadian writing,
*Canadian Accent: A Collection of Stories and Poems by Contem-
porary Writers from Canada* (1944). A sequel, "Canadian Accent
II," for which he chose work by Raymond Knister, Irving Layton,
Earle Birney, and Emily Carr, had to be abandoned for financial
reasons.

Amid all this activity on behalf of other Canadian writers, Gustafson continued with his own writing. *The Sewanee Review* published a group of his poems in 1940, and these were offprinted as *Poems* (1940). *Epithalamium in Time of War*, written for his sister's marriage in 1941, was printed privately, as was his *Lyrics Unromantic* (1942). His second major collection, *Flight into Darkness*, was published in 1944.

His editorial activities put Gustafson in contact with a great number of Canadian writers, and consequently, despite his expatriate situation, he was always in-the-know about literary matters in Canada. In 1945 John Sutherland asked him to be the New York correspondent for *First Statement*. Gustafson accepted and continued in that capacity when *First Statement* merged with *Preview* to become *Northern Review*. (He resigned in 1947 over the Sutherland-Finch affair.)[6] While Gustafson worked very hard for these magazines, gaining them American readers and reviews, he was never a partisan of any particular coterie. When it came to literary politics, he was national and international in scope. Intellectually, and temperamentally perhaps, he was probably closest to Patrick Anderson's *Preview* group (he had solid relationships with A.J.M. Smith and F.R. Scott), but Gustafson had always been his own man, dedicated to his craft and to the support of those poets whose work evinced a similar dedication.[7]

At war's end, Gustafson turned to writing full-time. He also turned to prose fiction, writing a number of short stories based on experiences from childhood and adolescence. "The Pigeon" won a *Northern Review* prize and was anthologized in Martha Foley's *Best American Short Stories* (1950). Previously, Foley had taken "The Human Fly" for her 1948 collection. *The Atlantic Monthly*, *The Canadian Forum*, and *Queen's Quarterly* all published Gustafson's short fiction.[8] Following these successes, Gustafson began work on a novel based on the life of his dynamiter-uncle, John Gustafson, set in a fictionalized Lime Ridge. Entitled "No Music in the Nightingale: An Ironic Comedy," this work occupied much of his time and energy throughout the 1950s, but it has never been published. The late 1950s also saw Gustafson edit his most popular anthology, *The Penguin Book of Canadian Verse* (1958; revised in 1967, 1975, and 1984).

This editorial work probably spurred him on to write more

poetry himself; also, his contacts with e.e. cummings, William Carlos Williams, W.H. Auden, and Stephen Spender in New York at this time might have been an influence. However, the primary reason for the redirection of Gustafson's creative energies back to poetry seems to have been the arrival of a benevolent muse. Her name was Elisabeth Renninger, and she became the "Betty" of his subsequent dedications. They married in 1958, and she has remained as constant in her power to inspire as she has in her companionship. Gustafson's good fortune in his marriage initiated an outburst of poetic creativity that resulted in the first full flowering of his genius. In 1960 he published two volumes: *Rivers among Rocks* was a retrospective collection of much of his early work and the poetry written in the previous decade; *Rocky Mountain Poems*, a sequence written in the mountains and the Yukon during a cross-Canada trip made with Betty in 1959, heralded new departures in style and approach. *Rocky Mountain Poems* won the Borestone Mountain Poetry Award in 1961. It was a turning-point volume for Gustafson and for modern Canadian poetry.

The cross-Canada trip also heralded Gustafson's return to his country and to his place of origin. In 1963, after a year travelling in Britain, Europe, and Scandinavia, he accepted a position in the English Department at Bishop's University and bought a house in North Hatley, Quebec, a resort town a short distance from Lennoxville. During the 1960s he continued to travel, visiting Britain, Czechoslovakia, Hungary, Greece, Egypt, Italy, and Turkey. He also became a music critic for the CBC, reporting annually on the Wagner festivals at Bayreuth, Germany. In 1966 he was appointed poet-in-residence at Bishop's and became a charter member of the League of Canadian Poets. He ended the decade, characteristically, with a volume of old and new poems, *Ixion's Wheel* (1969).

Gustafson's experiences in Czechoslovakia resulted in yet a new surge of poetry dealing with political and social events. "Nocturne: Prague 1968" (in *Theme and Variations for Sounding Brass* [1972]) was presented as a mixed-media event at Bishop's and then at Hofstra University, Hampstead, New York, in 1970. The following year, a Canada Council Senior Arts Award allowed him to visit Japan and the South Pacific, where he read his work in Hawaii and Australia. His first *Selected Poems* appeared in 1972, and in 1973 Mount Allison University honoured his achievements and contributions to Canadian literature with an honorary D.Litt. More honours followed the publication of *Fire on Stone* in 1974. This volume won the Governor General's Award for Poetry in English and the A.J.M. Smith Award for Poetry from Michigan State University.

Throughout the 1970s, Gustafson continued to travel and read his work abroad. With Al Purdy, he toured the Soviet Union as a Canadian Department of External Affairs delegate in 1976. *Soviet Poems: Sept. 13 to Oct. 5, 1976* was published in 1978, a year after his retirement from Bishop's. Since his retirement, Gustafson has continued to live in North Hatley, travelling whenever possible and publishing quality work at a rate any poet would envy. *Corners in the Glass* appeared in 1977, followed by *Gradations of Grandeur* (1979).⁹ Gustafson's publications of the 1980s include *The Moment Is All: Selected Poems, 1944–83* (1983); *At the Ocean's Verge: Selected Poems* (1984); *Directives of Autumn* (1984); a collection of poems entitled *Impromptus* (1984), most of which are taken from earlier volumes; two chapbooks, *Solidarnosc: Prelude* (1983) and *Twelve Landscapes* (1985); and *Winter Prophets* (1987). Gustafson also edited a fourth, revised edition of *The Penguin Book of Canadian Verse* (1984), and in 1989 Sono Nis Press of Victoria published two volumes of his *Collected Poems*. Also, in 1989, the National Film Board released a documentary on him, directed by Donald Winkler, entitled "Winter Prophecies: The Poetry of Ralph Gustafson." The 1990s are heralded by *Shadows on the Grass* (1991), and *Configurations at Midnight* (1992). Gustafson still writes his poetry in longhand, believing that ". . . poetry needs a sensuous touch."¹⁰

NOTES

¹ Ralph Gustafson, "Worthwhile Visitations," rev. of *Notes on Visitations: Poems 1936–1975*, by George Woodcock, *Canadian Literature*, No. 71 (Winter 1976), p. 91.

² I have taken most of the details of Gustafson's biography from Wendy Keitner's study *Ralph Gustafson*, Twayne's World Authors Series, No. 531 (Boston: Twayne, 1979).

³ Gustafson has been a music critic for the CBC since 1960 and possesses an internationally known and respected collection of piano recordings.

[4] Keitner, p. 25. It should be noted here as well that Louis Dudek and Michael Gnarowski's failure to include any articles that discuss this anthology and its revised editions, or Gustafson's other editorial activities during these years, renders their book *The Making of Modern Poetry in Canada: Essential Articles on Contemporary Canadian Poetry in English* (Toronto: Ryerson, 1967) seriously flawed.

[5] While the project never came to fruition, Smith used some of the material in his *The Book of Canadian Poetry: A Critical and Historical Anthology* (Chicago: Univ. of Chicago Press, 1943); see Keitner, p. 157.

[6] Sutherland's attack on Robert Finch, whose *Poems* (1946) had won the Governor General's Award for Poetry in English, in *Northern Review* (Aug.–Sept. 1947), resulted in a number of the magazine's editors and correspondents resigning and dissociating themselves from Sutherland's critical statements.

[7] Regarding his relationship with Smith, for example, Gustafson told Keitner: ". . . [We] share a deep concern for craftsmanship. My admiration for his work may have set an occasional limit to my exuberance about what was moving me but certainly I am not conscious of ever being 'influenced.' " Ralph Gustafson, letter to Wendy Keitner, 29 April 1973, Gustafson Papers, Queen's University Archives, Kingston, Ont.

[8] Gustafson's stories have been collected in two editions: *The Brazen Tower: Short Stories* (Tillsonburg, Ont: Ascham, 1974); and *The Vivid Air: Collected Stories* (Victoria: Sono Nis, 1980).

[9] Sono Nis Press first published *Gradations of Grandeur* in 1979, but without the author's revisions: these were incorporated in the 1982 edition, also published by Sono Nis.

[10] Marion McCormack, "A Poet's Laurels," *The Gazette* [Montreal], 4 March 1989, p. K10.

A.M. Klein (1909–72)

NOREEN GOLFMAN

IT IS TEMPTING to say at the outset that the facts of Abraham Moses Klein's life are probably the most interesting and strange of the Canadian modernist poets. Since Klein's death in 1972, the mystery surrounding his latter withdrawal from creative and public activity has not only intensified but it has also been the source of a celebrated debate during the 1974 University of Ottawa Klein Symposium when the rapscallion Irving Layton offered his own psychological interpretation of Klein's apparent inability to maintain a grip on life itself.[1] The curiosity directed at Klein's silent years is understandable, however, given the astonishing amount of energy that Klein was able to tap prior to this time. Indeed, no Canadian poet was as diversified, enterprising, and vigorous as A.M. Klein before the 1950s.

Born to Kalman and Yetta Klein in 1909 in Ratno, a town in the Ukraine, Klein entered the world at a significant moment for twentieth-century Jews.[2] Eastern European Jews like Klein's parents had been living with the ugly presence of anti-Semitism almost all their lives, but the terrifying and bloody pogroms of the 1880s eventually forced about four million Jews to flee their homes in search of safety in North America. In 1910, the infant Abraham Moses Klein arrived with his parents in Montreal, the French-Canadian city that would become the imaginative and moral centre of the poet's universe.

Klein grew up in the ghetto world of a burgeoning, cosmopolitan Montreal, surrounded by immigrants at once culturally bound together in need and hope of a secure future and alienated from the world of urban North America. Kalman, a devout, grey-bearded, learned Jew, offered his son the very model of old-world piety that Klein would come both to idealize and to wrestle with all his life. By his father and religious tutors Klein was thoroughly educated in the observances of Jewish orthodoxy, an orthodoxy with a particularly Chassidic flavour. Baron Byng High School (home to Layton, Richler, et al.) ushered Klein through new doors leading to fond attachments to Latin and English poets. This experience determined a new future for the bright student who steadily inclined to secular, especially literary, writing.

As David Lewis, Klein's life-long friend, told it, Klein first announced his intention to be a poet when the two walked home from Baron Byng one day.[3] Klein was then just sixteen years old, and already the romance of literary life was calling him away from rabbinical pursuits. The would-be poet did develop a fierce commitment to Zionism at this time, however, a commitment encouraged by participation in the youth organization Canadian Young Judaea. Klein became editor of the group's monthly magazine, the *Judaean*, in 1928, and he continued this responsibility until 1932. Thus began a career as editor and journalist.

When Klein entered McGill University in 1926, his long-term ambition, and eventual achievement, was a law degree. His obvious pleasures, however, involved studying economics with the notoriously wise-cracking Stephen Leacock and reading Chaucer, Spenser, and Milton with English professor George Latham. Characteristic of a lifetime of extracurricular passions, Klein wore several hats, "as a Zionist, a public debater, and an aspiring poet" (Caplan, p. 47). Probably the most significant experience for Klein involved his association with a group of friends who later came to be identified as the McGill School, a coterie of self-styled intellectuals who fashioned themselves as young Pounds, Eliots, and Yeatses. A.J.M. Smith, F.R. Scott, Leo Kennedy, and Leon Edel had been promoting modernism in *The McGill Fortnightly Review* in the mid-1920s. With the encouragement and support of these young men, Klein gained the confidence to identify himself as a literary figure with poetic dreams.

Although he never published anything in the *Fortnightly*, Klein did write several parodic pieces for the *McGill Daily* in 1927. That same year *The Menorah Journal* [New York] published his sonnet sequence "Five Characters." Klein was now a published poet at eighteen. In 1928 *Poetry* [Chicago] accepted his "A Sequence of Songs." Published work in *The Canadian Mercury* and *The Canadian Forum* soon followed. With David Lewis, Klein launched *The McGilliad* in 1930 — or the "McGill Yid" as he was fond of calling it — a campus magazine with a decidedly high-brow cosmopolitan flavour. A photograph of the editorial board of *The McGilliad* images a remarkably mature and serious-looking group of students whose gentlemanly gazes belie their youth (Caplan, p. 56).

In 1930 Klein entered the Law Faculty at the Université de Montréal. He continued to work on his poetry, collecting mostly unpublished lyrics in privately bound volumes: "XXII Sonnets" (1931), "Gestures Hebraic" (1932), "Gestures Hebraic and Poems" (1932), "Poems" (1932), and "Poems" (1934).[4] Less well known is the fact that during this period Klein was also experimenting with short fiction, writing stories with a pungent Jewish flavour. The Depression of the early 1930s, during which Klein studied law and wrote poems and fiction, strained the financial limits of Klein's family. After Kalman's death in 1933, Klein was charged with the responsibility of providing for the rest of the family. In 1934, he and his partner, Max Garmaise, opened a law practice that scarcely saw traffic. Yet Klein's experience with both the criminal world and the judicial system provided fresh satiric material for his poems and stories.

In 1935 Klein married Bessie Kozlov, and the pressures of looking after a family intensified. Determined to make it as a poet, if not as a successful lawyer, Klein doggedly persisted in his quest to be published. The American editors of *Opinion* and *The Menorah*

Journal encouraged that quest, putting Klein in contact with an influential group of admirers that included Ludwig Lewisohn, "one of the deans of American Jewish letters" (Caplan, p. 71). In 1936 two of Klein's longer pieces appeared in *New Provinces: Poems of Several Authors*, officially confirming his identity as a modernist poet. That year the Behrman's Jewish Book House accepted a manuscript that would come to be known as *Hath Not a Jew* .... Klein's first published collection of poetry would be distinguished by Lewisohn's Foreword announcing Klein as an "authentic" voice of Anglo-Jewish letters.

Despite the encouragement Klein must have felt by such acceptance, his law practice floundered, and the pressure to be financially solvent and widely recognized must have been trying. In 1938, perhaps partly as a pleasant diversion, Klein assumed the editorship of the prestigious *Canadian Jewish Chronicle*, a role that he would fulfil admirably until 1955 by writing weekly columns describing Jewish culture and political life with rhetorical gusto.[5] As if he did not have anything else to do, Klein also accepted the prominent Jewish businessman Sam Bronfman's offer to be his chief speech writer. As elected-president of the Canadian Jewish Congress for twenty years, Bronfman relied on Klein for tasks as varied as writing Congress correspondence to prefacing anonymously a special Seagram's publication.[6] Thus the 1930s ended with a spirited flourish for Klein whose energetic commitment to so many public roles actually increased in the next decade.

The successful reception of *Hath Not a Jew* ... in 1940 guaranteed Klein's next collection, which the Jewish Publication Society published as *Poems* in 1944. During the war years, Klein continued to work for Bronfman, edit the *Chronicle*, practise law, raise a family, write poetry, fiction, and drama, and associate with both the *Preview* and the *First Statement* writers in Montreal. *Preview*'s more European, traditionally modern interests were more congenial to Klein's moral-aesthetic temperament, however, although "more than anyone else, Klein managed to straddle both groups" (Caplan, p. 98). In 1944 Klein's mock-epic satire of the Third Reich leaders, *The Hitleriad*, was published by New Directions to mixed reviews. No disappointment, however, could match the profound grief occasioned by news of the Holocaust. Perhaps Klein's involvement with the CCF in 1944 was generated by a timely need to bring reason and honour to political life. Although he decided not to run for political office in the 1945 general election, Klein held allegiance to a party largely built by David Lewis and F.R. Scott. Meanwhile, he accepted an offer to be visiting lecturer in poetry at McGill, a post held until 1948.

In the late 1940s Klein turned his creative attentions to his Quebec environment. The successful result was *The Rocking Chair and Other Poems* of 1948, Klein's crowning poetic achievement and the winner of the Governor General's Award for Poetry in English. In 1949 political life called him again. This time Klein campaigned on a Labour-Zionist platform for the CCF in Montreal. His resounding defeat ended a short, albeit intensely committed, association with the political arena. No doubt an invitation to travel to the newly formed state of Israel in 1949 mitigated the humiliation of an election loss. That fortunate journey thus furnished the rich experience to be shaped as *The Second Scroll*, Klein's only published novel, an obviously Joyce-influenced quest for spiritual meaning in the modern age (1951). Joyce had been one of Klein's consuming passions since his McGill days. Before *The Second Scroll* appeared in print, Klein had written three provocative, albeit eccentric, pieces on *Ulysses*.

Although he was preparing a volume of *Selected Poems* for the Ryerson Press in the early 1950s, Klein never returned fully to creative, or public, life after *The Second Scroll*. Illness, mental depression, and eventually Bessie's death in 1971 contributed to Klein's own death in 1972, after almost twenty years of silence.

NOTES

[1] Ralph Gustafson, "Informal Reflections on the Klein Symposium," in *The A.M. Klein Symposium*, ed. and introd. Seymour Mayne, Re-appraisals: Canadian Writers (Ottawa: Univ. of Ottawa Press, 1975), pp. 81–84.

[2] The principal and indispensable biographical source for this discussion is Usher Caplan, *Like One That Dreamed: A Portrait of A.M. Klein*, foreword Leon Edel (Toronto: McGraw-Hill Ryerson, 1982). Further references to this work appear in the text.

[3] As told to David Kaufman in his film, *A.M. Klein: The Poet as Landscape*, Marlin Motion Pictures Ltd., 1978.

⁴ These privately bound volumes may still be found in the National Archives of Canada. The poems are available in *The Complete Poems of A.M. Klein*, ed. and introd. Zailig Pollock (Toronto: Univ. of Toronto Press, 1990).

⁵ See A.M. Klein, *Beyond Sambation: Selected Essays and Editorials 1928–1955*, ed. M.W. Steinberg and Usher Caplan (Toronto: Univ. of Toronto Press, 1982).

⁶ Bronfman's name was attached to the preface but Klein was the true author: Stephen Leacock, *Canada: The Foundations of Its Future* (Montreal: Gazette Printing, 1941), pp. [ix–xv]. See Caplan, p. 84.

Dorothy Livesay (1909–)

PAUL DENHAM

DOROTHY KATHLEEN LIVESAY was born 12 October 1909 in Winnipeg. Her mother was Florence Hamilton Randal Livesay, who wrote and published poems and stories, translated Ukrainian folk songs, and was conversant with the Canadian literary scene. Her father was John Frederick Bligh Livesay, a journalist, who was manager of the Western Associated Press and, in 1917, was one of the founders of the Canadian Press. Her younger sister was named Helen Sophia. In 1920 the Livesays moved to Toronto; they occupied a house in the Annex, the area north and west of the University of Toronto, and also built a country house, "Woodlot," to the west of the city near Clarkson, where they were neighbours of Mazo de la Roche. Dorothy attended Glen Mawr, a private girls' school, and in 1927 enrolled in modern languages (French and Italian) at Trinity College, University of Toronto.

During her first year at Trinity, she had her first book of poems, *Green Pitcher*, published and in 1929 won the Jardine Memorial

Prize for her poem "City Wife" (1929).[1] She spent her third year (1929–30) studying in France at the Université d'Aix-Marseille and, after receiving her B.A. from Trinity in 1931, spent a year at the Sorbonne, where she earned a Diplôme d'études supérieures in 1932, with a thesis on the influence of metaphysical and *symboliste* poetry on modern English poetry. The advent of the Depression, attendance in Toronto at lectures by the American anarchist Emma Goldman, and contact with volatile social conditions in Paris all contributed to her interest in communism.[2] By the time her second book of lyrics, *Signpost*, was published in 1932, she had lost interest in writing personal poems and was contributing strongly committed Marxist poems to the short-lived Toronto-based communist paper *Masses* (1932–34) and working in branches of the Progressive Arts Club. She studied at the School of Social Work of the University of Toronto during 1932–33, did field work with the Family Welfare Agency in Montreal, and then worked for a relief agency in Englewood, New Jersey. Returning to Canada in 1935, she wrote her long poems "The Outrider" [1935] and "Day and Night" (1936). The latter appeared in the first issue of *Canadian Poetry Magazine*.

She served on the editorial board of *New Frontier* (1936–37), a leftist journal whose purpose was "to acquaint the Canadian public with the work of those writers and artists who are expressing a positive reaction to the social scene."[3] She contributed several poems and stories to this journal and, when she moved to Vancouver in 1936, continued to work for it. In 1937 she married Duncan Cameron Macnair, and they settled in North Vancouver. In 1940 and 1942 their children, Peter and Marcia, were born. Together with her husband, Livesay helped organize a Vancouver branch of the Progressive Arts Club and the West End Community Centre.[4] She became disillusioned with communism, partly as a result of the Nazi-Soviet pact (August 1939), but continued to be involved in social and political affairs as well as literary ones. In 1941, with Alan Crawley, Anne Marriott, and Floris Clark McLaren, she helped found the little magazine *Contemporary Verse*, which for ten years provided almost the only Canadian outlet for modern poetry west of Ontario.

In 1944 her book of poems, *Day and Night*, containing several of her social poems from the 1930s, was published and won the

Governor General's Award for Poetry in English. In 1946 she went to Europe for *The Toronto Daily Star* and wrote a series of articles on post-war conditions. In 1947 another book of poems, *Poems for People*, won a second Governor General's Award for Poetry in English; in the same year, the Royal Society of Canada awarded her the Lorne Pierce Medal for her contribution to Canadian literature.

During the war, having actively opposed the treatment of Japanese Canadians in British Columbia as enemy aliens,[5] she wrote a long "poem for voices" on this subject, "Call My People Home," which was broadcast by CBC Radio in 1949 and published as part of a book of poems with the same title the following year. In the 1950s she collaborated with the composer Barbara Pentland on a chamber opera, *The Lake*, based on the experiences of Susan Allison, the first white woman settler in the Similkameen region of British Columbia.[6] It had one performance on CBC Radio in 1954 and is unpublished. In 1955 she published *New Poems* with Jay Macpherson's Emblem Books, and in 1957 Desmond Pacey edited her *Selected Poems*.

During the early 1950s Livesay taught in various capacities for the Extension Department of the University of British Columbia and the YWCA. She received a secondary teacher's diploma from the University of British Columbia in 1956 and then taught for two years in a Vancouver high school. In 1958 she went to the University of London for further study in methods of teaching English. While she was away, her husband died suddenly. She worked at UNESCO headquarters in Paris and then went to Northern Rhodesia (now Zambia), where she taught English for three years. Returning to Vancouver in 1963, she came in contact with that city's lively poetry scene and began writing again after a lapse of several years. *The Colour of God's Face* (1964; later revised as "Zambia") grew out of her African experiences. In 1966 she earned an M.Ed. at the University of British Columbia with a thesis on "Rhythm and Sound in Contemporary Canadian Poetry." Since then she has published several new books of poetry, most notably *The Unquiet Bed* (1967), *Plainsongs* (1969; revised and extended 1971), *Ice Age* (1975), *The Phases of Love* (1983), and *Feeling the Worlds: New Poems* (1984), as well as a book of linked stories, *A Winnipeg Childhood* (1973), which was expanded and republished as *Beginnings* in 1988, and a novella, *The Husband* (1990). Other recent books have made possible an extended view of her earlier development: *The Documentaries* (1968) collected some of her earlier long poems; *Collected Poems: The Two Seasons* (1972) made available many early and uncollected poems, though it is far from complete; *Right Hand Left Hand* (1977) is a collage of poems, stories, personal letters, documents, photographs, and journalism illustrating her life as a writer and activist during the 1930s, and *The Self-Completing Tree: Selected Poems* (1986) brings together "the selection of poems that [Livesay] would like to be remembered by."[7] Perhaps the best key to understanding Livesay's life and work is her new memoir, *Journey with My Selves* (1991). She served on the editorial boards of *Prism International* [Vancouver] and *White Pelican* [Edmonton], and in Winnipeg in 1975 she founded CV/II (*Contemporary Verse Two*), a journal of poetry and criticism. She has also written numerous reviews and articles on Canadian poetry: the most influential of these is "The Documentary Poem: A Canadian Genre."[8]

She has taught in various capacities at the University of British Columbia (1965–66), the University of New Brunswick (1966–68), the University of Alberta (1968–72), the University of Victoria (1973–74), the University of Manitoba (1974–76), the University of Ottawa (1977), Simon Fraser University (1979), and the University of Toronto (1983). In 1973 she was awarded an honorary D.Litt. by the University of Waterloo, and she is an honorary fellow of St. John's College, University of Manitoba, and of Trinity College, University of Toronto. In 1977 she was awarded a Queen's Silver Jubilee Medal. She is a founding member of the League of Canadian Poets, Amnesty International (Canada), and the Committee for an Independent Canada. Livesay now lives in Victoria, British Columbia. These days, she can write for only a half-hour at a time, due to carpal tunnel syndrome (stress-related damage to her wrist), but she still thinks it is necessary to "fight" and spends much of her time writing letters associated with her various political interests.[9]

NOTES

[1] A date in parentheses after a title indicates the year of that work's first publication. If first publication was considerably later than the year of compo-

sition, then the latter date, when available, has been indicated in square brackets. For detailed bibliographic information concerning the publishing history of Livesay's works, see Alan Ricketts, "Dorothy Livesay: An Annotated Bibliography," in *The Annotated Bibliography of Canada's Major Authors*, ed. Robert Lecker and Jack David, IV (Downsview, Ont.: ECW, 1983), 129–203.

² Dorothy Livesay, *Right Hand Left Hand*, ed. David Arnason and Kim Todd (Erin, Ont.: Porcépic, 1977), pp. 31–48, 58–60.

³ Editorial, *New Frontier*, I, No. I (April 1936), p. 3.

⁴ Helen Mintz and Barbara Coward, "The woman I am/is not what you see/move over love/make room for me," *The Grape*, 9–22 May 1973, pp. 10, 21; rpt. ("Being a Writer in the Thirties: An Interview with Dorothy Livesay") in *This Magazine*, 7, No. 4 (Jan. 1974), 20.

⁵ Dorothy Livesay, *The Documentaries* (Toronto: Ryerson, 1968), p. 32.

⁶ Barbara Pentland, "Dorothy Livesay: A Memoir," *Room of One's Own* [Dorothy Livesay Issue], 5, Nos. 1–2 (1979), 44.

⁷ Dorothy Livesay, *The Self-Completing Tree: Selected Poems* (Victoria: Porcépic, 1986), p. 3.

⁸ Dorothy Livesay, "The Documentary Poem: A Canadian Genre," in *Contexts of Canadian Criticism: A Collection of Critical Essays*, ed. Eli Mandel, Patterns of Literary Criticism, No. 9 (Chicago: Univ. of Chicago Press, 1971), pp. 267–81.

⁹ Liam Lacey, " 'I Was Always a Fighter,' " *The Globe and Mail* [Toronto], 27 June 1991, p. C1.

Anne Wilkinson (1910–61)

CHRISTOPHER ARMITAGE

ANNE WILKINSON'S strong sense of family tradition is manifest from the opening line, "These acres breathe my family,"[1] of "Summer Acres," the first poem in her first volume and in her *Collected Poems*. The eighty Beachcroft acres at Roches Point on the south end of Lake Simcoe in central Ontario had been acquired about eighty years previously by her grandfather Edmund Osler. The Osler family, in the persons of the Reverend Featherstone Lake Osler and his bride of two months, Ellen, had immigrated to Canada in April 1837. A Cornishman, he had given up a career in the Royal Navy to become a minister in the Church of England. At the urging of the Upper Canada Clergy Society, he reluctantly decided to immigrate to Ontario. Vigorously exercising his ministry, first at Bond Head south of Barrie and later at Dundas, the hard-working clergyman prospered. He and his wife had six sons and three daughters. Two of the sons became eminent lawyers;

another, William, was knighted for his services to medicine; and Edmund, financier and long-serving member of Parliament in Ottawa, was also knighted. Sir Edmund Osler was the poet's maternal grandfather. In "Summer Acres," the poet accurately describes herself: "September born, reared in the sunset hour, / I was the child of old men heavy with honour."[2]

Anne Cochran Gibbons was born on 21 September 1910 in Toronto, to Mary Elizabeth Lammond (Osler) and George Sutton Gibbons. Her father was from a family prominent in London, Ontario, and ran on the Labour-Liberal ticket in the 1917 election, only to be badly beaten. Playing around the spacious houses Eldon and Lornehurst, which belonged to an uncle and her paternal grandfather respectively, Anne spent her first eight years with apparent carefreeness in London, a city she described as "more prone to eccentric happenings than the reticent Toronto."[3] But the death of her father in 1919 resulted in Anne's return, with her mother, brother, and sister, from London to her maternal grandfather's mansion, Craigleigh, in Toronto. This large and imposing house stood on a thirteen-acre estate beside a ravine in Rosedale. Although her grandfather had been a world traveller, by the 1920s he was in his late seventies and preferred to stay home, nor would he permit his grandchildren to roam around Toronto. Thus, the household rituals of meals, visits by relatives, and the personalities of servants drew the attention of the alertly observant girl, who spent her ninth to her fourteenth years there. The importance of this period is reflected in her making it the subject of both the Epilogue to her informal history of her family, *Lions in the Way: A Discursive History of the Oslers*, and a substantial part of her autobiographical essay, "Four Corners of My World."[4] In the latter, she recounts how she was unable, shortly after Craigleigh's demolition following her grandfather's death in 1924, to rebuild it in her imagination: but time restored it to her memory in vivid detail. Meanwhile, her education proceeded informally and sporadically, much of it outside Canada. "Four Corners of My World" concludes with an account of two schools she attended while living at Santa Barbara in California: a nearby day-school run by three Canadian women and the more distant Ojai Valley School, a progressive institution that her mother had discovered through a magazine article by its eccentric founder and headmaster.

Erratic as her formal schooling may have been, she was encouraged to explore the world of books. Although in *Lions in the Way* she represents the male Oslers as having little time for music, theatre, or artists in person, she reveals the esteem in which books were held. The nursery at Craigleigh contained the standard children's classics by Hans Christian Andersen, Lewis Carroll, the Brothers Grimm, and Robert Louis Stevenson, as well as innumerable Victorian tales of piety. Her grandfather sometimes recommended books that were beyond her comprehension; thus she read Jane Austen and Thackeray "innocent of [their] irony and wit."[5] Not having learned that Kipling was unfashionable, she "wallowed" in his books until "India became the land of [her] waking dreams" (pp. 245–46). Dickens and Sir Walter Scott were "required reading for children of that era," though they provided less "blood and thunder" than *The Tower of London* and other tales by William Harrison Ainsworth (p. 246). Particularly significant in relation to the poems Anne was later to publish was her grandfather's reading aloud to the children "nursery rhymes, folk tales and ballads": "His deep bass voice still echoes in Poe's 'Raven' and 'Annabel Lee,' " which "filled us with pleasurable sadness, bringing the same mood as Arnold's 'Forgotten Merman' [sic]" (p. 246).

On 23 July 1932, Anne Gibbons married Frederick Robert Wilkinson. They had three children. The marriage was dissolved in 1953.

About the end of World War II, poems by Anne Wilkinson, then in her mid-thirties, began to appear in such periodicals as *The Canadian Forum*, *Contemporary Verse*, and *Northern Review*. Her first collection of poems, *Counterpoint to Sleep*, was published in 1951. A second collection, *The Hangman Ties the Holly*, was published in 1955. In 1956 the literary periodical *The Tamarack Review* came into existence in Toronto, with Wilkinson as one of its founding editors. In addition to her literary contributions, her generous financial help was acknowledged on various occasions as enabling the magazine to survive several of its first five years.[6] By its sixth year, she was dead; both the anthology *The First Five Years: A Selection from* The Tamarack Review (1962) and the periodical's final issue in 1982 are dedicated to her memory.

In addition to two books of poetry, she published two prose works: *Lions in the Way* (1956) and *Swann and Daphne* (1960), a fairy tale for children. These four books, which demonstrate her imaginative range and technical diversity and which appeared during the fifth decade of her life, emphasize the loss caused by her death at the age of fifty and at the height of her literary powers. A major collection entitled *The Tightrope Walker: Autobiographical Writings of Anne Wilkinson*, edited by Joan Coldwell, was released by University of Toronto Press in 1992. She died of cancer in Toronto on 10 May 1961. Ivon Owen, a fellow editor of *The Tamarack Review*, observed in his obituary notice in that magazine:

> It was perhaps impossible to know Anne Wilkinson slightly: you knew her well or she remained a stranger, a beautiful but unapproachable young woman (for neither middle age nor illness touched her face) . . . . [T]o her friends the things that mattered about Anne were the warmth of her affection, her delight in words . . . , and — most vivid memory of all — the sound of her laughter. These things, and latterly the manner in which she endured a succession of cruel blows, were known directly only to a small circle . . . . [Her four books] are eloquent of another vital element in her nature: the constant presence in her mind of the childhood that the young Anne Gibbons had lived so intensely, a childhood of a sort rare in Canadian experience — rare, paradoxically, both in its restless shiftings of locale and in its pervading atmosphere of permanence and continuity.[7]

NOTES

[1] Anne Wilkinson, "Summer Acres," in *The Collected Poems of Anne Wilkinson and a Prose Memoir*, ed. and introd. A.J.M. Smith (Toronto: Macmillan, 1968), p. 3.

[2] Wilkinson, "Collected Poems," p. 4.

[3] Anne Wilkinson, "Four Corners of My World," *The Tamarack Review*, No. 20 (Summer 1961), pp. 28–52; rpt. in Wilkinson, *Collected Poems*, p. 190.

[4] See above, note 3.

[5] Anne Wilkinson, *Lions in the Way: A Discursive History of the Oslers* (Toronto: Macmillan, 1956), p. 245. Further references to this work appear in the text.

⁶ See I[von]. M. O[wen]., "Anne Wilkinson 1910–1961," *The Tamarack Review*, No. 20 (Summer 1961), p. 27; and Robert Weaver, Editorial, *The Tamarack Review*, No. 41 (Autumn 1966), p. 4.

⁷ Owen, p. 27.

Irving Layton (1912–)

WYNNE FRANCIS

IRVING LAYTON was born near Neamtz, Roumania, on 12 March 1912. In 1913 his family moved to Montreal, where Layton lived until 1969, when he moved to Toronto. He was educated at Alexandra Public School, Baron Byng High School, Macdonald College, and McGill University, from which he obtained a master's degree in economics and political science in 1946. His first book of poems, *Here and Now*, appeared in 1945. Since then he has published close to fifty volumes of poetry, more than a dozen short stories, and more than eighty articles and reviews. He has also edited several anthologies; and he has published two collections of his voluminous correspondence and an autobiography.

Layton has won numerous prizes and awards, including a Canada Foundation Fellowship (1957), several Canada Council Fellowships and Arts Awards, and the Governor General's Award for Poetry in English (1960). He has acted as a visiting professor

(1978) and adjunct professor (1988 and 1989) at Concordia University and as poet-in-residence at the universities of Guelph (1969), Ottawa (1978), and Toronto (1981) and at Concordia University (1989). He has received honorary degrees from Bishop's and Concordia universities; and, upon his retirement in 1979 from his position as full professor at York, he was awarded a doctor of letters degree by that university. He was made an Officer in the Order of Canada in 1976. In 1981 he was nominated, by admirers in Italy, Korea, and Canada, for the Nobel Prize for Literature; he was nominated again by Italy in 1983. Most recently, in 1991, the International Festival of Authors held an evening of poetry readings in honour of Layton in Toronto.

Critics and translators have made Layton's poetry available in Italian, Greek, Spanish, Portuguese, Russian, German, Roumanian, and Korean. His work has been particularly well received in Italy, where he is frequently invited to lecture and read. Three volumes of his poems have been illustrated by Italian painters. A special translation of *The Cold Green Element* appeared in Italy in 1974 as *Il freddo verde elemento*, with an introduction by Northrop Frye.

Layton was married to Faye Lynch in 1938. There were no children from this marriage. In 1946 he married Betty Sutherland; they had a son, Max, and a daughter, Naomi. In 1961 he began living with Aviva Cantor; one son, David, was born of this union. His marriage to Harriet Bernstein, in 1978, was dissolved in 1981, after the birth of a daughter, Samantha. He is now married to Anna Pottier.

No biography has yet appeared to flesh out the facts of Layton's life. He himself, however, has seen to it that his readers know about those aspects of his childhood and youth that are important to his poetry. In his Foreword to *The Collected Poems of Irving Layton* (1971), he stated, "A poet has his images and symbols handed to him very early in life; his later poems are largely explorations he makes into the depths of his unconscious to unravel their meanings."[1] He proceeded, in that same Foreword, and in numerous subsequent prefaces, articles, and interviews, to record a selection of early impressions and experiences that have now become familiar to his readers. Thus we have learned that Layton was born circumcised (a messianic sign); that he was the youngest of eight children in the orthodox, working-class Lazarovitch family; and that he grew up, cheerful and pugnacious, in an impoverished immigrant district in Montreal. His father, he has told us, was a retiring, scrupulously pious man ("an ineffectual visionary"), who prayed in the back room and made goats'-milk cheese in the kitchen. His mother was a robust, resourceful, and vituperative woman, who opened a grocery store in her front room in order to provide a living for the family. Layton has given us colourful descriptions of the crowded flat where the children slept four-in-a-bed — except for "Issie" (the youngest), who slept with his mother until he was thirteen. He has told us of the anti-Semitic jibes and insults to which the family was subjected and how, as a small boy, he pounded his "magic broomstick" on the ceiling to silence the rowdy, drunken upstairs neighbours. We have a vivid portrait, too, of Strul, the detested brother-in-law, for whom the young Layton had a reluctant admiration and against whose example he had to struggle to avoid following in the footsteps of a colourful, boorish, and very successful peddlar.

Layton remembers most of his schoolteachers as being insensitive and dull. He makes two exceptions: Miss Benjamin of the sixth grade, who inspired his first love poem, and Mr. Saunders, the high-school teacher who stirred his young pupil's interest in poetry by giving a spirited reading of Tennyson's "Ballad of the Revenge."

The facts on which such anecdotal memories are based are not nearly as important as their mythic potential. It is as myths that they function both in Layton's real life and in his work — myths that serve both to shape his responses to later experiences and to structure his poetic rendering of them. The world, for Layton, still wears Strul's face; the obtuse critics and unimaginative academics he encounters are all versions of his insensitive schoolteachers; his mother's warm flesh, and Miss Benjamin's cleavage, are forever linked in his mind with love and poetry.

Of the 1930s (his own twenties), Layton has had less to say; but the significant facts (or their mythic projections) are all reflected in his early poems and stories. He was well known in Montreal as a stormy, radical orator. He sustained that reputation throughout the years (1933–39) he spent at Macdonald College, on the outskirts of Montreal. It was during these years, also, that he adopted the name Irving Layton, in lieu of Israel Lazarovitch. His first unhappy marriage, in 1938, soon disintegrated. In 1942 he joined the

Canadian army, from which (being considered temperamentally unsuited to army life) he was honourably discharged eleven months later.

From 1942 on, Layton's biography merges with Canadian literary history. His meeting with Louis Dudek and John Sutherland and his subsequent association with the poetry magazine *First Statement* have been documented.[2] He himself has told us how he came to write "The Swimmer" in 1943, the poem that caused him to realize that poetry was his true vocation.[3] His first two volumes appeared in the 1940s under the imprint of First Statement Press.

For the next five decades, from the 1950s through to the 1980s, Layton's life story is inextricably bound to his books: first, because he writes so directly out of his personal experience that a reader may trace, in his writings, his changing family relationships, his friendships and enmities, his divorces and love affairs, his travels, his politics, his obsessions and anathemas; and second, because, since he put poetry before all else, his personal fortunes have been largely dependent upon the success of his writing, or at least upon the public reaction to his books.

From 1945 to 1960, Layton earned a meagre living, first by tutoring and doing odd jobs such as proofreading, then by teaching in high schools during the day and, as a part-time lecturer, in colleges in the evenings. By such means, he managed to support his wife, Betty, and their two children and to finance the publication of his first fifteen books. Financial hardship apart, teaching was something Layton enjoyed and at which he was very successful. He was to remain a teacher throughout his life, both in his profession and in his role as poet-prophet.

Layton's books drew little attention from critics until the mid-1950s. By this time, however, he had gained some notoriety for challenging gentility and philistinism among Canadian readers and reviewers. His poems were known chiefly for their social realism and frank celebration of sex. About 1955 critics began to concede that his poetry had considerable merit beyond its sensational aspects. By 1957 he had received sufficient public and critical attention to attract a Canadian commercial publisher: McClelland and Stewart brought out his award-winning collection *A Red Carpet for the Sun* in 1959.[4] Thereafter both his literary and his personal fortunes began to soar.

In the 1960s Layton became a public figure known to millions of Canadians whether or not they had ever read his poems. His dynamic personality and provocative views were aired with remarkable frequency by all the mass media, and he was much in demand across the country for personal appearances, interviews, panel discussions, and readings. Reviewers in even the smallest newspapers played their part in publicizing him by loudly applauding or denouncing each of his books as they appeared. The result was that Layton acquired a public image that, while it enhanced the sales of his books, also deflected the attention of more serious literary critics. Distracted by Layton's aggressive personality and repelled by the publicity "circus," such critics were slow to come to grips with his poetry as such. If Layton suffered neglect early in his career, he has suffered since 1960 from overexposure.

Many of his friends (and his enemies) in the 1960s hoped that the publicity "bubble" would soon burst. But Layton continued to astound his public and confound his critics throughout the 1970s. Responding to Israel's military success in 1967, he began to emphasize the pride of being Jewish. This, combined with a renewed interest in the Holocaust, prompted him to write several books of poems in which his aim was to reclaim Jesus for Jews and to denounce Christians as the chief instigators of anti-Semitism. This "campaign," much advertised and publicly defended by Layton, drew outraged protests from some sectors of Canadian society; but the uproar over *For My Brother Jesus* (1976) and *The Covenant* (1977) took place largely outside the literary community. It served mainly to keep the spotlight on the man and his ideas, rather than on the poetry, though Layton protests that no such distinction exists.

Layton continued to make news in the later 1970s. His marriage to the young Harriet Bernstein, the birth of their child, the breakdown of their marriage, their divorce, and the ensuing litigation over Layton's right to visit his baby daughter, all received news coverage. And these events were also the main topics of two of his collections of poetry, *Europe and Other Bad News* (1981) and *The Gucci Bag* (1983).

Because of such a persistent and highly publicized fusion of his life and his poetry, the many Canadians who read Layton, or read of him, have strong opinions about the poet and his work. He is surely the most admired, the most scorned, the best loved, the most detested, the most exhilarating, and the most exasperating poet Canada has ever spawned. And the most talented and prolific. Perhaps he is also great; but it may take Canadians a long time to admit it, if only because Layton himself has always thought so and has told us so, again and again. Among other things, he is our self-appointed gadfly; and we, whether we like it or not, are his beloved enemy, an indispensable foil against which he continues to measure himself and to find us wanting.

At eighty, Layton has not finished with us yet. In the last ten years, he has published *A Wild Peculiar Joy: Selected Poems 1945–82* (1982), *Shadows on the Ground* (portfolio, 1982), *The Gucci Bag* (1983), *A Spider Danced a Cosy Jig* (edited by E. Cameron), *Where Burning Sappho Loved* (bilingual Greek-English edition, 1985), a book of love poems, *Dance with Desire* (1986), *A Tall Man Executes a Jig* (portfolio, with Salvatore Fiume, 1985), *Final Reckoning: Poems 1982–86* (1987), *Fortunate Exile* (1987), *A Wild Peculiar Joy: Selected Poems 1945–1989* (1989), and a selected bilingual Italian-English edition of this last book, *Tutto sommato: poesie 1945–1988* (1989). *Fornalutx: Selected Poems 1928–1990* was published in 1992. In addition to his poetry, Layton has published two volumes of his correspondence: *Wild Gooseberries: Selected Letters 1939–1989* (edited by Francis Mansbridge, 1989), and *Irving Layton/Robert Creeley Correspondence* (1990). His autobiography, *Waiting for the Messiah*, was published in 1985. Given Layton's continued energy and output, it looks as if he will have his way: "I want to go into the sunset with both pitchforks blazing."[5]

NOTES

[1] Irving Layton, Foreword, in his *The Collected Poems of Irving Layton* (Toronto: McClelland and Stewart, 1971), n. pag.

[2] Wynne Francis, "Montreal Poets of the Forties," *Canadian Literature*, No. 14 (Autumn 1962), pp. 21–34.

[3] Irving Layton, Preface, in his *The Laughing Rooster* (Toronto: McClelland and Stewart, 1964), p. 19.

[4] In 1952, at the instigation of Raymond Souster, Layton had begun an intense correspondence with Cid Corman, Robert Creeley, and numerous other

young American poets. The letters reveal that he was very intent upon impressing them with his own poetry and with that of Dudek and Souster and that he was not at all receptive to Black Mountain poetics. The result of the correspondence is to be measured rather in terms of publications. Layton was the first Canadian poet to be featured in Corman's poetry magazine, *Origin*, and he guest-edited a Canadian issue of that magazine (No. 18 [Winter–Spring 1956]). He was listed as a contributing editor to Creeley's *Black Mountain Review* (1954–57), which also published several of his poems. Creeley's Divers Press brought out *In the Midst of My Fever* in 1954. In 1956 another young American, Jonathan Williams, published *The Improved Binoculars* in a handsome edition with an enthusiastic introduction by William Carlos Williams. *A Laughter in the Mind* (1958) also appeared under the imprint of Williams' select Jargon Press. None of these books, nor any of the eight other titles that Layton published in Canada during that decade, shows any influence of the Pound-Williams-Olson tradition to which the correspondence with the Americans had exposed him. All during this period, Layton was developing his own style and his own theory of poetry.

By a quirk of fate, Jonathan Williams' publication of *The Improved Binoculars* served to launch Layton on his public career. Lorne Pierce of Ryerson Press had agreed to distribute a thousand copies of this book in Canada under the Ryerson imprint. As fate would have it, the proofs arrived late on Pierce's desk; it was while the books were actually waiting at customs that the Ryerson board balked at what they read in a Layton poem. A Methodist publishing house, they felt, simply could not lend its name to a book containing such images as ". . . the blood and balls / of Christ" ("The Poetic Process" [p. 90]). (In later collections, the phrase has been changed to ". . . the blood and gall / of Christ" [*The Collected Poems*, p. 156].)

Layton's disappointment and fury at the withdrawal of Ryerson's support boiled over into every available news outlet. His public denunciation of the timidity and prudery of the Canadian publishers in general evoked a challenge from Jack McClelland. The result was that Layton acquired an important Canadian commercial publisher; the rest is literary history. After the publication of *A Red Carpet for the Sun* (1959), Layton's connection with the American poets dwindled into insignificance.

5 Irving Layton, Foreword, in his *Droppings from Heaven* (Toronto: McClelland and Stewart, 1979), p. 13.

P.K. Page (1916–)

JOHN ORANGE

PERHAPS the most noticeable characteristic of P.K. Page's life has been her breadth of experience. Since her father was a career soldier, the family settled in a number of places in Canada, and, after she married a diplomat, she lived in various locations around the world. It is no wonder, then, that her writings and drawings present a wide variety of images and reflect a great deal of movement, while, at the same time, they seem to search backward and forward for what could be called (metaphorically) "home."

Patricia Kathleen Page was born on 23 November 1916 in Swanage, Dorset, to Rose Laura (Whitehouse) and Lionel F. Page while her father was on a tour of duty in Britain. He had come to Canada in 1903 and had tried farming and brokerage before taking a commission in the Thirty-Fifth Central Alberta Horse prior to the outbreak of the First World War. He had joined the Fifth Canadian Battalion in 1914 and then worked his way up the ranks,

138

while serving in France and Belgium, to lieutenant colonel in command of the Fiftieth Battalion in 1917. When Patricia was two years old, the family returned home to Red Deer, Alberta. By the time she was old enough to begin school, the family had relocated to Winnipeg, where Patricia attended River Heights Public School for six years. In the late 1920s when her father took command of Lord Strathcona's Horse (Royal Canadians), the family moved to Calgary, and her education was completed at St. Hilda's School for Girls, except for one year spent in an experimental educational system in England when her father was sent to staff college in Sheerness. Since, in Alberta, grade eleven was sufficient to qualify for university, Page ended her formal education at the age of seventeen, feeling that she had all she needed or wanted of school, at least for the time being.

Her parents had what she calls a "memory for rhythmic utter-ances,"[1] so she grew up in an environment where poetry was quoted often and with enthusiasm. She grew into writing quite naturally in her teens. At that time, she was called "Patsy," though, to avoid teasing from her friends, she called her writing self "P.K." (Besides, she like the letter *K* a great deal; to her it seemed to hold magic.)[2] It was during a year's stay in England in 1934 (the family had moved again, this time to Halifax) that she had a poem called "The Moth" published in *The Observer* [London], 2 Dec. 1934, p. 35.

When her father was appointed district commanding officer the next year in Rothesay, New Brunswick, near Saint John, Page began to look for work. From time to time, she worked with D.B. Holly reading and writing dialogues for a CBC Radio series. She also reviewed children's books and was persuaded to join a friend who was developing a children's theatre in Saint John. In order to save this new little theatre royalty expenses, Page wrote a play for them called *Silver Pennies; or, The Land of Honesty*, which was performed in 1935 around the same time *The Canadian Bookman* published her poem "The Chinese Rug" (17, No. 5 [June 1935], 73). She acted in theatre productions and worked as a salesclerk in the book section of a department store in Saint John.

While living in Rothesay and working in Saint John in the later 1930s, Page made a number of contacts with people who encour-aged her writing. She responded to an advertisement for a poetry contest in New York, only to learn later that all the contestants who entered won. On the list of local winners was the name and address of John Sutherland, who was convalescing from tuberculosis in nearby Hampton. Page drove out to meet him, and thus they began an important friendship.[3] Two friends from the theatre persuaded her to join the Canadian Authors Association with them, and it was at a convention just outside Montreal that Page met Anne Marriott, who mentioned that Alan Crawley was starting a poetry magazine out west and that she ought to send him some poems. *Canadian Poetry Magazine* and *Saturday Night* were publishing Page's poems in 1939 and 1940, and Crawley was very encouraging and helpful to her when she sent him poems in the fall of 1941 for the first numbers of *Contemporary Verse*. She also tried her hand at a short story while she was living in the Maritimes, and the publisher to whom she sent it suggested that it was really an outline for a novel. Consequently she spent some time developing a novel called *The Sun and the Moon*, which she began sending to publishing companies in 1941. Macmillan wrote back that they would like to publish the novel but could not because of the paper shortage.

The turbulence of the war had scattered her family during this period. While her father was commander of "Z" Force in Iceland and her brother served as midshipman in the North Atlantic, Page lived with her mother in New River Beach, New Brunswick. The British took over the facilities in Iceland after four months, and her father returned home. Page set out in the fall of 1941 for Montreal. She did clerical and research work and lived in a boardinghouse on Sherbrooke Street. Soon she was introduced to Patrick Anderson at a party, and he invited her to a meeting of writers interested in starting a new journal called *Preview*. Out of this association, Page met F.R. Scott, Neufville Shaw, and eventually other Montreal writers such as A.J.M. Smith, Ronald Hambleton, Leo Kennedy, and A.M. Klein. The *Preview* group made up each number of their magazine by discussions leading to consensus, and Page, who was now a member, learned a good deal about poetry from their debates. She not only had outlets in *Preview* and in Alan Crawley's magazine, but also in *The Canadian Forum*, *Poetry* [Chicago], and in John Sutherland's new magazine, started later in 1942, called *First Statement*.

The next few years were tremendously important and productive. Macmillan surprised Page with a telegram saying that they were ready to publish *The Sun and the Moon*. By this time, the novel embarrassed her, and she mentioned withdrawing it to a friend who convinced her that since it was honestly felt when it was written, she should publish it. Page agreed to go ahead with it, but she decided to hide behind the pseudonym Judith Cape. Besides publishing the novel in 1944, Page published a group of poems in a book called *Unit of Five* along with Ronald Hambleton, James Wreford, Louis Dudek, and Raymond Souster. She also won the Oscar Blumenthal Prize for a group of five poems published in *Poetry* [Chicago].

In the summer of that year, she returned to Halifax because her father, now Major General Lionel Page, D.S.O., was dying. In the fall, she moved with her mother to Victoria, where she acted as regional editor for *Northern Review*, an amalgamation of *Preview* and *First Statement*. (She had done a good deal of the production work on *Preview*, and her leaving contributed to the death of that publication.) In 1946 her first book of poems, *As Ten, as Twenty*, was published by Ryerson Press in Toronto. A group of five poems published in *Contemporary Verse* the same year earned Page the Bertram Warr Award.

In the spring of 1946, she moved to Ottawa to begin work with the National Film Board, where she did research and wrote scripts for films and filmstrips for a wide variety of government departments and agencies. When William Arthur Irwin, a political reporter for a number of newspapers and later an editor for *Maclean's*, became the chairman of the NFB in 1950, he met Page and they were married that December. Three years later Arthur Irwin embarked on a diplomatic career when he was appointed Canadian high commissioner in Australia.

During her three-year stay in Australia (1953–56), Page continued to write, and she also published her second book, *The Metal and the Flower* (1954), which won the Governor General's Award for Poetry in English. Her husband's next posting was as ambassador to Brazil, and, when she accompanied him there in 1957, a combination of factors caused her to stop writing poems and stories, though she did keep a journal. She learned to speak Portuguese, which took up a good deal of her time alongside her other duties, but mostly she was simply overwhelmed by the extraordinary beauty of the country and the wonder of its people. "Well, I think Brazil gave me a whole dimension or emphasized a dimension that I had, I don't know how to explain it," she once said, "but I honestly felt in a kind of way that my consciousness was altered."[4] Her previously secondary interest in drawing now became her major interest, and she did not publish any poems between 1956 and 1967. Instead, she became fascinated with problems of spatial perception and design. She studied drawing with Frank Schaeffer, and, by 1960, she had an exhibition in Toronto and had some drawings reproduced in *The Tamarack Review*. This is not to suggest that her interest in poetry had changed by any means. In fact the president of Brazil invited Page and two other women poets to address the Academia Brazileira de Letras (in Portuguese), partly as a way of getting women writers recognized by that group, and she was received very well.

When Arthur Irwin was named ambassador to Mexico and Guatemala (1960–64), Page's interest in drawing and painting increased. She spent each autumn of 1959 and 1960 in New York while her husband attended the General Assembly meetings of the United Nations; consequently, she took the opportunity to study etching at Pratt Graphics and at the Art Students' League. On Saturdays she would travel to Mount Vernon for lessons with Charles Seliger, and she also learned a great deal at the Marion Willard Gallery. She has tried crayon, rapidograph, oil, water colour, egg tempera on wood, and other techniques in her art. When she lived in Mexico, her increased knowledge and skills led to a number of exhibitions in that country. She was also represented in an exhibition at the National Gallery in Ottawa. Since then, her drawings and paintings (exhibited under the name P.K. Irwin) have been purchased by a number of galleries, including the Art Gallery of Ontario, and she has exhibited and published drawings in a variety of places in Canada.

In 1964 Page and Irwin settled in Victoria, and soon after that she began to write poetry once again. *Cry Ararat! Poems New and Selected* was published in 1967, and it included reproductions of a number of Page's drawings. Throughout the 1970s she published in various magazines, mostly in the West, and continued to experiment in new drawing and painting styles and techniques (for example, she did a series of geometrical drawings that were published together with poems by Mike Doyle in a portfolio entitled *Planes* [1975]). Margaret Atwood collected Page's short stories and reprinted them along with Page's novel as *The Sun and the Moon and Other Fictions* in 1973. The next year, Page began to conduct writers' workshops for three weeks each summer at New College, University of Toronto, and she published another volume of poems, *P.K. Page: Poems Selected and New*. She was appointed a member of the Canada Council Advisory Arts Panel for 1976–79 (though she never felt the need to apply for a Canada Council grant herself), and she taught a credit course in creative writing at the University of Victoria in 1977. That same year, she was made an Officer of the Order of Canada. She was also a part of a contingent of Canadian poets to tour Britain, and she made some recordings of her poems for the League of Canadian Poets.

Her growth, both intellectual and technical, has accelerated since the 1970s. Her interest in the Sufi poets of the Middle East sharpened at the beginning of the 1970s, and her interest in a breadth of topics from physics and brain structure to angels has continued. She edited a book of short poems called *To Say the Least: Canadian Poets from A to Z* (1979), and her collection of new poems *Evening Dance of the Grey Flies* (1981) indicates a lightening of her style and a shift of interest towards more personal and intensely felt issues. Ageing and death (her mother died at the age of ninety in 1982), lost time, change, and the transitory nature of experience are set in opposition to visions of the universal and permanent and true that come with a way of seeing offered by and through art. The garden of "home" is still a distinct possibility in Page's writing, and its definition appears to be coming clearer as time and change seem to speed up in her life.

In 1985 she put together a new selection of her work for Oxford University Press entitled *The Glass Air: Selected Poems* (revised, with new poems added, in 1991), in which she arranged her poems chronologically and added a number of newly published works along with her two essays on the creative process and some of her drawings. Two years later she published the journal that she kept during her stay in Brazil, *Brazilian Journal* (1987), a fascinating record of the psychology of displacement and the sense of wonder that can result. This journal was awarded the B.C. Book Awards

Hubert Evans Prize in 1988. In the last few years Page has published several works for children: a fairy tale, *A Flask of Sea Water* (1989); a second children's book, *The Travelling Musicians* (1991); and *Wisdom from Nonsense Land* (1991), a book her parents wrote and illustrated for their children in 1918, for which Page wrote the afterword.

Since 1985, Page has received honorary doctorates from the universities of Victoria, Calgary, and Guelph, and from Simon Fraser University. NFB director Donald Winkler made a documentary about her in 1991: *Still Waters: The Poetry of P.K. Page.* Page and her husband live in Victoria.

NOTES

[1] Robert Enright, interview with P.K. Page, in *Modern Canadian Poets: A Recorded Archive* (Toronto: League of Canadian Poets, 1982).

[2] Judy Keeler, "An Interview with P.K. Page," *The Canadian Forum*, Sept. 1975, p. 33.

[3] Michael Heenan, "Souvenirs of Some; P.K. Page Responding to a Questionnaire," *Canadian Poetry: Studies, Documents, Reviews*, No. 10 (Spring–Summer 1982), p. 103.

[4] Keeler, p. 34.

Miriam Waddington (1917–)

MIRIAM WADDINGTON was born in Winnipeg in 1917, one of four children of Russian-Jewish immigrants. Her father, Isidore Dworkin, had come to Canada in 1910 and was running his own meat-curing business in Winnipeg when he met and married Mussia Dobrusin, who had emigrated from Russia to work as a nurse in Moose Jaw. The Dworkin home became a centre for many Jewish and Yiddish authors, and, as Isidore Dworkin had leftist political sympathies, for a number of political activists as well. The language spoken in the home was Yiddish, though the poet remembers her mother reciting Russian pieces by Pushkin, more for her own delight than for the children's, as they did not speak Russian.[1] But the sound of the rhymes and the folkloric content that she somehow derived from these tales later exerted an influence on her poetry, as did Yiddish, a living, idiomatic language: conversational directness has always been one of the aims of her style of writing.

She has also translated poems by the Yiddish poet J.I. Segal.[2] But she has an uncomfortable recollection associated with that language, stemming from Canada's often hostile reaction toward Jewish immigrants; as a young girl, she felt ashamed having to tell her younger twin brothers in Yiddish what was being said to them by classmates and teachers, for when they first went to school, they knew no English.

Her first interest in poetry was fostered at school when a teacher singled out her efforts after having asked the class to write some poetry. Encouraged by this teacher to continue writing, she composed some derivative ballads. It is perhaps significant that she attempted poems in standard metrical arrangements, for the poet herself feels that a poet is probably born with certain technical gifts that might be sharpened by practice, but which remain as a base for the poet's writing throughout her/his career.

During the Depression her father's business failed, and in 1931 the family moved to Ottawa, where Miriam attended high school. It was at this time that some of her early poems appeared in print in such publications as *Canadian Girl* and *The Citizen* [Ottawa]. She also won the poetry prize in a competition organized by the Arts and Letters Club, the judge being Duncan Campbell Scott.

In 1936 she began studies in English literature at the University of Toronto, where she continued to publish poetry, as well as articles and reviews, in the student paper *The Varsity*. During her undergraduate years, she did not view her own poetry with great seriousness, although she did meet other young aspiring writers in Toronto at the time, including Anne Marriott, Raymond Souster, and Margaret Avison.

She graduated in 1939 and was married the same year to a journalist, Patrick Waddington, who later worked for the CBC. While her interest in literature had been stimulated by her studies at the University of Toronto, there was no possibility at that time for a woman or a Jew (let alone a Jewish woman) being hired to teach at the university. Instead she took a job with *Magazine Digest*, working on translations from French and German. Soon irked by the hack nature of this work, she left the magazine within a year and returned to the University of Toronto to study for a diploma in social work. She had decided that English literature would not change the world and that she did not want to live in a library. After receiving her diploma in 1942, she became, in her own words, "a romantic middle-class social worker"[3] and joined an agency. Subsequently, she undertook advanced study at the Pennsylvania School of Social Work in Philadelphia and returned to Montreal in 1945 to teach at the School of Social Work at McGill University.

During this period of her life, she was beginning to concentrate more on her writing; she was encouraged by having poems accepted for the January 1943 issue of *First Statement*, whose editor, John Sutherland, she first met during a visit to Montreal. It was Sutherland who was responsible for getting her first volume of poems into print: *Green World* (1945) was published by First Statement Press and hand-printed by Sutherland himself. During the next few years, Ryerson Press asked her to submit manuscripts, and eventually that press published her next two volumes, *The Second Silence* (1955) and *The Season's Lovers* (1958).

After her divorce in 1960, Miriam returned to Toronto with her two sons. Although she joined another agency there, she was becoming dissatisfied with the direction social work was taking in the 1960s. Her fuller commitment to writing was nurtured by a Senior Fellowship in Creative Writing which she received from the Canada Council for 1962–63. In 1964 she was offered a position to teach English and Canadian literature at York University, where she has been professor emeritus since 1983.

During her first years of teaching at York, she also studied for an M.A. in English literature at the University of Toronto. Her master's thesis on A.M. Klein was published in 1970. Some further volumes of poetry emerged from this period: *The Glass Trumpet* (1966) and *Say Yes* (1969), culminating in a collection of new and selected poems, *Driving Home* (1972), which won the J.I. Segal Award in 1973.

In recent years, she has travelled extensively, making personal journeys to recover, investigate, and experience elements of her family and ethnic history — most notably in Russia, Poland, and Israel. These places have figured in her later writing, together with her sense of Canadian-ness. She collected her poetic ruminations about Canada and Canadians in *Call Them Canadians*, a book of photographs published by the National Film Board in 1968 for which she supplied the text. During a stay in England, she published a small gathering of poems, *Dream Telescope* (1972), the title poem of which had originally been printed in one form in *Say Yes*. This same poem was reprinted again, in slightly revised form, as part of the slim volume *Mister Never* (1978). In 1976 she published a collection of poems, *The Price of Gold*. Three other collections of poems have followed: *The Visitants* (1981), *Collected Poems* (1986), which won the J.I. Segal Award in 1987, and *The Last Landscape* (1992). Waddington has also published a collection of stories, *Summer at Lonely Beach and Other Stories* (1982), and a book of essays, *Apartment Seven: Selected Essays* (1989), as well as editing an anthology, *Canadian Jewish Short Stories* (1990). Her manuscripts have been acquired by the Public Archives in Ottawa.

NOTES

[1] Some of this biographical information was given to the author in an unpublished interview with Miriam Waddington, 20 Sept. 1980.

[2] See Michael Yates, ed., *Volvox: Poetry from the Unofficial Languages of Canada . . . in English Translation* (Port Clements, B.C.: Sono Nis, 1971), pp. 155–64.

[3] Miriam Waddington, Introd., *John Sutherland: Essays, Controversies, and Poems*, ed. Miriam Waddington, New Canadian Library, No. 81 (Toronto: McClelland and Stewart, 1972), p. 7.

Margaret Avison (1918–)

DAVID A. KENT

MARGARET AVISON was born on 23 April 1918 in Galt (now Cambridge), Ontario, one of three children of Mabel (Kirkland) and the Reverend H. Wilson Avison. The Methodist church, however, soon sent her father to Western Canada (first Regina, then Calgary), and so she received her primary education on the Prairies. Avison has since described one consequence of this experience: "The landscape around southern Alberta permanently defined space for me."[1] She grew up an obedient child, taught by her parents "to read the Bible, to pray, to love, to enjoy," and driven by a powerful "Will To Be Good."[2] In her early teens, though, she witnessed the "real hunger, real want," caused by the Depression, and in a profound (but, she later realized, misplaced) act of sympathy, she "stopped eating" and became ill with what we would probably now call anorexia nervosa ("I Couldn't," p. 92); she required three years of treatment. Over the following twenty or thirty years, she recalled in 1968, her religious faith waned. Christ became merely an ethical ideal, abstract and uninvolved with life, and the Bible grew "more and more opaque" ("I Couldn't," p. 91). She dismissed the idea of a personal, loving God. Although she continued to engage in forms of "Christian service,"[3] her church-going stopped for over twenty years.

In about 1931, the family of five (including a brother, Ted, and a sister, Mary) returned east and settled in Toronto, where Avison has remained ever since (in one interview she describes herself as an inveterate "city mouse").[4] After high school, she entered Victoria College, University of Toronto, in 1936. At Victoria she had the benefit of such teachers as E.J. Pratt and Northrop Frye, and she became involved in the student publication *Acta Victoriana*. In this magazine can be found some of her earliest poems, reviews, and short stories.[5] Her parents moved to Ottawa in 1938, but she remained at school and, with the help of a bank loan, completed her arts degree in 1940. That year she also found the first of a long series of temporary jobs: file clerk at the North American Life-Insurance Company. Her working life since has been characterized by frequent dislocations and reorientations, in marked contrast to her continuing, though unostentatious, dedication to poetry. After the insurance company, she worked for Gage publishers, proof-reading and helping to Canadianize American texts. This association eventually led her to the writing of the elementary text *History of Ontario*, published in 1951. From 1943 to 1945, she acted as librarian and research assistant and, latterly, Information Secretary at the Canadian Institute of International Affairs. After the war, she worked in the Registrar's Office, University of Toronto, and on Saturday mornings taught soldiers who had returned to university for a degree. This was the first of her several experiences in teaching.

During the 1940s and 1950s, Avison also did freelance editing work, wrote book reviews (almost exclusively for *The Canadian Forum*), and occasionally published her poems in such periodicals as *Contemporary Verse*, *The Canadian Forum*, and *Poetry* [Chicago]. At one point, for a period of two years, she acted as nursemaid to a family with four children, and a highlight of this relationship was a long trip through France. Although she paid increasing attention to her writing, she could still experience the frustrations of not having enough time for poetry. She therefore confessed to Alan Crawley in a letter of 14 June 1952:

> I feel rotten about the frittering I seem to do earning a living, reading maybe too much and too rapidly, writing first drafts of poems now and then, when little pools of quiet occur, and then never going back to polish as they require. And never putting the loose pages of them in order or keeping track of what should be salvaged, what would come out after enough working over, what should be thrown away and forgotten. It is a state of confusion and unseemliness that grows worse with time . . . .[6]

In 1953 she met Cid Corman and soon after began corresponding with him.[7] At about the same time, she travelled to Indiana University to take two summer courses, one in linguistics and the other with John Crowe Ransom on Thomas Hardy's poetry. After having her poems published in the prestigious *Kenyon Review*, she won a Guggenheim Fellowship for 1956–57, which allowed her to travel to Chicago. Here she put together most of the poetry comprising *Winter Sun*, the winner of the Governor General's Award for Poetry in English when it was published in 1960.

Included in her literary activities of this period were her translations of Hungarian poetry[8] and the ghostwritten *A Doctor's Memoirs* (1960), the autobiography of A.J. Willinsky. She also earned a living one year by writing abstracts of dissertations in social work done at the University of Toronto. In 1963 she returned to the University of Toronto to do graduate work in English literature and completed her M.A. in 1964 with a thesis on Byron. At this time, she also attended a writers' workshop at the University of British Columbia together with American poets such as Charles Olson, Robert Creeley, and Denise Levertov. Other changes were afoot, however. In a letter to Cid Corman, published in *Origin* in 1962, she seemed to sense some radical change coming: "There is some corner I have to turn yet, some confronting I have to do . . . ."[9] Her "long willful detour into darkness" ended on 4 January 1963 when "the Jesus of resurrection power" spoke to her, "making Himself known at last, sovereign, forgiving, forceful for life" ("I Couldn't," pp. 93, 91). Avison's sudden conversion to a full-bodied

Christianity led her out of the "living death" ("I Couldn't," p. 93) she, in retrospect, sees she was experiencing. She had been attending sermons on biblical interpretation for two years but had initially been impelled to return to church after reading William James's *The Varieties of Religious Experience*. Then while reading the Gospel of Saint John, and in particular Chapter xiv ("You believe in God, believe also in me"), she was suddenly moved to "take the challenge";[10] she gave up everything in a radical act of faith. Two months of compulsive writing followed, during which she wrote most of the poems that make up *The Dumbfounding*, her second volume of verse, published in 1966.[11]

Avison continued her graduate work for another three years, completing all the examination requirements for the Ph.D. but not the thesis. For two years (1966–68), she taught courses at Scarborough College (everything from seventeenth-century literature to modern), but she abandoned her studies and teaching in 1968 to seize the opportunity of joining the Presbyterian Church Mission at Evangel Hall in downtown Toronto. She worked in this storefront church for four years. For a time, she taught poetry to the patients at the nearby Queen Street Mental Hospital. As George Bowering once observed, in this double vocation she imitated Christ — "a scholar who worked among the outcast."[12] She continued publishing poems in small magazines and did more translations from Hungarian. She was also writer-in-residence at the University of Western Ontario during 1972–73. After an interlude in the Radio Archives of the CBC, she began working for the Mustard Seed Mission's Canadian office (where she continued to work until the autumn of 1986).

Her third book of poetry was published in 1978. *sunblue* reveals Avison fully emerged as a devotional poet in the English tradition and has confirmed her position as a major religious poet. In 1982 McClelland and Stewart reissued her first two collections in a single volume, *Winter Sun/The Dumbfounding: Poems 1940–66*. In 1984 Avison gave a collection of books, periodicals, letters, and some manuscripts (mostly by other writers) to York University. These materials, while not as plentiful as might be hoped, will nevertheless be a valuable resource for future research on her work.[13] Early in 1985 it was announced that Avison had been made an Officer of the Order of Canada. In the autumn of the same year, she was awarded an honorary D.Litt. by York University. In 1989 Avison published her fourth book of poems, *No Time*. A collection of her *Selected Poems* appeared in 1991. Recently, Avison donated all her unpublished poems to the University of Manitoba, on the condition that they never be published. She continues to write.

NOTES

[1] Harry der Nederlanden, "Margaret Avison: The Dumbfoundling [sic]," interview, *Calvinist Contact*, 19 Oct. 1979, p. 1. Any details about biography not documented below were kindly supplied by Margaret Avison. I am grateful to Ms. Avison for reading the completed essay and saving me from several errors and misplaced emphases.

[2] Margaret Avison [Angela Martin, pseud.], "I Couldn't Have My Cake and Eat It," in *I Wish I Had Known* . . . (Grand Rapids, Mich.: Zondervan, 1968), pp. 90, 88. Further references to this work appear in the text. I am indebted to Francis Mansbridge's fine work, "Margaret Avison: An Annotated Bibliography," in *The Annotated Bibliography of Canada's Major Authors*, ed. Robert Lecker and Jack David, VI (Toronto: ECW, 1985), 13–66, which I was allowed to consult prior to its publication and which notes this previously unknown source.

[3] The phrase is from Lawrence M. Jones, "A Core of Brilliance: Margaret Avison's Achievement," *Canadian Literature*, No. 38 (Autumn 1968), p. 51.

[4] John Bolette, Claudette Jones, and Mike Caroline, "A Conversation with Margaret Avison," videotaped interview, Scarborough College, 1971. Available for viewing in the audio-visual department of the University of Toronto library.

[5] Avison's contributions to *Acta Victoriana* during her undergraduate years (1936–40) include ten poems, three short stories, two short essays, and two movie reviews.

[6] Letter to Alan Crawley, 14 June 1952, Alan Crawley Papers, Queen's University Archives, Kingston, Ont. Quoted with the permission of the author.

[7] There are five letters from Avison to Cid Corman, written during 1953, housed in the Corman Collection, Harriet Irving Library, Univ. of New Brunswick, Fredericton, N.B. I am grateful to Michael Darling for alerting me to the existence of these letters.

[8] Avison's translations are listed in Mansbridge, pp. 24–25.

[9] Letter to Cid Corman, *Origin*, 2nd ser., No. 4 (Jan. 1962), p. 10.

[10] Nederlanden, p. 3.

[11] See Merle Shaine, "Some of Our Best Poets Are . . . Women," *Chatelaine*, Oct. 1972, p. 104.

[12] George Bowering, "Avison's Imitation of Christ the Artist," *Canadian Literature*, No. 54 (Autumn 1972), p. 60.

[13] See David A. Kent, "A List of Books and Periodicals Given to York University by Margaret Avison (August, 1984)," available from York Univ. Archives, Scott Library.

Louis Dudek (1918–)

TERRY GOLDIE

LOUIS DUDEK was born on 6 February 1918 in Montreal, the city where his activities as poet, critic, and editor have always centred. As Ralph Gustafson succinctly puts it, "Louis Dudek was born in Montreal; lives in Montreal; always returns to the harbour of his birthright and local knowledge."[1] Both his parents were of Polish descent, though his father had been born in Russia, his mother in England. They met and married in Canada and had three children, Louis and two daughters.

From an early age, Dudek was interested in poetry. Wynne Francis records that at fifteen he engaged in a poetry competition with his sister and was judged the victor by their parish priest.[2] Whether or not he felt this proved his ability, it is an event he has recalled more than once. Several other factors in Dudek's youth seem to have been relevant to his later development. His father had various labouring jobs, in which he was often held back by poor

English. This experience of economic hardship and social dis-advantage shaped Dudek's early concern for the working class. The linguistic environment in Dudek's home, Polish with a growing presence of English, may have sown the seed for Dudek's lifelong interest in bilingualism and multilingualism.

Dudek's mother died in 1926, and an aunt was brought out from Poland to look after the children. The psychological effects of this change on an eight-year-old must have been major, though any theories about their specific nature can only be speculative. Still Susan Stromberg-Stein suggests that these effects exerted a strong influence on Dudek's poetic sensibility.[3]

As a youth, Dudek clung very closely to his Roman Catholic origins. He broke with the religion in his late teens, but has never turned to the strident opposition to it that might be expected: "I'm not an anti-Catholic. I'm a lapsed Catholic. Be a believer in what you know. Life is a myriad-sided existence. Believe in it."[4] Wynne Francis provides the following analysis:

> Growing up in a working-class milieu during the depression years, Dudek came to believe that religion was incapable of measuring the complexities of modern life, that it took inade-quate account of both the beauty and the horror of natural existence, and that it was restrictive and inhibiting in its view of mankind. Poetry on the other hand offered an increasingly appealing way of assessing life.[5]

During 1936–39 Dudek attended McGill University, where he became an associate editor of *The McGill Daily*, the first of many editing roles he has had. After graduation, he supported himself by freelancing as a journalist and advertising copywriter, though he continued to publish poetry in the *Daily* and to associate with its staff. In 1940 he met another young poet, Irving Layton; and in 1942 Layton introduced him to John Sutherland, who had just begun a new little magazine, *First Statement*. Dudek has always emphasized the limitations of his involvement with the magazine, but his position on the editorial board and his contributions of poems and critical articles were an important part of the magazine and of his own literary development.

In 1943 Dudek married Stephanie Zuperko (with whom he has

one son, Gregory), and the couple left for New York. Dudek intended to study journalism and history at Columbia University. Instead, a variety of influences led him to enter the master's program in English, for which he completed a thesis entitled "Thackeray and the Profession of Letters." During this same period, he was beginning to be recognized as a poet. His work was included in the Ryerson anthology *Unit of Five* (1944), edited by Ronald Hambleton; and in 1946 Ryerson published his first book, *East of the City.*

In 1951, after teaching English at the City College of New York and working on his Ph.D. dissertation, "The Relations between Literature and the Press," Dudek returned to Montreal to a teaching position at McGill. Although Dudek had continued to contribute to *First Statement* and its successor, *Northern Review*, he had become increasingly disaffected with Sutherland's conservatism and thus was attracted to a new magazine, *Contact*, edited by another *Unit of Five* alumnus, Raymond Souster.

The purpose of *Contact* is aptly defined by Frank Davey in *Louis Dudek & Raymond Souster*:

> *Contact* was, then, like *First Statement*, *Direction* and *Enterprise*, a definite expression of literary discontent. Both Souster and Dudek saw the few existing Canadian periodicals as inadequate both to their personal publication needs and to the hopes they had for the future direction of Canadian writing. While they reacted to this situation differently — Dudek by working behind the scenes, Souster by direct action — the message which they projected through *Contact* was clear: Canadian poetry magazines were conventional and parochial; Canadian writers were isolated and technically naive; international writing was rapidly leaving a static Canadian literature behind.[6]

Souster's own comment shows just what form this direct action would take. His magazine would be "an outlet for experiment and a franker discussion of the directions poetry is to take, not articles on Lampman and the movies."[7]

Dudek's involvement was, as Davey notes, primarily behind the scenes, but the vibrant character of *Contact* is in many ways representative of his own work in the period. The 1950s were Dudek's most prolific years as a poet. In 1952 his Ryerson chapbook, *The Searching Image*, was published, as well as *Cerberus* (with Irving Layton and Raymond Souster) and *Twenty-Four Poems* — both by Contact Press, a new publishing venture started by Dudek, Layton, and Souster. In later years, Contact published the following books of poetry by Dudek: *Europe* (1954), *The Transparent Sea* (1956), *En México* (1958), and *Laughing Stalks* (1958).

Even with this outpouring, Dudek maintained other interests. In 1957 he began publishing his own magazine, *Delta*, which he continued, solely under his control, until 1966. As well, he created the McGill Poetry Series, first publisher of Leonard Cohen. In 1967, the year that Contact Press folded, Dudek began Delta Canada with the publication of his own *Atlantis*. Delta Canada subsequently published his *Collected Poetry* (1971) and the works of many others, including R.G. Everson and F.R. Scott, both under Delta Canada and its later imprint DC Books. Dudek was divorced from Stephanie in 1965, and married Aileen Collins (the "C" in DC Books) in 1970.

Dudek has always been a critic as well as a poet, and, since the 1960s, the former occupation has perhaps overshadowed the latter. In 1960 *Literature and the Press: A History of Printing, Printed Media, and Their Relation to Literature*, a revision of his Ph.D. dissertation, was published, and in 1967 a series that he presented on CBC Radio was printed as *The First Person in Literature*. The best reflection of Dudek's achievement as a critic is *Selected Essays and Criticism* (1978), a collection of forty-eight pieces from throughout his career. Even given this number, it is by no means complete. Particularly of note among the exclusions are the various cultural reactions he wrote for *The Gazette* [Montreal].

Until his retirement in 1984, Dudek continued to lecture on modern poetry as Greenshields Professor of English at McGill University. Outside the university, he has spoken on the same subject to such audiences as the Canadian Council of Teachers of English and the Royal Society of Canada. A collection of these speeches has been published as *Technology and Culture* (1979).

For a period, Dudek's published poetry was primarily limited to occasional appearances in magazines. The exceptions were *Epi-*

grams (1975), a diffuse collection of very short pieces, and *Selected Poems* (1975). In the early 1980s Dudek was particularly active, however, publishing *Cross-Section: Poems 1940–1980* (1980), a collection of previously unpublished short poems, *Poems from Atlantis* (1980), a reprint of passages from *Atlantis*, and a special edition of *Open Letter*, entitled *Louis Dudek: Texts & Essays* (1981), which is primarily a collection of Dudek's prose but also includes an interview and some drafts from *Europe*, *Atlantis*, and *Continuation 1*. *Continuation 1*, a long poem, was published in 1981. He had previously published parts of it in *Collected Poetry* and in *The Tamarack Review* (Summer 1976). His latest works are a collection of essays, *In Defence of Art* (1988), a book of selected poems, *Infinite Worlds* (1988), and another collection of poems, *Small Perfect Things* (1991). Dudek's accomplishments have been recognized with several awards over the last few years, including an honorary diploma from Dawson College in Montreal (1984), an honorary doctorate from York University (1983), and admission to the Order of Canada (1984).

NOTES

[1] Ralph Gustafson, "Louis Dudek," in *Contemporary Poets of the English Language*, ed. Rosalie Murphy (London: St. James, 1970), p. 309.

[2] Wynne Francis, "A Critic of Life: Louis Dudek as Man of Letters," *Canadian Literature*, No. 22 (Autumn 1964), p. 7.

[3] Susan Stromberg-Stein, "A Biographical Introduction to Louis Dudek's Poetry," M.A. Thesis McGill 1977, pp. 9–11.

[4] Susan Stromberg-Stein, interview with Louis Dudek, 16 Oct. 1975. See Stromberg-Stein, p. 25.

[5] Francis, p. 7.

[6] Frank Davey, *Louis Dudek & Raymond Souster*, Studies in Canadian Literature, No. 14 (Vancouver: Douglas & McIntyre, 1980), p. 15.

[7] Raymond Souster, letter to Louis Dudek, 23 June 1951, as quoted by Michael Gnarowski, *Contact 1952–1954: Being an Index to the Contents of Contact, a Little Magazine Edited by Raymond Souster, Together with Notes on the History and the Background of the Periodical* (Montreal: Delta Canada, 1966), p. 3.

Al Purdy (1918–)

LOUIS K. MACKENDRICK

ALFRED WELLINGTON PURDY was born on 30 December 1918, near Wooler, Ontario, a hamlet north of Trenton. His forebears were Loyalists who had fled from upstate New York; his father was a graduate of the Guelph Agricultural College and a fruit farmer who died when his son was two. Purdy's mother subsequently moved to Trenton, dedicating herself to raising the boy; his childhood is warmly and vividly recalled in his memoir *Morning and It's Summer* (1983). He attended the Dufferin Public School in Trenton, Albert College in Belleville, and the Trenton Collegiate Institute, where his first poem was published in the school magazine, *Spotlight*. At sixteen, Purdy discontentedly left school after grade ten to perform odd jobs, his inveterate, untutored, and omnivorous habit of reading already firm. He began riding cross-Canada freight trains during the Depression, an anticipation of his persistent inclination to travel. In 1937 he went to Vancouver in this way but, depressed and homesick, immediately returned home.

As one solution to his intermittent employment, Purdy enlisted in the RCAF, serving for six years through promotions and demotions: he was principally stationed at Trenton, Vancouver, and Woodcock, on the Skeena River in northern British Columbia, with shorter terms at Picton, Toronto, and Ottawa. On 1 November 1941, he married Eurithe Parkhurst of Belleville; the Purdys have one son, Alfred. At this time Purdy was publishing poetry in *The Vancouver Sun*. In 1944 a chapbook, *The Enchanted Echo*, was published in an edition of five hundred copies by Clarke and Stuart of Vancouver, at a cost to him of $200. However, he could not afford the book's storage costs, and 350 copies were reportedly destroyed by a warehouse worker. By the end of the war Purdy's poetry was being published in *The Canadian Forum*, a continuing association, and in the *Canadian Poetry Magazine*, for which he also wrote occasional reviews.

Upon his military discharge Purdy operated a taxi business, with some discretionary bootlegging, in Belleville. In 1950 he moved to Vancouver and began five years' employment with the Vancouver Bedding Ltd., a mattress factory, into which he introduced the Vancouver Upholsterer's Union. In 1955 *Pressed on Sand* appeared from the Ryerson Press, and his first verse-play was accepted and produced by CBC Toronto. The Purdys moved to Montreal, and on the way to Europe with friends Purdy stayed with Irving Layton, with whom he had corresponded. Through Layton he met Louis Dudek and, in the summer of 1956, Milton Acorn. He was working heatedly on poems, poems for voices, plays, and adaptations, supported by Eurithe's job with the CPR. The slim *Emu, Remember!* was issued in 1956; he attempted many verse-plays for CBC Montreal, and two were accepted and aired (1956, 1957). He was later to start, but never finish, a novel based on his Montreal experiences.

In 1957 the Purdys moved to Ameliasburg, Ontario, in Prince Edward County, where Purdy began building an A-frame house near Roblin Lake; construction was piecemeal from salvaged lumber and funded with proceeds from his Montreal plays and unemployment insurance monies. His poetry was appearing somewhat more widely; irregularly he helped Dudek with his journal, *Delta*, and with Acorn he started a little magazine, *Moment*, in the fall of 1959; the year also saw the release of *The Crafte So Longe To Lerne*. In 1960 Purdy received the first of his Canada Council grants, with which he planned to write another verse-play — which instead became *The Blur in Between* (1962) — and return to the Skeena. His breakthrough collection, *Poems for All the Annettes*, appeared in 1962 from Dudek and Peter Miller's Contact Press. His occasional personal, literary, and travel pieces, to be selected in *No Other Country* (1977), began to be printed, and his reviews were seen in such periodicals as *Canadian Literature, Evidence*, and the *Canadian Author and Bookman*. For "The Country North of Belleville," printed in *The Tamarack Review* (Spring 1963), he was awarded the University of Western Ontario's President's Medal in 1964 for the best poem published in a magazine by a Canadian. He visited Mexico and Cuba in 1964 as well, and *Evidence* printed a selection of nine of his poems. Purdy's talent had matured and was beginning to be recognized.

Another Canada Council grant, in 1965, permitted Purdy's trip to Baffin Island, and McClelland and Stewart, his principal publisher thereafter, issued *The Cariboo Horses*, which won the Governor General's Award for Poetry in English in 1966. His poems were included in A.J.M. Smith's *Modern Canadian Verse in English and French* (1967); his representation in later standard Canadian anthologies was now to become automatic. Since that time Purdy's life has assumed some regular patterns. Short-term grants and arts awards from the Canada Council were given almost regularly. His subsequent honours included the Centennial Medal in 1967, the A.J.M. Smith Award in 1974, an award from the Academy of Canadian Writers in 1977, the Jubilee Medal in 1978, investiture into the Order of Canada in 1982, and the Milton Acorn Memorial People's Poetry Award in 1991. His travels continued: he visited Greece, Italy, and England in 1968–69, Hiroshima in 1971, South Africa in 1973, Peru in 1975, the Soviet Union, along with Ralph Gustafson on a writers' exchange program, in 1978, and the Galapagos Islands in 1980. In 1970 he was a visiting professor at Simon Fraser University; from 1971 to 1973 he taught creative writing at the Banff School of Fine Arts, and in 1972–73 he was poet-in-residence at Montreal's Loyola College. For 1975–76 he was writer-in-residence at the University of Manitoba and the same at the University of Western of Ontario in 1977–78 and the University of Toronto in 1987.

Purdy's publications have continued with exceptional frequency. What might be noted are highlights other than individual volumes of new poems. In 1969 Purdy edited the anthology *Fifteen Winds* as well as Milton Acorn's *I've Tasted My Blood*. His *Selected Poems* were published in 1972, and a major selection of his work was included in Eli Mandel's *Poets of Contemporary Canada, 1960–1970* (1972). *The Poems of Al Purdy*, a selection with an auto-biographical introduction, appeared in 1976, continuing the confirmation of his major contemporary rank. In 1978 *Being Alive: Poems 1958–1978*, a selection assisted by Dennis Lee, and 1982's *Bursting into Song: An Al Purdy Omnibus* continued the recognition of his body of work. *The Bukowski/Purdy Letters* (1983) was another, hitherto unknown, side of his multifarious productivity. Purdy's *Collected Poems*, winner of the Governor General's Award for Poetry in English, appeared in 1986 and *The Purdy-Woodcock Letters* in 1988. In 1990 Purdy published his first novel, *A Splinter in the Heart*. That year he also published a new collection of poems, *The Woman on the Shore. Yehl the Raven* appeared in 1991, and *Point of Transfer: The Selected Plays of Al Purdy* was published in 1992.

Purdy is at present a recipient of the Canada Council's Senior Arts Awards. He gives readings, makes wild grape wine, and continues to publish admirably undiminished poetry. He has edited, introduced, or selected the work of such other writers as Charles Bukowski, Milton Acorn, Doug Fetherling, Fraser Sutherland, George Woodcock, Peter Trower, C.H. Gervais, and Andrew Suknaski. He has assembled two anthologies of the work of younger poets and a collection of Canadian opinions of the United States, and has published over two-dozen individual books of selected and new poems. His status is a matter of popular and critical record, and his continuing contemporaneity is unquestioned, making it difficult to credit him as one of the older masters of the modern Canadian poetic tradition. Purdy divides his time, with his wife Eurithe, between their houses in Ameliasburg, Ontario, and Sydney, British Columbia. He has written ". . . 40 000 words of a memoir" and has the plot of another novel in mind, but, says Purdy, "I don't know that I want to spend my formative years on it."[1]

NOTE

[1] H.J. Kirchhoff, "Purdy's First Literary 'Marathon,' " *The Globe and Mail* [Toronto], 6 Nov. 1990, p. C1.

Raymond Souster (1921–)

BRUCE WHITEMAN

FROM THE STANDPOINT of the outside observer, the facts of Raymond Souster's life seem as ordinary as his literary activities have been extraordinary. He was born 15 January 1921 in Toronto, and, with the exception of the last four years of the Second World War, he has never lived elsewhere. Humberside, Sunnyside, and High Park in west-central Toronto are to him what Gloucester was to Charles Olson: extensions of his skin and the objects of his local pride. He was born there, he went to school there (attending Indian Road Public School, Runnymede Public School, and Humberside Collegiate, with a stint at the University of Toronto Schools), and he has lived there with his wife Rosalia (they married in 1947) since his discharge from the air force in August 1945.

Souster graduated from high school in 1939 and followed his father into the banking business. Family members were not then permitted to work for the same bank, but Souster's father had a friend whose son was also interested in working for the bank, so the two sons went to work in a nicely engineered exchange — Souster for the Imperial Bank, and the friend's son for the Standard Bank where Ray's father worked. The Imperial later amalgamated with the Bank of Commerce, and Souster has worked there his whole life. Though banking may seem an unpoetic vocation, Souster has never felt that his job compromised in any way his life in poetry:

> You asked about how I make a living — for better or for worse it's the banking business, has been since I was 18 except for a four year hitch in R.C.A.F. And not as deadly as you might think — if nothing else one meets a lot of people — and people are my main interest.[1]

Though he never saw combat, the war years were vital to Souster, and the war influenced his poetry and fiction more than any other single event. He enlisted in November 1941, was given the trade of equipment assistant or storekeeper, and was sent to Technical Training School at St. Thomas, Ontario. From there, he was posted to Sydney, Nova Scotia, Scoudouc, New Brunswick, and finally to England. Towards the end of the war, he returned to Dartmouth, Nova Scotia, where he was discharged.[2]

The name of one of Souster's magazines, *Contact*, summarizes well the extent of his involvement in Canadian literature. He has known, or been involved with, most of the important poets in Canada and many in the United States, since the Second World War. He has been a magazine editor, a publisher, and an editor of anthologies and school texts; and he was a founding member and the first chairperson of the League of Canadian Poets. The sheer range of his contacts is astonishing: from John Sutherland and the *First Statement* group in the 1940s, to the Souster group (one could almost put it) of the 1950s (Louis Dudek, Irving Layton, Peter Miller, Kenneth McRobbie, and others), to the poets who published in the American magazines *Origin* and *The Black Mountain Review* (Charles Olson, Cid Corman, Robert Creeley, and their students), to the young Canadian poets of the early 1960s (George Bowering, Frank Davey, Margaret Atwood, Victor Coleman, and many others). Souster corresponded with them, encouraged them, published their poems and their books, and organized public readings for them. Through all of these activities, he had a great influence on the direction of Canadian poetry during roughly the period from 1950 to 1966.

Souster's own introduction to poetry was at the University of Toronto Schools when he was twelve years old, and he has written a poem about it:

My first introduction to poetry:
our form-master on the blackboard
breaking up one of the stanzas
from William Campbell's *August Reverie*
into principal and subordinate clauses.[3]

A number of his poems were published in the editorial pages of *The Toronto Daily Star* when Souster was a teenager; but his earliest mature poem to appear in print was "Nocturnal," which Earle Birney accepted for the August 1940 issue of *The Canadian Forum*. His earliest publication in book form was in *Unit of Five* (1944), and he later told the story of how that group-book came about.[4] From this beginning, he went on to publish more than thirty books and pamphlets in the next four-and-a-half decades. Among these are three volumes of selected poems (in 1956, 1964, and 1972); his collected poems have been published in six large volumes, between 1980 and 1989, by Oberon. Since his retirement from banking in 1984, Souster has devoted himself to poetry, publishing *Jubilee of Death: The Raid on Dieppe* (1984), the *Flight of the Roller Coaster: Poems for Children* (1985), *It Takes All Kinds: New Poems* (1986), *The Eyes of Love* (1987), *Asking for More* (1988), and *Running Out the Clock* (1991). Two of his books and one of his poems have won awards. *The Colour of the Times: The Collected Poems of Raymond Souster* won the Governor General's Award for Poetry in English in 1964; *Hanging In* won a City of Toronto Book Award for 1979; and the poem "The Farm Out the Sydenham Road," first published in *The Tamarack Review*, won the University of Western Ontario President's Medal for 1967. Souster was also awarded a Centennial Medal in 1967. He was poet-in-residence at University College, University of Toronto, in 1984–85.

On the whole, Souster's contributions have been remarkable,

and, if one considers the fact that he has never had a Canada Council award, nor ever enjoyed the chunks of unoccupied time that a university teaching post can afford, they seem even more astonishing. He is a modest man and would doubtless claim that he has done no more than many other poets; but few can match the breadth of his accomplishments. The poets, of course, have been quick to recognize them:

. . . somehow when I read you I am moved. I am moved by your subject matter, and I am moved by the way that has induced you to conform to it as the very foundation head of your art. . . . Have confidence in yourself. You've got it.[5]

Yours is an original voice — there's absolutely nothing like it in Canada.[6]

And you with yr little machine in yr basement make the most LUCID magazine — in the world![7]

NOTES

[1] Raymond Souster, letter to Charles Olson, 30 Aug. 1954, in Bruce White-man, ed., "Raymond Souster's Letters to Charles Olson," *Canadian Poetry Studies, Documents, Reviews*, No. 9 (Fall–Winter 1981), p. 78.

[2] Raymond Souster, "About Myself (Some Facts and Near-Facts on Raymond Souster)," ts., Raymond Souster Papers, Thomas Fisher Rare Book Library, Univ. of Toronto.

[3] Raymond Souster, Introd., *Vapour and Blue — Souster Selects Campbell: The Poetry of William Wilfred Campbell Selected and Introduced by Raymond Souster* (Sutton West, Ont.: Paget, 1978), p. xiii.

[4] Raymond Souster, *Rain-Check* (Ottawa: Oberon, 1975), p. 9.

[5] William Carlos Williams, letter to Raymond Souster, 28 June 1952, *Island*, No. 1 (Sept. 1964), p. 47.

[6] Irving Layton, "Crêpe-Hanger's Carnival," CIV/n, No. 7 (1954), p. 27.

[7] Charles Olson, letter to Raymond Souster, 17 Jan. 1958, Lakehead Univ. Library.

Eli Mandel (1922–92)

DENNIS COOLEY

ELI MANDEL WAS BORN in Estevan, Saskatchewan, on 3 December 1922, to parents who had emigrated from Ukraine in their early teens, his father from Kiev and his mother from Odessa. His father, a grocer in Estevan, struggled to survive in a marginal economy that soon turned to disaster during the Dirty Thirties. The family lived in what Mandel remembers as "just a ramshackle part of town" on the edge of the Souris Valley, riddled with abandoned mines and tunnels.[1] The valley has come to figure prominently is some of his more recent work, notably *Out of Place* in 1977, but it appears covertly from the outset in his first book publication in *Trio*, where the cave, a major symbol, recurs in the next two books, as source of oracular powers and sexual mysteries. "That was a magical part of my childhood, the valley," Mandel remembers. "It was cowboy country . . . it was mythic country." The edge of the valley represented "a definite break" between the town and a symbolic space "which I don't understand. I really don't . . . . It's a haunting image that remains powerful for me" (Cooley). The valley also contained, at Roche Percee, southeast of Estevan, an outcropping of rocks on which Natives had once carved petroglyphs, which in Mandel's childhood and, later, adulthood spoke strangely and strongly to him.

Much of his childhood was filled with reading adventure stories about Tarzan and Doc Savage and with all the fantasies, taboos, and fevered sexuality that infuse such childhood. Mandel's boyhood life was informed, too, by

the whole panoply of 19th century versification ranging as it does from the impossibly sublime to the intense[ly] inane. . . . In that poor shabby house surrounded by the devastated land and indeed in very peril of our lives, the high-minded sentimentality of those words moved across my mind like a vision of real human possibility.[2]

Mandel recalls those days when in the midst of a rough prairie his imagination began to take on literary contours that would turn him away from the place:

. . . living in Estevan I didn't even know I lived there. The life of the mind and the life of the body had been radically separated, compartmentalized. Mentally, I was being brought up as a genteel Victorian boy, with a quaint though serious touch of middle-European Yiddish gentility to boot. (AT, p. 73)

In 1935 Mandel's family moved to Regina where his father reestablished himself in the grocery business, and Eli finished the last grade of public school before going to Central Collegiate. In high school he was influenced by one of his teachers, Mr. Fife — "Great God, I liked him very much" (Cooley) — who introduced him to the Romantics and who encouraged bright young students to write and to read Canadian literature.

After graduation Mandel worked in a Regina pharmacy for two years. Then his parents, free from debt, and feeling an enormous respect for learning, were able to send Mandel to Regina College to study pharmacy. But he didn't enjoy the technical work and in 1943, after his first year, left to join the army. He arrived overseas on his twenty-first birthday and served in the Royal Army Medical Corps and in supply command, with a short, wild stint in a motorcycle training unit.

When the war ended, Mandel enrolled for six months in Khaki College in England. It was a heady experience for him: he took four courses and began to publish poetry in the school paper. At the time, he began reading recent British literature — MacNeice, Eliot, Yeats, Joyce — and, what proved to be just as important, continental writers — Dostoevsky, Mann, and above all Kafka. This opened an influence that figured prominently at the time in his writing and that has continued in abated ways since.

He was deeply affected by war, too, particularly the appalling death on a spectacular scale and the personal loss of friends and relatives. Heartsick, he made his way back to Saskatchewan in June 1946 to pick up his life: "I was going back to talk to my aunt about her son [his cousin, Jack Mandel, who died in the war] and realized the revulsion I felt. It was looking at those [graves] that I got sick . . . in seeing all the dead and then having to talk about the dead."[3] The terrible sense of cultural and personal desolation he felt figures in the early poem "Estevan, Saskatchewan" and, together with the influence of his European literary models, gives rise to the black romanticism that characterizes the first stage of his writing, in which the poet presents himself as tormented outsider who would heal a sick world.

Mandel enrolled in the fall of 1946 at the University of Saskatchewan, from which he received a B.A. in 1949 and a M.A. in 1950. While there he was strongly influenced by Carlyle King, "a great fighter for Canadian literature" (Cooley), by the novelist Edward McCourt, and by John Lothian, a Shakespeare scholar and another Scotsman who, like Mr. Fife, championed Canadian literature. When Mandel did come across modern Canadian poetry he was ecstatic:

I think that my writing Canadian poetry, that is writing poetry in Canada, became possible when I realized that people were doing it, and doing it well. When I came back from Europe . . . I was reading Auden, Hopkins, Yeats, I was reading Eliot and so on and terribly excited by it and believing I could do something. I remember in the library at Regina coming across a book called *Go to Sleep World* by Raymond Souster . . . and I read it and I said, "Wow this is the real stuff." That meant a great deal to me.[4]

In 1949 Mandel married Miriam Minovitch, who came from Moose Jaw and who was herself studying at the University of Saskatchewan. After Mandel completed his Master's degree in the next year, they left for a three-year stay at the University of Toronto where, in his own words, Mandel was "very erratic and very high strung" as a Ph.D. student (Cooley). He excelled nevertheless and began to publish poems in literary journals, the first, "Train Wreck," in *Northern Review*. He soon published a batch of poems in *Contact* at Raymond Souster's invitation and, on further invitation, a larger group in *Trio* (which included Gael Turnbull and Phyllis Webb) in 1954. His career as a poet was well underway.

In the fall of 1953 he took a position at Collège Militaire, Royal de Saint-Jean, where until 1957 he taught, worked on his dissertation on Christopher Smart, and wrote poetry and where, in 1955, his daughter Evie was born. In 1957 he completed his doctorate and that fall moved to the University of Alberta in Edmonton where, with one year's interruption, he held an academic appointment until 1967. At first he found it "rather dreary" (Cooley), perhaps because he had become accustomed in the East to the company of Irving Layton, Phyllis Webb, F.R. Scott, Louis Dudek, Leonard Cohen, and James Reaney, and he took some time to establish new literary connections in Edmonton. He soon, however, struck up a fine and fertile relationship with the novelist Henry Kreisel, whom he greatly values. While he was in Edmonton, Mandel's academic and literary life blossomed. In response to an enquiry from Roy Daniells, a poet and professor at the University of British Columbia, he put together a new manuscript, *Fuseli Poems*, for which he received a Canada Foundation Fellowship in Writing and which, in 1960, appeared to favourable reviews and to a near miss in the awarding of the Governor General's Medal.

After spending 1963–64 at York University, Mandel returned to Edmonton for another three years, where he continued to work productively. *Black and Secret Man*, which was not as well received as *Fuseli*, came out in 1964, and in 1966 his *Criticism: The Silent-Speaking Words*, based on a series of CBC Radio talks and distilling his current thinking on poetry, appeared. The book illustrated a dimension to Mandel's literary life that has been constant — the active interplay of poetry, criticism, and literary theory, his criticism being especially concerned with the value and meaning of poetry in the twentieth century.

In 1967 Mandel divorced his first wife, married Ann Hardy, and returned to Toronto to York University. His swaying between Toronto and Edmonton, the forays east and the returns west — often sporadic but by the mid-1970s increasingly sustained — marked something more than the occasions of an academic's life. They signified and perhaps intensified Mandel's vacillation between two cultural worlds: one which in a sense he was born into; another which since the end of the war, during the first years of studying and then teaching in the East, he had been moving more and more into.

In the same year that he moved east, he published *An Idiot Joy* (1967), a major accomplishment for which he received the Governor General's Award for Poetry in English, one of those fine occasions when jurors identify a crucial book. His inclusion in Gary Geddes' influential Oxford anthology *15 Canadian Poets* in 1970 gave his work greater impetus, for it provided added visibility and access to readers. Those opportunities Mandel soon put to good use. One of his first projects as critic was to publish in the Coles Canadian Writers and Their Works series, edited by William French of *The Globe and Mail* [Toronto], a book on Irving Layton, a poet for whom Mandel has always had a great admiration. Another important consequence of his new contacts came in the form of a series of poetry anthologies he edited and coedited in the late 1960s and the early 1970s. Mandel's astute knowledge of contemporary poetry, his openness to the new, his knack for recognizing talent, and his generosity in celebrating it led him to produce several breakthrough anthologies, among them *Five Modern Canadian Poets* (1969) and (with Ann Mandel) *Eight More Canadian Poets* (1972).

In 1973 Mandel began to consolidate some of his writing with the publication of *Crusoe: Poems Selected and New*. He also moved into new territory during the 1970s by drawing on memories and dreams of the Prairies. Margery Fee at the time asked him, "Do you think of yourself as a Canadian poet?" His reply pointed to an archaeological drive to origins, however mediated:

> Not particularly. I think of myself now as a prairie poet, a writer whose being was formed by the experience of living on the prairies as a boy. I think the first six to ten years are absolutely essential. There's no way of escaping that. (Fee, p. 8)

He added that *Stony Plain* (1973) "is right because this is a book that's going back to roots, towards the prairies" (Fee, p. 8). In his own poetry, this rethinking led in 1977 to a striking long poem, *Out of Place*, about his literal and his spiritual return to birthplace, to Estevan in particular and to the Prairies in general. His turning back to his origins almost certainly was related to an enabling poetics he began to develop in the 1960s. In "Writing West: On the Road to Wood Mountain," an essay central to understanding his shifts, he speaks — this is 1977 — of the muse of Estevan and of "divided men seeking to make themselves whole" (*AT*, p. 77) by imaginatively recovering their lost selves. The way back to the authentic, Mandel was coming to believe, might lie through a more direct and simple language. In this view the writer is "not so much in place, as out of place and so one endlessly trying to get back, to find his way home, to return, to write himself into existence, writing West" (*AT*, p. 69).

Signs of that redirection emerged elsewhere in *Another Time*, a collection of essays published in 1977. The collection was divided into three parts: "Reflections," "Writing West," and "Writers and Writing." The relative strengths of the sections provide a good indication of the new centres Mandel was arriving at. The first part, "Reflections," contains the essays that are most European in their subjects and procedures, and it is the weakest. Compared to other essays in the collection, these ones tend to be vague, stylistically tortured, semantically dull — as if the intellectual basis that lay beneath his earliest writing had lost its power and could no longer command his best thinking. The third part, "Writers and Writing," presents a variety of essays, the most interesting of them in what they reveal about Mandel's own practice being "Modern Canadian

Poetry," "Ecological Heroes and Visionary Politics," and "Banff: The Magic Mountain." The second section, "Writing West," is the strongest and includes the fine essay I've already mentioned, "Writing West: On the Road to Wood Mountain," which meditates on his own Prairie childhood, explores the poetic example of Andy Suknaski, and speculates on moving into an aesthetics that is more vernacular and immediate.

More recently Mandel has travelled abroad, as scholar and as poet, to read and lecture. And in his writing he has begun to draw on those experiences and to find new forms adequate to them. *Life Sentence* (1981) combines in intriguing ways excerpts from his travel journals together with poems the occasions gave rise to. In 1981 Mandel published a second and updated selected, *Dreaming Backwards*, in the new Spectrum series begun by General Publishing. The Yeatsian title, which for years he had intended to use, declares his continued respect for an earlier rhetoric and for literature as an institution.

Although Mandel has long been an important and esteemed academic, he has become, from the mid 1970s, roughly, more and more involved in the literary community in Canada, and less and less active in the internal structures of the university. Teaching can be, he has found, an impediment to writing because ". . . real teaching is a drain . . . [and] you end up having used up that creative energy which would have gone into your writing" (Fee, p. 2).

Nevertheless, Mandel has led a productive life and has worked on many fronts. As teacher, editor, critic, lecturer (in person and on the radio), anthologist, workshopper, conversationalist, reviewer, writer-in-residence (City of Regina during 1978–79, University of Rome in 1983), visiting professor (University of Victoria during 1979–80, University of Calgary during 1984–85), correspondent, fan, he has shaped the literature he himself has contributed to, so much so that it might be most accurate to describe his role in Canadian literature as being, in the best sense of the term, that of a man of letters.

In 1986 he published a new collection of his essays, *The Family Romance*. Many of its pieces derive from talks he has given in recent years. The new role as public figure is somewhat surprising because in the past Mandel never cultivated a public personality. Nor for many years did he cultivate relationships with other poets, thinking ". . . it doesn't matter to me very much to see and talk to other writers. On the whole I don't like it" (Fee, p. 7). He has until recently been so withdrawn that he has known two of his esteemed colleagues at York — Miriam Waddington and Frank Davey — primarily through their appearances in print. In many ways a shy man, one who never could feel comfortable promoting his own work, Mandel has mainly gone his own way, working privately and attending to friends on private occasions. He reads intently, alone with his thoughts until he presents them in some public forum. Even so Mandel has become increasingly conspicuous as a literary guru. He is especially prominent and instrumental as lecturer at conferences, where invariably he gives a compelling address or reading. Never one to rest with approved texts, suspicious of their authority and the status that has been thrust upon them, he courts the new, seeks to mediate our collective writing, but always in the light of the old.

Mandel served as Professor of English and Humanities at York University until his retirement. He has three children, two by his first marriage — Evie and Charles — and one from his second — Sara. He died in 1992.

NOTES

¹ Dennis Cooley, personal interview with Eli Mandel, 14 March 1982. Further references to this work appear in the text.

² Eli Mandel, *Another Time*, Three Solitudes: Contemporary Literary Criticism in Canada, Vol. 3 (Erin, Ont.: Porcépic, 1977), p. 72. Further references to this work (*AT*) appear in the text.

³ Mark Lowey, " 'The best book is coming,' " *Calgary Herald*, 25 Nov. 1984, p. B3.

⁴ Margery Fee, "An Interview with Eli Mandel," *Essays on Canadian Writing*, No. 1 (Winter 1974), pp. 2–13. Further references to this work appear in the text.

Milton Acorn (1923–86)

ED JEWINSKI

UNTIL a complete biography of Milton Acorn is written, much of the man's life will continue to be mixed with a mythology of his own making. Indeed, Acorn often changed, altered, or exaggerated parts of his life and family history to impress upon his readers human beings' need to be socially and politically responsible and, therefore, to be politically self-conscious. At every opportunity, Milton Acorn dramatized his own life as an inescapable commitment to politics.

By mythologizing his life, his family heritage, and his personal history, he hoped to counter public complacency. To dramatize a family history full of heroes fighting for freedom, liberty, and equality, he claimed to have had a relative (a grandfather named Edward Carbonell) who, during the French Revolution, attempted to set up a communal state.[1] To show he had a right to speak about the plight of Native Canadians, he proclaimed that "Indian blood" was in his family line, thanks to his great-grandmother, who was part Micmac, part Malecite.[2] Most interestingly, Acorn also claimed that, as a young man, he had fathered an illegitimate child whom, despite many efforts, he was never able to contact again.[3] He writes to the boy in one poem, "Letter to My Redheaded Son," but the poem could equally suggest a mythic son, a child orphaned in the world, a lost boy who symbolizes the isolation of every child of the poor in a social world that does not give due respect to the individuals born into that society.

Acorn deliberately entwined facts and fictions to give force to his visions of social justice and responsibility. This habit of mythologizing his own past had a deep purpose: he wanted to reveal that his feeling of identification with the poor and the oppressed and the outcast was profound and sincere and "natural" to the blood. From his perspective, it seems, claiming a direct line with those who were treated unfairly forced others to accept him as the indisputable speaker for those he wished to help. The tactic usually worked; its end result was that few Canadian readers would dispute that Milton Acorn, above all, is the "People's Poet."

Acorn's "conventional life" is, however, as interesting as his "mythological" one. Milton James Rhode Acorn was born in Charlottetown, Prince Edward Island, on 30 March 1923. One of five children, he had an elder brother, Robert, and three sisters, Helen, Katherine, and Mary. His father was a ship's carpenter, and his mother, a homemaker. He was born into a solid working family, and he never forgot it. The working-class background influenced much of his writing: from the very beginning he understood and attempted to express the feelings and attitudes of workers. As a young man he managed only a grade eight education. When the Second World War began, he signed up early with the Canadian Forces and was sent to Camp Borden, near Toronto, for military training. The hasty program, however, was utterly impractical and inadequate as he soon discovered. Once on the troop ship and on his way to Europe, he was still too inexperienced to prepare for the sudden and sharp reports of depth charges that were to protect the ship, which seemed in danger of being torpedoed. The ship survived, but Acorn's brief military service had ended before the boat even arrived in Europe. The head wound he suffered was severe enough that for most of his life he received a disability pension from Veterans Affairs.

On his return to Prince Edward Island, he became an apprentice carpenter, following a trade that allowed him to travel wherever he wished, for skilled labour was always in demand. In 1956, he moved to Montreal, the site of two significant developments for him. The first is that he became active in politics and published his early poems in a political magazine, *New Frontiers*. The second is that he met a number of poets who influenced his writings, particularly Al Purdy, who later contributed a short but insightful account of Acorn's early career in an Introduction to *I've Tasted My Blood: Poems 1956–1968* (1969).

The Montreal period of Acorn's career is extremely important, for it convinced him to abandon his trade as a carpenter for poetry. Living in a small cheap room on St. Antoine Street, receiving little support, and having little money, he elected to dedicate himself to writing. Despite the hardships and handicaps, he privately printed his own first book, actually a small mimeographed pamphlet entitled *In Love and Anger* (1956). At about the same time, he and Al Purdy coedited and published a small magazine called *Moment*. The magazine was simply "produced on a mimeograph machine"[4] in Purdy's Linton Street apartment, but its contents were significant for its time. Two of Acorn's short polemical essays so forcefully articulated central principles of the new poetry emerging from Montreal writers that Louis Dudek and Michael Gnarowski included them in *The Making of Modern Poetry in Canada: Essential Articles on Contemporary Canadian Poetry in English*.

While editing *Moment* and presenting his views in prose, Acorn also published his own poetry. Two notable works were completed during this period: *Against a League of Liars* and *The Brain's the Target* (both 1960). Al Purdy, the closest of friends and the best of Acorn's critics, helped by providing food, living expenses, and support for publication — it was Purdy who encouraged Ryerson Press to accept the manuscript of *The Brain's the Target*, thereby granting Acorn the opportunity to reach a larger audience, one that could then convey a sense of Acorn's commitment to the working class.

In 1960, Acorn moved to Toronto, where he attended the Contact Poetry Readings series while, at the request of Raymond Souster, he prepared his next manuscript. There, he met Gwendolyn MacEwen (who was nineteen to his thirty-seven), and they married in 1962. After a fiasco of a marriage, which lasted only a few months before ending in divorce, Acorn went to Roblin Lake, near Belleville, where he stayed with Al Purdy and his wife Eurithe. Meanwhile, Raymond Souster published Acorn's *Jawbreakers* (1963) and *The Fiddlehead* released a special "Milton Acorn Issue," which contained fifty-eight poems. At the age of forty, he was finally seeing his work extensively published.

In 1964, Acorn moved again, this time to Vancouver. He immersed himself in politics, helping to found an underground magazine called *Georgia Straight* and peddling issues of this outspoken and political magazine in the streets. He attended public readings to support "communist" causes and expended energy trying to raise funds for political activity.

Not really experienced in the ways of political power and more the idealist than the practical politician, Acorn tried to assist young writers like bill bissett in gathering funds for the cause. In their optimism, these writers protested American imperialism in Vietnam by reading poems and speaking about the need for universal justice. Acorn and bissett thus raised forty-eight dollars and, as Acorn put it, mailed the money to one of the Trotskyist factions, not really having any sense of what to do with the cash once they had raised it. They were careful to earmark the funds "For Medical Aid," but they received only the return query: "What's Medical Aid?"[5]

As Al Purdy has repeatedly pointed out, Acorn, at the best of times, was a member of every socialist group and a card-carrying member of none.[6] Essentially committed to equality, freedom, and human dignity, and fundamentally opposed to all forms of oppression, Acorn read the socialist-communist-Trotskyist-Maoist-nationalist writers in his own way, and he never yielded to any platform, nor accepted anything that opposed his principles of economic and social equality for all. Convinced that Canadians were largely complacent and unjust primarily because of their lack of a deep sense of social equality, he deliberately mythologized himself into a communist, a Stalinist, a Trotskyist, a Maoist — a member of any leftist group that would challenge the established ideals of easy, complacent small-L liberalism.

In the late 1960s, Acorn returned to Toronto, living there in a variety of small cheap hotels and rooming houses populated by the poor and the transient. Much of his attention as a writer went to describing the life of the boardinghouse world. In 1969, his first successful book was published, the book long anticipated by those who knew his work: *I've Tasted My Blood: Poems 1956–1968* (1969). When the book did not receive the Governor General's Award for Poetry in English, a number of fellow Toronto poets protested the procedures of the entire adjudication process. The major charge was that the system was fundamentally influenced by an American voice, a voice that rejected the best Canadian art in favour of a writer who leaned toward American models of writing. Although the charge was not completely fair, the issue of Canadian nationalism and Canadian independence in the arts was strong enough to involve writers like Irving Layton, Joe Rosenblatt, Eli Mandel, and Margaret Atwood. In protest, these writers collected funds for an award and granted Acorn the title of "The People's Poet," a title he proudly carried for the rest of his life. Since Acorn's death, other poets, notably Al Purdy, have received the Milton Acorn Memorial People's Award.

Unabashedly committed to the people, Acorn published his next book with the title *More Poems for People* (1972) to acknowledge a fellow socialist poet, Dorothy Livesay. He was now a highly visible figure at the famous Bohemian Embassy. His reputation was that of an eccentric well known for his politics and his drinking bouts in such places as Grossman's Tavern and the Waverley Hotel. Despite the public posture, however, Acorn was hard at work — he began to write, collect, and unify the material of *This Island Means Minago* (1975). For the first time he focused the majority of a single collection almost exclusively on his native province, Prince Edward Island. The book won him the Governor General's Award for Poetry in English.

Still a fundamental socialist in the broadest sense, Acorn attempted in his next book to give a sense of overt nationalism to his work. In *Jackpine Sonnets* (1977), he drew on an old form, expanded and wrenched it, as have many modernist poets like Hopkins, Yeats, and Lowell, and welded the form to his social and political perspective.

In 1981, he returned to Prince Edward Island. One short, rather uneven work appeared: *Captain Neal MacDougal & The Naked Goddess* (1982). The next year, Al Purdy edited a second substantial collection of Acorn's poems, producing *Dig Up My Heart: Selected Poems 1952–83* (1983).

Then at sixty-three, on 20 August 1986, Acorn died of heart disease and diabetes in his hometown of Charlottetown. His last books, *The Whiskey Jack* (1986), *A Stand of Jackpine* (1987), *The Uncollected Acorn* (1987), *I Shout Love and Other Poems* (1988), and *Hundred Proof Earth* (1988) were published posthumously.

Despite his often turbulent life and intense political commitment, Acorn was not denied public honours. In addition to the title "People's Poet" of 1970 and the Governor General's Award in 1975, he was granted an honorary Doctor of Laws Degree from the University of Prince Edward Island in 1977 and was elected a lifetime member of the League of Canadian Poets in 1985. Eventually, therefore, the myth did become the man.

NOTES

[1] In "An Interview with Milton Acorn," by Terry Baker, Aileen Le Roux, and James Deahl, *Intrinsic!*, Nos. 7 & 8 (Spring 1979), p. 171, Acorn recounts the story of his relative. In an interview by Bruce Meyer and Brian O'Riordan entitled "In the Cause of the Working Class," in *In Their Words: Interviews with Fourteen Canadian Writers* (Toronto: House of Anansi, 1984), p. 128, Acorn admits to "romanticizing that a lot."

[2] Acorn's claim to Native ancestry is made in many places. Most notably, Eli Mandel (*Eight Canadian Poets* [Toronto: Holt, Rinehart, Winston, 1972], p. 38) writes: "I have heard him claim to be Indian, descendent of an old Maritime tribe."

[3] In "In Memorium: Milton Acorn 1923–1986," *The League of Canadian Poets Newsletter*, No. 54 (Nov. 1986) [inside cover], James Deahl records that a son was given up for adoption.

[4] Al Purdy, "In Memorium," *Books in Canada*, Oct. 1986, p. 16.

[5] See James Deahl, "Interview with Milton Acorn," *Writers' Quarterly*, 8, Nos. 3–4 (1986), 5.

[6] Al Purdy, Introd., *I've Tasted My Blood*, by Milton Acorn (Toronto: Ryerson, 1969), p. x.

James Reaney (1926–)

RICHARD STINGLE

JAMES CRERAR REANEY was born on 1 September 1926 on a farm in South Easthope township near Stratford, Ontario, a farm to which he regularly returns and which remains for him the physical centre of his world. It and the surrounding area of Southwestern Ontario are the imaginative centre of his writing as well, since almost all his poems, stories, and dramas are articulations of that section of Canada, with the exception of some pieces set in Winnipeg and Toronto.

Reaney is the only son of Elizabeth Henrietta Crerar and James Nesbitt Reaney, though he has a younger brother and sister by his mother's second marriage. The Reaneys were Scots-Irish and the Crerars (a Macintosh name) Highland Scots who settled in Perth County in the last century. Through his mother, Reaney is also descended from Germans from Hessen-Darmstadt who came in the same period to the adjoining county of Waterloo. Though mainly

Presbyterian and Plymouth Brethren in background, Reaney's parents were also involved during his childhood with an Independent Gospel Hall and a missionary-oriented Congregationalist church that had not entered Church Union in 1925.

Reaney attended Elmhurst School, South Easthope (1932–29) and Stratford Collegiate and Vocational Institute (1939–44). He studied English language and literature (with Honours options in Greek, Latin, and History) at University College in the University of Toronto, receiving his B.A. in 1948 and his M.A. in 1949. His life at college centred on the Modern Letters Club and a circle of friends that included Colleen Thibaudeau (a fellow poet, short-story writer, and his future wife), Hugh Kenner, Robert Weaver, Phyllis Bloom (now Gotlieb), Marion Walker, Evelyn Maguire, Milena Matuska, Margaret Dale, Kurt Dahl, and Paul Arthur. At the Royal Conservatory of Music was John Beckwith, the musician who has collaborated with Reaney in many productions, from "The Great Lakes Suite" of 1950 to *Crazy To Kill: A Detective Opera* of 1989. Among his friends at Victoria College, University of Toronto, were Alan Brown, Ronald Bates, Margaret Gayfer, Robert Patchell, and myself; at Trinity College, University of Toronto, Arthur Millward. Reaney read papers on Edith Sitwell, Virginia Woolf, and Evelyn Waugh to several college literary clubs, made puppets that he used to enact *Menaechmi* and a Molière play, wrote and made witty drawings for *The Undergrad* and *here and now* and won the Norma Epstein prize for poetry and short stories in 1948. He published beyond the university in *Canadian Poetry Magazine*, *The Canadian Forum*, *Northern Review*, *Contemporary Verse*, and *Driftwind*. In 1947, his short story "The Box-Social" was a campus scandal that was picked up by *The Globe and Mail* [Toronto], which led in turn to publication of the story and two others for a mass audience in *New Liberty Magazine*.

In 1949, Reaney published *The Red Heart*, his first collection of lyrics, for which he received the Governor General's Award for Poetry in English. President A.H. Gillson of the University of Manitoba appointed him directly to teach creative writing, and among those who studied with him were John Hirsch, Adele Wiseman, and Tom Hendry. Among colleagues who were friends as well were Victor Cowie, Jack Woodbury, Chester Duncan, and myself. Important influences on Reaney in this period, when he was working out a cultural approach to the teaching of Canadian literature, were Kenneth McNaught in History and John Warkentin in Geography and his reading of Marshall McLuhan, whose first book, *The Mechanical Bride*, he read in the early 1950s. By 1969 this cultural approach was to issue in an undergraduate course in Canadian Literature and Culture at the University of Western Ontario devised and taught by a team led by Reaney and including Donald Hair, Ernest Redekop, James Good, Bruce Lundgren, and myself. It was also to lead to Reaney's graduate course in Ontario Literature and Culture at Western and to four of the six Ph.D. theses completed under his direction between 1975 and 1983. Reaney outlines this graduate course in "An ABC to Ontario Literature and Culture."

Married in 1951 and with two sons, James Stewart (1952) and John Andrew (1954), Reaney realized the need to secure his professional position with further qualifications, and, in any case, he wanted to study with Northrop Frye. In 1957, he returned to the University of Toronto, where he completed requirements and wrote his thesis, "The Influence of Spenser on Yeats," under Frye's supervision, and received the Ph.D. in 1959. In those years, he took full part in student affairs as President of the Graduate English Club, developed friendships with fellow poets like Jay Macpherson and Eli Mandel, published *A Suit of Nettles* (1958), for which he received his second Governor General's Award for Poetry in English, and wrote his first play, *The Sun and the Moon*, which was not to be performed until 1965.

Reaney and his family returned to Winnipeg, where their daughter Susan Alice Elizabeth was born in 1959, the year in which *Night-Blooming Cereus*, with music by Beckwith, was first performed on CBC Radio. It was performed again in 1960, this time with *One-Man Masque* (with Reaney acting the role) at Hart House, University of Toronto. Reaney received the Massey Award in 1960, for *The Killdeer*, and moved to London, Ontario, to join the Department of English of Middlesex College, University of Western Ontario, and to begin the strenuous life he has led for over three decades as editor, dramatist-director, and teacher. As editor he published, and for a considerable time hand-set, his own magazine, *Alphabet: A Semi-Annual Devoted to the Iconography of the Imagination* (1960–71), in which he wished to relate documentary and myth and in which writers, critics, and visual artists could find an outlet. He published poets of varying kinds — Jay Macpherson, Margaret Atwood, Al Purdy, Milton Acorn, bpNichol — and kept in touch with writers across Canada. He published art work by Londoner friends Tony Urquhart and Greg Curnoe and, with Jack Chambers, issued an emblem book, *The Dance of Death at London, Ontario* (1963). *Twelve Letters to a Small Town* appeared in 1962, after its performance with Beckwith's chamber-music setting on CBC in 1961.

As a dramatist, Reaney has been prolific. Though most of his plays have been published, some remain in script. Pamela Terry directed the first performances of *The Killdeer* (1960) and *The Easter Egg* (1962). For the third time, Reaney was given the Governor General's Award, this time for two works, *Twelve Letters* and *The Killdeer and Other Plays* (1962). John Hirsch directed his first children's play, *Names and Nicknames*, at the Manitoba Theatre Centre, Winnipeg, in 1963, with Martha Henry and Douglas Rain in the cast, and Reaney himself put on three marionette shows at the Western Fair in London in 1965. He has discussed the importance of this experience in "Stories on a String: It All Started in London, Ontario, in the Mid-1960s (Part 1)." From 1964 to 1966, Reaney was resident author for Summer Theatre at Western, with Keith Turnbull as artistic director and Paul Thompson (later of Theatre Passe-Muraille in Toronto) as technical director. In the 1965 series, Turnbull directed *The Sun and the Moon*; in 1966, Reaney directed *Listen to the Wind*, the play that reveals a new shaping of dramatic form that was to become characteristic of Reaney's plays. Certainly, its effect is clear on *Colours in the Dark*, directed by John Hirsch at Stratford in 1967, with Henry, Rain, and Heath Lamberts in the cast. In the same year, Reaney rented several floors of a building in downtown London for Alphacentre, a sort of community centre of the arts. Here Reaney held Saturday sessions for his Listeners' Workshop in which children and adults took part in acting out sections of the Bible. The importance of this group for Reaney's later relations with adult actors is made clear in several of his articles: "Ten Years at Play" (1969), "Kids and Crossovers" (1976), and "Your Plays Are Like Movies — Cinemascope Ones" (1979). The death of John Andrew in 1966 darkened this otherwise radiant period.

In his sabbatical year (1968–69) in Victoria, Reaney worked on a play based on the murder of the Donnellys in Lucan, Ontario, a story that had fascinated him in his childhood and intermittently since then. On his return to London, he devoted himself to research in the archives at Western and to writing and rewriting *The Donnellys*, the play that finally turned into a trilogy presented at Tarragon Theatre under Turnbull's direction. *Sticks and Stones* appeared in 1973. *The St. Nicholas Hotel* followed in 1974 and won for Reaney the Chalmers Award in 1975 and an honorary D.Litt. from Carleton University. *Handcuffs*, which completed the trilogy, was performed in 1975; in 1976 Reaney was made an Officer of the Order of Canada. In 1978 he was elected to the Royal Society of Canada, and in 1979 he accepted an honorary D.Litt. from McMaster University.

In these years, Reaney and Turnbull devoted themselves to their theatre company, NDWT, centred at Bathurst United Church in Toronto, though still frequently using the Drama Workshop at the Department of English at Western, as it had done for workshops preceding the premieres of *The Donnellys*. The company took *The Donnellys* on a national tour in 1975, an account of which is given by Reaney in *14 Barrels from Sea to Sea* (1977). On the company's return, it performed *Baldoon* (1976) and toured Ontario with it and then performed *The Dismissal* (1977), *Wacousta!* (1978), and *Gyroscope* (1981). Reaney and some company members have assisted local amateurs to mount complex, masque-like plays commissioned to celebrate local anniversaries: *King Whistle!* (1979) at Stratford; *Antler River* (1980) at London; *I, The Parade* (1982) at Waterloo. *Traps* (1980) was put on by Theatre Beyond Words. Another company, Comus Music Theatre of Canada, at long last performed *Shivaree*, the opera by Reaney with Beckwith, in 1982. *Cloudshadows* (1981) is in some respects a return to the dramatic design of the early plays. *Canadian Brothers, or the Prophecy Fulfilled* extended Reaney's adaptation of John Richardson's novels that he had begun with *Wacousta!*; it was premiered at the University of Calgary on 24 November 1983.

While continuing his work on plays and operas, Reaney wrote important works in many other genres. In "Some Critics Are Music Teachers" (1982), an essay contributed to a festschrift for Frye, he makes clear the importance to him of the contrapuntal criticism of his early teacher. "The Brontës: Gothic Transgressor as Cattle Drover" advances a hypothesis about the origin of the Heathcliff-Rochester figure in the novels of the Brontës. *Imprecations: The Art of Swearing* (1984) is a satiric poem of linked narratives drawn from his own experiences, which also are the basis for a children's story, *Take the Big Picture* (1986). His earlier venture in this genre was *The Boy with an R in His Hand*, which is set in the Toronto of 1826. *Take the Big Picture* is contemporary in theme and setting and is clearly autobiographical in many sections.

When in high school, Reaney had been fascinated to learn that Ann Cardwell was the *nom-de-plume* of a Stratford writer who had published *Crazy To Kill* (1941). In 1989, he arranged for a new edition of this murder mystery and wrote an introduction for it. He also used it as the basis for a libretto that John Beckwith set to music. This opera, *Crazy To Kill: A Detective Opera*, was premiered at the Guelph Festival on 11 May 1989. *Serinette*, a new opera with music by Harry Somers, was premiered at Sharon Temple on 7 July 1990.

Reaney's intense commitment to work in so many areas led to nervous prostration for some time in 1988, and he decided to retire from teaching in 1989. Now he dedicates all his energies to writing, to collaborating with others in staging his works, and to working closely with students of drama at Western. His works in progress include an opera in collaboration with Harry Somers and, with John Beckwith, a musical play on the Brontës.

Robert Kroetsch (1927–)

ANN MUNTON

ONE MUST START, as Robert Kroetsch tells us, "with an invocation / invoke"[1] myth, memory, the muse. Beginnings are crucial and magical for the poet. Roy Kiyooka tells him, "the new myth of beginnings. . . . It's the Western Canadian myth: the artist from the distant place, from the bookless world." Kroetsch answers, "I'm from a farm, . . . way hell and gone out in Alberta."[2] The beginnings — rural, western, fictive, vacant, replete — recur in the writing. Documents are also important. The official ledger recording Kroetsch's arrival is probably in some obscure room of an Alberta government building in downtown Edmonton. A more informal recording would be found in the traces of a farmhouse celebration. And so the story begins. Some specifics are as follows.

The paternal side of Kroetsch's family ("a widow and her sons, six or seven"[3]) embarked aboard the *Pauline* on the mythic journey for the New World, arriving in New York in June 1841.[4] The maternal side remained in Germany a while longer, where Kroetsch's maternal great-grandmother, Anna Weller, was born in 1849 (*FN*, p. 65). From New York the Kroetsch family travelled north and settled close to Belmore in Bruce County, Ontario, the site for the family sawmill. Here, in 1856, Kroetsch's grandfather Henry Kroetsch was born, and in turn Kroetsch's father, Paul Kroetsch, was born in 1893. A further westering notion overtook the family in the first years of Alberta's provincial infancy. In 1905 began the movement of the Kroetsch family to take up farming in rural Alberta. The Wellers preceded them by four years, via another route. One of Kroetsch's maternal great-grandfathers fought on the Union side and was wounded in the American Civil War. Also drawn westward, he established a homestead in Minnesota, whence his two sons and their families continued on to the district of Alberta in 1901. Kroetsch's mother, Hilda Marie Weller, was born there in 1903 at Spring Lake, a small community in central Alberta. Hilda Weller and Paul Kroetsch were married in 1925 and settled on a farm in Heisler, just a few miles south of Hilda's birthplace.

> [Heisler] was a very small town with only 200 people. It was a shopping centre and there were grain elevators. And there were coal mines nearby. They were little family coal mines on the Battle River. So Heisler was both a farming and coal mining community.[5]

The Kroetsches had five children. Their first child, and only son, was born on 26 June 1927 — the poet, Robert Kroetsch.

Kroetsch grew up in rural Alberta and reportedly was "spoiled rotten from the day of [his] birth."[6] Surrounded by sisters, aunts, uncles, and cousins, he had an immediate sense of the extended family. In fact, farm and family are probably the two most important formative influences on him. The farm was large and worked primarily by horses. "[T]here was a high definition of male and female activity, and lots of hired help working."[7] Prevented from doing the indoor male work because of allergies, and the indoor female work because of the sexual boundaries, Kroetsch spent his time in the solitary, outdoor activities of gardening, fixing fences, and rounding up cattle in the fall. In retrospect, these become

tremendously significant pursuits. Planting trees, a reversal of the
pioneer norm, and raising a bountiful garden, Kroetsch eagerly
received the winter seed catalogues, worked intimately with the
earth of his home place, and bridged the traditional male/female
divisions. Riding the fence lines or searching out lost cows in Battle
River coulees, Kroetsch was free to feed his imagination and dream
the beginning stories.

And stories were a crucial aspect of family life. "Women cooking
and canning together, visiting. Men working together, drinking
together" (Hancock, p. 36). The gossip and tall tales of kitchen and
prairie pub provide Kroetsch with an enveloping oral tradition.
Stories of the journey to the New World, the first homesteaders
and ground-breakers, gave way to stories of immediate surround-
ings and folk: "That kind of storytelling in a small community is
how you invent each other — give each other a character" (Mac-
Kinnon, p. 4). Kroetsch tells of being unable to contend in person
with his famous storytelling father and thus slipping off upstairs
to write (Hancock, p. 36; MacKinnon, p. 6).

These oral stories were Kroetsch's early measure, because the
family library consisted of only three or four books: "One of them
was on looking after horses. . . . One was on wild flowers. . . . One
was on threshing machines" (Hancock, p. 37). He read through
the stacks of pulp magazines found in the hired man's room: "*Ten
Story Western, Air Aces*. Stories about Doc Savage" ("Taking the
Risk," in *RK*, p. 65). He borrowed books from a travelling library
and sent off by mail for others, but there was something incon-
gruous about the fiction he found:

> I remember reading voraciously as a boy, and the fictional boys
> I read about were always doing things I couldn't begin to do,
> because we didn't have the big oak trees or whatever. And that
> sense of alienation made me feel that first I had to go see — I
> didn't really believe you could construct a world without huge
> wheat fields.[8]

The solution was twofold. First of all, you invent your own stories
with wheat fields instead of oak trees. Second, you locate books
with resonances deeper than geographic similitude.

Kroetsch attended Heisler Public School, a small school with four
grades to a room, from 1932 to 1944. He graduated in 1945 from

the Red Deer High School. When only in grade four, he happened by accident on two books that were unlike all the others he had read so far. As he tells it in "Taking the Risk," he had exhausted his class's meagre library resources and, upon exploring the wealth of the next room, discovered Joseph Conrad's *The Nigger of the "Narcissus"* and Henry James's *The Turn of the Screw* (*RK*, p. 65). The impact, over time, was profound. Another aspect of rural schooling that became significant was the means of transportation. On the long and leisurely horse-and-buggy or horse-and-cutter rides to school, Kroetsch became both an acute observer of the passing scene and seasons and an inventor of complete story worlds. "To this day," he tells us, "I can't walk from my parked car to my office without inventing a story" ("Taking the Risk," in *RK*, p. 66).

Majoring in English and philosophy at the University of Alberta in Edmonton (1945–48), Kroetsch concentrated on nineteenth-century literature, but the stories surrounding him now were those of hardship and bravery told by the returning veterans. Prompted by machismo, and in an attempt to match such daring and discover the experience beyond books necessary for the would-be writer (Hemingway was now the acknowledged exemplar), Kroetsch took off promptly upon graduation for the North — that last of Canadian frontiers. He worked first as a labourer on the Fort Smith portage and then for two shipping seasons on the riverboats on the Mackenzie River. In 1951 he briefly worked for a catering company on Hudson Bay, and then from 1951 to 1954 he was the civilian Director of Information and Education for the United States Air Force in Goose Bay, Labrador.

After six years spent primarily in the North, at the age of twenty-seven Kroetsch returned to graduate school. He attended the Bread Loaf School of English at Middlebury College in Vermont during the summer of 1954 and again in 1955 and 1956, completing his M.A. degree there. From 1954 to 1955 he attended McGill University, studying the development of English prose with Hugh MacLennan:

I'd discovered in six years of not only seeking but finding experience that I had one hell of a lot to learn about literature. About writing. About the experience of fusing of words with experience. ("Taking the Risk," in *RK*, p. 67)

During this time Kroetsch began work on a novel about his experiences on the Mackenzie River, and in 1955 *Maclean's* published his first story of note, "That Yellow Prairie Sky." (His earliest short stories, "The Stragglers" and "The Toughest Mile," were published in *The Montrealer* in 1950.)

While at Middlebury College Kroetsch met Jane Lewis, whom he married in 1956. They have two daughters — Laura Caroline Kroetsch, born in 1964, and Margaret Ann (Meg) Kroetsch, born in 1966. Kroetsch and his wife separated in 1974 and subsequently divorced. From 1956 to 1961 Kroetsch attended the University of Iowa, participating in the Writers' Workshop there, as many Canadian writers have done. Among his professors were George P. Elliott and Harvey Swados. Kroetsch received his Ph.D. in 1961, for the unpublished novel "Coulee Hill," and from 1961 until 1978 he was on the faculty in the English Department at the State University of New York at Binghamton. In 1962 he returned briefly to the Mackenzie to research *But We Are Exiles*, published in 1965 when he was in his late thirties. Primarily a novelist in these first years, Kroetsch next published his "Out West" series of three interrelated novels: *The Words of My Roaring* (1966), *The Studhorse Man* (1969) (which won the Governor General's Award for Fiction in English), and *Gone Indian* (1973). *Badlands* followed in 1975, *What the Crow Said* in 1978, and most recently *Alibi* in 1983. Experience in a broad sense and the home place continue to be important in these novels, as Kroetsch develops from a realistic approach to fiction to a more fabulist one, exploring, often in a surreal or postmodernist manner, tall tales and myths. These interests are reflected also in Kroetsch's critical activities. In 1974 he founded, with William Spanos, the important critical journal *Boundary 2: A Journal of Postmodern Literature*. A special issue of *Open Letter* (1983) and *The Lovely Treachery of Words: Essays Selected and New* (1989) collect the critical essays that Kroetsch has written since 1971.

Near the end of his sojourn in the United States, Kroetsch again began to feel the pull of the prairies. His early story, "That Yellow Prairie Sky," examined his home place from the perspective of "that western problem that goes back to the homesteaders: do I stay or do I leave?"9 Twenty years later, Kroetsch revised this sentiment so that he could embrace both possibilities. He was writer-in-residence at the University of Calgary in the fall of 1975 and at the universities of Lethbridge and Manitoba from 1976 to 1977. In 1978 he returned permanently to the Canadian West as a professor in the English Department at the University of Manitoba in Winnipeg. Kroetsch's daughters remained in the United States with their mother. In 1982 he married writer and teacher Smaro Kamboureli; their marriage has ended.

Kroetsch's physical return to the West coincides with his beginning to write poetry seriously. Fifteen years intervened between the publication of his first poem and the publication of his first book of poetry, during which time he published five novels and a travel book, *Alberta* (1968), and edited the anthology *creation* (1970). In the years since that first book of poetry, the published work is more evenly divided between poetry and fiction, with the addition of a steady stream of critical essays.

Kroetsch says he wrote his first poem in Iowa at the age of thirty-two, and single pieces began to be published in little magazines in the early 1960s. His first published poem, "Letter to a Friend's Wife," was published in 1961; his first collection of poetry, *The Stone Hammer Poems: 1960–1975*, was not published until 1975. There followed *The Ledger* (1975), *Seed Catalogue* (1977), *The Sad Phoenician* (1979), and *The Criminal Intensities of Love as Paradise* (1981). Then in 1981 Kroetsch published *Field Notes*, the title of which came to designate his ongoing long poem. *Field Notes* consists of the five previously published book-length poems, plus four others. In 1983 he published *Letters to Salonika*. In 1985 he published the five-part *Advice to My Friends*, and in 1986 the ten-part *Excerpts from the Real World*, both continuations of *Field Notes*. In 1986 he also published a reprint of *Seed Catalogue*, which contains further poems for *Field Notes* and, in 1989, *Completed Field Notes: The Long Poems of Robert Kroetsch*.

More clearly autobiographical than his novels, the early poetry is profoundly regionalist in Eli Mandel's sense of focusing on first place:

> ... surely ... the essence of what we mean by a region [is] the overpowering feeling of nostalgia associated with the place we know as the *first* place, the *first* vision of things, the *first* clarity of things.[10]

Kroetsch captures this essence in his absorption with beginnings; memory replaces history as a means to tell the past; the storyteller is revered; and tall tales demonstrate a "humour in the ludicrous." In the most recent poetry, Kroetsch explores the borders of possibility in language, form, and process.

Although the facts with which we can qualify the myth of Robert Kroetsch are those which he himself chooses to reveal, they are nevertheless related to the poems. Shirley Neuman, for instance, examines the actual strategies of autobiography in two articles.[11] Autobiographical aspects have loomed larger in Kroetsch's later works, specifically in the poetry, and are intrinsically associated with major concerns: language, place, doubleness, boundaries. In fact, there are many biographical significances that become apparent in the poetic patterns. Kroetsch's sojourn in the United States, for example, probably allowed him the distance and perspective necessary to tackling the crucial questions of home place and belonging (*nostos*), alienation and exile. In fact, it allowed him to act out the familial westering journey and to embody the doubleness of his parents' geographic sensibilities:

> My father was from Ontario — so he came west [at age 16] with a deep sense of nostalgia for Ontario — he preferred its rich green, rural landscape. My mother was born in Alberta and its landscape was the world she was used to. I felt that I grew up with a kind of double vision. (MacKinnon, p. 3)

The unique division of labour in the prairie town of Heisler further emphasized the duplicitous view:

> They [the coal miners] lived a strange life and the fact that they went underground contributed to my double vision. The farmers working on the surface would give me a kind of surface metaphor while the coal miners working below the surface would provide the underworld metaphor. (MacKinnon, pp. 3–4)

The doubleness is reinforced by an erotic tension of the sexual boundaries implicit in Kroetsch's childhood world. The ambiguity of the garden space is amplified in the endless ambiguities of Kroetsch's poetry and the continual pushing of boundaries.

The temptation of silence is also constantly present, while, ironically, language is one of Kroetsch's major concerns; and even this doubling of silence and speaking can be related to biography: to the silence of his geographical place, the seductive unspokenness of a primal landscape, and to the death of his mother when he was only thirteen. Kroetsch explains,

> . . . I think part of my move to autobiography was daring to say that my mother died when I was so young and I was very close to her: I think some of the female presence in my book [*Badlands*] is almost a parody of the absence which is really what the book is about. . . . [O]ne of the things that I can see happening, in the next few years as I go on writing, is a kind of enunciation. I can feel even my long poem, *Field Notes*, drawing toward that.[12]

The enunciation of silence or the voicing of the unvoiced is central to the poetry as both subject and process. There is also Kroetsch's literal silencing as a unilingual citizen of world literature: his parents refused to speak German after the day of his birth.

Autobiographical patterning thus seems to structure the poems: duplicity, the pull between belonging and leaving, a westering movement, the search for home, absence, loss, the seasonal growth cycle. Patterns of return are found: in *Seed Catalogue*, when a cousin of Kroetsch's returns to Anna Weller's birthplace, first descendant to do so, nearly a century after her birth, he comes carrying death, "a cargo of bombs" (*FN*, p. 65), and meets his own. Kroetsch returns to Germany himself many years later and meets his double in the Frankfurt *Hauptbahnhof*, recorded in the poem of that title. He takes his two American-born daughters to Greece, birthplace of his second wife and home of muses and oracles, recorded in "Delphi: Commentary." He seeks crucial and magical beginnings in "Mile Zero" and "Spending the Morning on the Beach."

Myth, memory, the muse.

NOTES

[1] Robert Kroetsch, "Seed Catalogue," in his *Field Notes 1–8: A Continuing Poem* (Don Mills, Ont.: General, 1981), p. 56. Further references to this work (*FN*) appear in the text.

2 Robert Kroetsch, "Taking the Risk," in *Robert Kroetsch: Essays*, ed. Frank Davey and bpNichol [*Open Letter*, 5th ser., No. 4 (Spring 1983)], p. 65. Further references to this collection (*RK*) appear in the text.

3 Robert Kroetsch, *The Crow Journals* (Edmonton: NeWest, 1980), p. 37.

4 Robert Kroetsch, "Mile Zero," in his *Advice to My Friends* (Don Mills, Ont.: Stoddart, 1985), p. 36.

5 Brian MacKinnon, " 'The Writer Has Got To Know Where He Lives': An Interview with Robert Kroetsch," *Writers News Manitoba*, 4, No. 1 (Feb. 1982), p. 3. Further references to this work appear in the text.

6 Geoff Hancock, "An Interview with Robert Kroetsch," *Canadian Fiction Magazine*, Nos. 24–25 (Spring–Summer 1977), p. 36. Further references to this work appear in the text.

7 Shirley Neuman and Robert Wilson, *Labyrinths of Voice: Conversations with Robert Kroetsch* (Edmonton: NeWest, 1982), p. 21.

8 Robert Kroetsch, "A Conversation with Margaret Laurence," in Robert Kroetsch, James Bacque, and Pierre Gravel, *creation*, ed. Robert Kroetsch (Toronto: new, 1970), p. 62.

9 Kroetsch, "A Conversation," p. 54.

10 Eli Mandel, "Images of Prairie Man," in *Another Time*, Three Solitudes: Contemporary Literary Criticism in Canada, III (Erin, Ont.: Porcépic, 1977), p. 50.

11 Shirley Neuman, "Allow Self, Portraying Self: Autobiography in *Field Notes*," *Line*, No. 2 (Fall 1983), pp. 104–21; "Figuring the Reader, Figuring the Self in *Field Notes*: 'Double or Noting,' " *Open Letter* [Robert Kroetsch: Reflections], 5th ser., Nos. 8–9 (Summer–Fall 1984), pp. 176–94.

12 Neuman and Wilson, p. 22.

Phyllis Webb (1927–)

JOHN F. HULCOOP

PHYLLIS WEBB WRITES with her left hand, a fact most biographers might, understandably, overlook:

> I cannot write with my right.
>
> I grasp what I can. The rest
> is a great shadow.[1]

The would-be Webb biographer should be something of a palmist — work with what is offered, grasp what one can, acknowledging that the rest (what one might like to but cannot write) is and must remain "a great shadow":

> is there a shadow following the
> hand that writes
> always? or for the left-handed
> only?

(WB, p. 13)

What the biographer is offered to read is not a life but a hand (and, like Virginia Woolf, Webb writes a difficult, sometimes illegible, hand):

> . . . read
> my palm's lines:
> This is my life
> . . . .
> This is the story
> I've indented my flesh with.
> Read if you can those crooked paths.[2]

In "a radio scandal for four voices in verse and prose" entitled "YOU SURE LOOK FUNNY WHEN YOU WRITE" and projected as part of (or perhaps alternative to) a long, unpublished poem called "The Left Hand Exercise,"[3] *left* is ironically identified with "the unconscious / . . . the female element, and / . . . Satan and / . . . all misery, evil and death." Certainly, any would-be biographer of Webb will have to confront all these issues in one form or another — sometimes political, sometimes religious, and sometimes both simultaneously, as in the serious and divinely comic poem that begins "Death, Judgement, Heaven, Hell, / and Spring. The Five Last Things, / the least of which I am" (*WB*, p. 82).

Webb's "sinistrality"[4] may, illegitimately, strike the innocent reader of her work as the least of what she is; such a reader, looking, even longing for a conventional — right-handed — "life," one that will explain or provide a key to the work, will expect to begin conventionally with Webb's family. And such a right-minded reader will be disappointed because the poet (or her persona) states quite frankly that "My family is the circumstance I cannot dance with."[5] Like Elizabeth Bennet (at the beginning of *Pride and Prejudice*), Webb's would-be biographer is left (again, that word) without a partner in the attempt to choreograph the steps of her life: never a *pas de trois* or a *pas de famille*; most often a *pas seul*; occasionally a *pas de deux*. "Oh Lord Krishna DANCE / Shiva DANCE . . ." (*WL*, p. 6). Shiva is the principle of generation; his followers are allowed to participate in the great "game" or lila of life by dancing; but in the lila of Webb's life — which is poetry: the sometimes "flagrant musick of the old lore" (*WL*, p. 36) — folk-dancing, family-dancing — is not the style.

And yet "the subject family, the repeated // word ready to pounce out of the thunder" (*WL*, p. 46) lurks, an ever-present sub-text to the *prima materia* of Webb's dream-work.[6] Like the speaker in "I Daniel" who does "not want to keep / the matter in my heart // for the heart of the matter / is something different" (*WL*, p. 35), the poet dreams her dream and delivers its coded messages (*WL*, p. 37): censored material, transformed and so disguised, pounces like

> . . . the cats restless, hungry
> in view of winter, in view of cold
>
> cold as the curse of mere matter, *Mère*
> matter . . . .
>
> (*WL*, p. 46)

Webb herself remarks on "the dominance of male figures" in the "Portraits" section of *Wilson's Bowl* (*WB*, p. 9) where amongst Socrates, Dostoevsky, Rilke, Pound, Vasarely, and Kropotkin, lurks "Father":

> . . . his long beautiful
> hands holding the reins
> just so, horse dancing.
>
> (*WB*, p. 33)

And rival siblings masquerade as "conjunctive and / peaceable" in an ironic "Suite of Lies,"[7] the unpublished drafts of which are a startling revelation of the bitterness inherent in "suite."[8]

> Nothing can be undone, least of all
> the darkness of history and the fact
> of one's birth.
> Those are the major premises that come
> to us to be gathered.[9]

Phyllis Jean, youngest of Mary and Alfred Webb's three children, was born on 8 April 1927 (she has two brothers).

> I grew up on an island — Vancouver Island. I was born in
> Victoria . . . and my one ambition as a teenager was to get off
> that island . . . and on to the mainland. . . . And then by half
> way through my life my ambition was to get back on an island,
> preferably a Gulf Island, and everything just kept turning up
> Salt Spring. So here I am, and I've been here for twelve years
> now.[10]

Though she's lived in Vancouver, Edmonton, Toronto, Montreal,
London, Paris, and San Francisco, the pull has always been back
to the West Coast. "I think it is the sea. It is my original landscape,[11]
and I think that really profoundly pull[s] me. . . . And it's so quiet
here and peaceful . . . I feel safe on this island. I feel protected from
people" (Munton, p. 10). From a 1944 poem, published in her
school magazine and describing the "mad, wild ocean,"[12] to her
most recent volume, *Water and Light*, the importance of West
Coast seascapes in her work has been consistent and obvious. In a
CBC Radio talk, she fondly recalled "the summers of my childhood
. . . spent at Brentwood on the Saanich Peninsula of Vancouver
Island," swimming and boating: "most of my summer hours were
watery ones. Either in the water or on it."[13] In the 1960s, soon after
publishing *The Sea Is Also a Garden*, Webb gave six more talks, at
least three of which — "Swimming," "Marine Life," and "Afloat
on Waters" — relate to the aqueous summers of her childhood.[14]
Northrop Frye has asserted that

> Every good lyrical poet has a certain structure of imagery as
> typical of him as his handwriting, held together by certain
> recurring metaphors, and sooner or later he will produce one
> or more poems that seem to be at the centre of that structure.
> These poems are in the formal sense his mythical poems, and
> they are for the critic the imaginative keys to his work.[15]

Webb is, of course, a great lyrical poet; and the recurring images
and metaphors that structure her poetic thought are often directly
related to the islands, the water, and the light of the West Coast
that exercise a moon-like pull on the tides of her being.

Webb's parents separated before she was ten; she was raised
mainly by her mother and mainly in Victoria, where she attended

St. Margaret's, a school for girls, from grades seven to twelve. In 1949, she graduated from the University of British Columbia with a B.A. in English and philosophy. "I've always been a very questioning person . . . ever since I was a child" (Munton, p. 6), Webb has stated; and, while several critics and interviewers have alluded to her "relentless questioning of life's purpose," few have shown the good sense of Eleanor Wachtel who sees that Webb's questioning affirms "a philosophic as well as a poetic stance."[16] "I have always had to seek a meaning," Webb says,

> I was not handed it at birth — what Laing calls ontological insecurity. . . . I had never thought of phil. (phyl) as the study of death when I was studying it; but of course the search for meaning, for grounding, is made necessary by death. When my eye took in the Socratic question — "For is not philosophy / the study of death?" — it was as if my whole past interest in phil. was lit up.[17]

Such a reflection renders indisputable the significance of the following lines from one of her more notorious poems:

> . . . But there's no shame
> in this concept of suicide.
> It has concerned our best philosophers
> . . . .
> In the end it brings more honesty and care
> than all the democratic parliament of tricks.[18]

"I think I became a Canadian and claimed my country when I was seventeen and arrived at political consciousness."[19] Its arrival was hastened by the Second World War. Though Webb was only twelve when it began (in 1939), the war

> was one of *the* formative experiences of my youth. It all came mainly through radio broadcasts and talk among people; also, my oldest brother, Walter, was in the war — he joined up at seventeen, and was overseas. But the horror and insanity of war, and of politics, turned me to socialism in my seventeenth year.[20]

At twenty-two, the youngest candidate in the Commonwealth (Wachtel, p. 11), Webb fought for the CCF in a provincial election — and lost; but the campaign introduced her to F.R. Scott, chairman of the CCF from 1942 to 1950, and the man who would exercise the greatest influence on her life for the next decade. As well as founding the League for Social Reconstruction, Scott was an energetic advocate of civil liberties and minority rights.[21] He was also an established literary figure, having had a hand in starting *The McGill Fortnightly Review*, *The Canadian Mercury*, and *Preview*, and having published his first collection of poems, *Overture*, in 1945. Scott not only encouraged Webb to move to Montreal, which she did in 1950, but also introduced her into the literary circles that revolved about both *Preview* and *First Statement*. Though she had already been writing for some years, Webb herself dates the beginning of her own literary career from the move to Montreal.[22] In 1951 she contributed poems to *The Cataraqui Review*, *Northern Review*, and *Contemporary Verse*, adding PM *Magazine* and *Contact* to her list of publishers in 1952, CIV/n and *Forge* in 1953.[23] In 1954, Contact Press published *Trio* containing first poems by Eli Mandel, Gael Turnbull, and Phyllis Webb.

"Almost a Jesus / I walk on waters white with a glass stride / and mimeograph the snow with feet behind me. . . ." These lines, from "Ottawa River — Winter,"[24] owe the mimeographing metaphor to one of Webb's three major occupations in 1950–57. During this time she held at least six secretarial positions, mostly at McGill but also at the London School of Economics in England. London and Paris Webb once regarded as the "two major 'moves' of my life."[25] She travelled to England in 1954: "Almost the first thing I did when I arrived was to go to Ireland. I find that significant"[26] — presumably from both a political and literary point of view. It was, of course, a "literary pilgrimage to do homage to Yeats and Joyce";[27] but it was also, perhaps, a rejection of the imperialistic "mother-country" in favour of the symbol of an on-going fight for independence. After the publication of *Even Your Right Eye* in 1956, a Canadian Government Overseas Award financed Webb's move to Paris where she stayed for almost two years (1957–59), captivated primarily by the French Theatre of the Absurd, by Pirandello, Adamov, Sartre, Artaud, and other writers.[28] "I lived in Paris during a series of political crises. At one point civil war threatened.

I was a witness . . . to violence and even was once involved in it. I was never able to forget that a brutal Colonial War was in progress." In a series of articles written for the *Victoria Daily Times* in August 1959, Webb describes her Parisian garret, the Cité Universitaire, the cafés she frequented, the riot in which she was involved, and fencing: "I had never expected to become a fencing fan but in Paris I did. I liked the mock dance of death, the civilization of rage . . . it epitomized the French."[29]

In addition to stenography and poetry, Webb's other major occupation during this period was the rapidly expanding contribution she made to the CBC, first radio and later television. It consisted largely of talks on general topics, of reviews for *Critically Speaking*, of hour-long programs like those on the letters and journals of Rilke and Van Gogh, as well as reports on specific events like the Canadian Writers' Conference at Queen's University in July 1955. Here Webb also delivered an important paper on "The Poet and the Publisher," in preparing which she had tabulated responses from sixteen Canadian poets (in addition to some notable academics and publishers) to a questionnaire of her own devising.[30] Extensive freelance work continued after her return to Vancouver in order to teach at her old *alma mater* (1959–63) and culminated in her being offered a full-time job with the CBC in 1964. She began by running the network's *University of the Air*, but subsequently proposed, along with William A. Young, that her program and his (*The Learning Stage*) be amalgamated into a single series to be called *Ideas*. This program, still running in 1992, is the most important and successful program of its kind ever aired on CBC Radio. Webb became its executive producer in 1967, in which year, between April and July, she also hosted thirteen programs for CBC television. For these historic programs, Webb interviewed at least thirty Canadian poets from F.R. Scott, Dorothy Livesay, and A.J.M. Smith to Margaret Atwood, bpNichol, and bill bissett.

Before joining the staff of the CBC, Webb lived in San Francisco for a year (1963–64), having received a Canada Council Junior Arts Award, partly in recognition of her third volume, *The Sea Is Also a Garden* (1962). One of the American poets with whom she became close friends whilst in San Francisco was Robert Duncan whom she had met, along with Charles Olson, Allen Ginsberg, Robert Creeley, and Denise Levertov at the epoch-making poetry conference held at the University of British Columbia in 1963.[31] Although Webb published *Naked Poems*, a landmark volume in her literary career, in 1965, she wrote very little during the five years she was employed full-time by the CBC (Wachtel, p. 12). Not that the experience was unfruitful; quite the contrary, since it brought her into contact with a large number of artists and intellectuals — Paul Goodman, R.D. Laing, N.O. Brown, and Glenn Gould for most obvious examples — whose special interests not only added new dimensions to Webb's work but, in some cases, actually helped to generate it.[32]

Suffering from nervous exhaustion, Webb took a long leave of absence from the CBC in 1967, returning to the West Coast where, for the first time, she stayed on Salt Spring Island. Already, she had begun to brood upon and write a large work centring on the life of the Russian anarchist-geographer, Prince Peter Kropotkin; and, before resuming work in Toronto, she visited Russia. Crossing the Atlantic again in 1968, she worked in England with R.D. Laing, controversial psychiatrist and sometime-poet, on his Massey lectures, *The Politics of the Family*. The following year, a Major Arts Bursary from the Canada Council enabled her to resign from the CBC. She headed west almost immediately. And, apart from a year as writer-in-residence at the University of Alberta, in Edmonton (1980–81), has lived in Vancouver, on Salt Spring Island, or in Victoria ever since. The change from east to west did not, however, put an end to Webb's CBC connection. In addition to her fairly regular reviews for *Critics at Large* and *Critics on Air* (programs produced by John Merritt, who had the foresight to preserve his Webb tapes) and her frequent poetry readings for Robert Weaver's *Anthology*, she submitted major scripts in 1970, "Waterlily and Multifoliate Rose: Cyclic Notions in Proust," in 1971, "The Question as an Instrument of Torture," and in 1972, "Calamities and Crystals: Fate and the Unconscious." Another 1972 program, "Rejoice in the Lamb: The Offering of Christopher Smart," won Webb and her producer, Robert Chesterman, an Ohio Radio Award.[33]

For Webb the poet this was an equally productive period. Between the spring of 1970 and the summer of 1973, she published the seven "Poems of Failure," the five sections of "A Question of Questions," the eight "Letters to Margaret Atwood," plus eight more individual poems.[34] The first *Selected Poems 1954–65*, with its controversial book-design by David Robinson, appeared in 1971 and resulted in Webb's being honoured by the B.C. Library Association in 1972 as "the writer who had made the greatest contribution to the poetry of B.C. in the past five years." In 1972, the year she returned to Salt Spring Island, she also met Ben Metcalfe about whom she wrote a long article for *Maclean's*.[35] Then she fell more or less silent, having what she has described as "a severe break-down" in June of 1974.[36] In 1975 she refused a "Doctor of Laws *honoris causa* in recognition of her outstanding contribution to Canadian Literature," even though the President of Simon Fraser University, Pauline Jewett, wrote personally to Webb urging her to change her mind and accept. "It wasn't until the mid-1970s, when some physiological symptoms (hypoglycaemia, thyroid) were diagnosed and treated, that 'the terrible abyss of despair' receded" (Wachtel, p. 9).

Dating back to 1970, Webb's interest in petroglyphs brought her two new friends: Lilo Berliner and Beth Hill (*Talking*, p. 130). Lilo Berliner's other-worldly correspondence with the distinguished anthropologist Wilson Duff — whose work inspired and shaped the celebrated 1975 exhibition of *images: stone: b.c.: Thirty Centuries of Northwest Coast Indian Sculpture*[37] — began in 1973 and ended late in 1975 when Duff committed suicide. Earlier that year, he had sent some poems to "Lilo, my 'twin' ": "The title poem, 'There Is No Such Thing as Going Too Far,' disappeared into the xeroxed face of a stone mask with closed eyes. . . . This was one of the great twin masks . . . reunited for the exhibition," its double having been brought back from Paris by Duff himself (*Talking*, p. 144).[38] Before doubling the act of "self-recognition" she clearly saw in Duff's self-killing (and Duff had seen in the great twin masks), Lilo Berliner deposited her correspondence with Duff on Phyllis Webb's front doorstep (*Talking*, pp. 129–49). This was in January 1977. By February, Webb was already at work on a sequence of poems that would eventually constitute the central and title-section of *Wilson's Bowl*. It is dedicated to the "memory of Lilo, who walked into the sea" (*WB*, p. 61). Three more years elapsed before *Wilson's Bowl* was published, but Webb was beginning to resume the world. She taught Creative Writing at the University of British Columbia and then at the University of Victoria during 1976–79; went to Edmonton as writer-in- residence, 1980–81; and published three books in 1982: *Talking, Sunday Water: Thirteen Anti Ghazals*, and *The Vision Tree: Selected Poems*. This last won her the Governor General's Award for Literature in English. In 1984 Webb published *Water and Light*; her most recent work is a collection of previously unpublished poems, *Hanging Fire* (1990). From 1989 to 1991 she was adjunct professor of Creative Writing at the University of Victoria. Since the late 1980s Webb has been "trying to retire," but she continues nevertheless to produce new work.[39]

Much has been made of Webb's self-isolation, her existential sense of despair, her early preoccupation with suicide, the glass-like fragility of her body and mind (see Wachtel, p. 9).[40] Exactly the same distorting emphasis exists in the pre-1970s criticism of Virginia Woolf, the writer with whom — in so many respects — Webb most deserves to be compared.[41] Yet the continuity of Webb's public life as a broadcaster and teacher is self-evident. She has also given countless poetry readings all over the country, as well as winning for herself unique recognition from the Canadian poetry community.[42] Her social and political interests, from the age of seventeen on, have cast her in a series of diverse but related roles: first as a socialist and CCF candidate, then as a theoretical anarchist, as a member of the B.C. Civil Liberties Union, in which role she successfully agitated in 1962 for the more frequent employment of women announcers by the CBC, later, as the founder of the Salt Spring Island chapter of Amnesty International, and, in her own typically non-conformist way, as a feminist of growing commitment and increased artistic affirmation. Though feminist critics have not, as yet, zeroed in on Webb with the intensity that marks their devotion to Woolf and Nicole Brossard, nevertheless, the feminist movement has been instrumental in compelling Canadian critics to revise their estimations of Phyllis Webb.[43] The last two lines of the final poem in *Wilson's Bowl* — "and the great dreams pass on / to the common good" — are surely more indicative of Webb's most passionate concerns than any two lines one might quote from earlier volumes.

None of which is intended to deny that the woman who loves islands and lives alone is a woman of great reserve. She has resolutely rejected any suggestion that she write her own autobiography, explaining her rejection on the same grounds she explains her inability to write novels or short stories (suggesting that her vision is profoundly metaphoric rather than metonymic).[44] Nor is this insistence on the continuity of Webb's public life and social interests an attempt to obscure the clarity of the "mad gardener's" exploration of the underwater world of dreams: an intensely private and often a- or even anti-social world of displacements and discontinuities. Much of Webb's work, like that of P.K. Page and Jay Macpherson, belongs in what Frye calls "the archetypal phase" of literature. In this phase, ". . . the work of literary art is a myth, and unites the ritual [social enactment] and the dream [private experience]. By doing so it limits the dream: it makes it plausible and acceptable to a social waking consciousness."[45] "A lozenge of dream / sticks on [the poet's] / tongue" (WL, p. 48). The incomprehensibility of the dream's private symbolism is limited by an act of ritualization, a rite of enactment that is also the act of writing: "The pull, this way and that, ultimately into the pull / of the pen across the page" (WL, p. 18). The pen of the left-handed poet is pulled from left to right across the page and, in the process (the rite of writing/righting), limits are placed upon the dream, the private is made accessible to public view, and the anti-social impulses of the world of the shadow are metamorphosed into what is acceptable to the "social waking consciousness." The dreamworld is always radical and subversive, as the ironic writing-voice of "I Daniel" knows: "It was only politics, wars and rumours, / in the vision or dream" (WL, p. 42). Politically speaking, the dreamworld is left-wing, subversive of the establishment; the wakingworld of social consciousness tends to be, because it *is* (like the church) established, more right-wing. And the poet has always been identified with a bird flying (by the nets itemized by Stephen Dedalus) *on both wings*.[46] "Wings, uprush of inspiration, brush / past the broken shell of my ear," says the poet in a poem (WL, p. 32) that begins with swans and plays intertextual games with right-winged Yeats's sexist sonnet ("Leda and the Swan"). Sometimes a swan, sometimes the "varied thrush, the orchard oriole, / the crying dove" (WL, p. 29), and sometimes "The Common Crow, ill-tempered and always hungry / infested with matter" (WL, p. 31): the poet flies by in many forms. But whatever form she may take, she does "not want to keep / the matter in [her] heart" — she would prefer poetry, made public, revealed and revealing (apocalyptic). And thus "the great dreams," which are always private, "pass on / to the common good" — which is always social and, maybe, always socialist, leftist.

NOTES

[1] Phyllis Webb, "Poems of Failure 1," Note, in her *Wilson's Bowl* (Toronto: Coach House, 1980), p. 13. Further references to this work (*WB*) appear in the text. This first footnote is the place to acknowledge my considerable debt of gratitude to Phyllis Webb, without whose generous help this study could not have been written. All poems, published and unpublished, all letters and excerpts from interviews are quoted with the permission of the poet.

[2] Phyllis Webb, untitled ts. ["I turn my hand"], Webb Manuscripts Collection, National Library of Canada, Ottawa. I wish to acknowledge the help of Ms. Linda Hoad, the Manuscripts Librarian, and M. Claude LeMoine, Curator of the Literary Manuscripts Collection, and to thank both for their kind assistance.

[3] Phyllis Webb, "File: Drafts of The Left Hand Exercise 21pp 40pp (poem)," ts. dated "Sept. 1969," Webb Collection. The number of pages, initially 20, has twice been amended, first to 21 and then to 40. This is an extremely important draft, including much material subsequently incorporated in the "Kropotkin Poems." The lines "Is there a shadow following the hand that writes always / or for the left-handed only?" appear at the bottom of page 1. The quotation in the text above appears on the penultimate page (unnumbered) of the ts.

[4] Phyllis Webb, "The Left Hand Exercise," ts. 4, Webb Collection. The word is used by A. Blau in *The Master Hand: A Study of the Origin and Meaning of Right and Left Sidedness in Its Relation to Personality and Language* (New York: U.S. Army Medical Library, 1946), quoted in Michael Barsley, *The Other Hand: An Investigation into the Sinister History of Left-Handedness* (New York: Hawthorn, 1966), and by Webb in ts. 6.

[5] Phyllis Webb, "Sunday Water: Thirteen Anti Ghazals," in her *Water and Light: Ghazals and Anti Ghazals* (Toronto: Coach House, 1984), p. 9. Further references to this work (*WL*) appear in the text.

[6] Phyllis Webb, an incomplete, undated poem entitled "Mother" in ts. with marginal ms. notes, Webb Collection. One marginal note is the phrase "Mater materia."

[7] Phyllis Webb, *Selected Poems 1954–1965*, ed. and introd. John F. Hulcoop (1971; Vancouver: Talonbooks, 1972), p. 154.

[8] Probably the first version of "A Suite of Lies" is scribbled on the bottom of a handwritten letter (to the poet from Anita Merritt). The illegibility of some words suggests that the draft of this extremely reticent series of poems was written at high speed: it included images of blood, pain, crying out, and desolation, which do not appear in the published version.

[9] Phyllis Webb, "Continuum," *Saturday Night*, Feb. 1966, p. 17.

[10] Ann Munton, personal interview with Phyllis Webb, Jan. 1983, pp. 6–7. It gives me particular pleasure to thank Munton, formerly a student of mine, for permission to quote from this interview. Further references to this work appear in the text.

[11] Defining regionalism, Eli Mandel names "the place we know as the *first* place, the *first* vision of things, the *first* clarity of things," in his *Another Time* (Erin: Porcépic, 1977), p. 50. In this sense, Webb is a regional poet: the West Coast seascapes are her *"first* place," her *"original* landscape."

[12] Phyllis Webb, "Ego," ts., Webb Collection. A ms. note at the bottom of the page states "Published school magazine 1944."

[13] Phyllis Webb, "Summer," undated ts., Webb Collection. In a letter to John Hulcoop, 9 July 1964, Webb refers to having "recorded my memories of summer childhood" for the CBC.

[14] Phyllis Webb, "Swimming," "Marine Life," and "Afloat on Waters," undated tss., Webb. Collection. The other three talks are entitled, "Summer Romance," "Flowers and Gardens of Summer," and "The Sun." The relationship between these talks, the literary texts that Webb was currently teaching in her freshman English class at the University of British Columbia, and some of the poems in *The Sea Is Also a Garden*, would not be difficult to establish.

[15] Northrop Frye, *The Bush Garden: Essays on the Canadian Imagination* (Toronto: House of Anansi, 1971), p. 179.

[16] Eleanor Wachtel, "Intimations of Mortality," interview with Phyllis Webb, *Books in Canada*, Nov. 1983, p. 9. This is one of the very best interviews with Webb published to date. Further references to this work appear in the text.

[17] Phyllis Webb, letter to John Hulcoop, 31 July 1986. The two lines quoted are from Webb's own poem "Socrates" (*WB*, p. 27).

[18] Webb, *Selected Poems 1954–1965*, p. 104.

[19] Phyllis Webb, *Talking* (Montreal: Quadrant, 1982), p. 13. Further references to this work (*Talking*) appear in the text.

[20] Phyllis Webb, letter to John Hulcoop, 10 Oct. 1970. Compare Webb's assertion that the Second World War was "one of *the* formative experiences" of her youth with Timothy Findley's memories of how the same war infiltrated his consciousness and affected his youth, in "Frame of Fire: A Portrait of

Timothy Findley," a program for CBC Radio, written by John Hulcoop and produced by John Merritt, 26 March 1983.

²¹ During the 1950s, Scott successfully conducted two major court cases against the Quebec government of Maurice Duplessis: (1) from 1946 to 1959, the famous Roncarelli restaurant case; (2) in 1957 the infamous Padlock Law case.

²² Phyllis Webb, ". . . in Montreal, I started to write seriously," *The Province [Weekly] B.C. Magazine*, 6 April 1957, p. 17.

²³ The 1952 dates that Cecelia Frey cites for Webb's first contributions to CIV/n are incorrect in "Phyllis Webb: A Bibliography," in *The Annotated Bibliography of Canada's Major Authors*, ed. Robert Lecker and Jack David, VI (Toronto: ECW, 1985), 398. Speaking with authority as one of the magazine's founders, Aileen Collins states that the ". . . first issue of CIV/n . . . appeared in 1953"; see Aileen Collins, ed., CIV/n: A Literary Magazine of the 50s (Montreal: Véhicule, 1983), p. 8.

²⁴ Phyllis Webb, "Ottawa River — Winter," ts., Webb Collection.

²⁵ Phyllis Webb, letter to John Hulcoop, 3 Nov. 1970. Webb might not still hold this view since her move back to the West Coast, from Toronto, may well prove to be the "major" move of her life.

²⁶ Phyllis Webb, letter to John Hulcoop, 24 Jan. 1981.

²⁷ Phyllis Webb, "A Dublin Delight," ts., talk for CBC Radio (1954), p. 1.

²⁸ Phyllis Webb, letter to John Hulcoop, 10 Oct. 1970. See also "Progress Reports to the Awards Committee of The Royal Society of Canada," Jan. and July 1958, Webb Collection, under the heading "Canada Council."

²⁹ Phyllis Webb, "Echoes of Paris," tss., *Victoria Daily Times*, 3, 4, 5, 6, 7, and 10 Aug. 1959. The first quotation is from the first talk, "Paris"; the following is from "Fencing."

³⁰ Phyllis Webb, "The Poet and the Publisher" originally subtitled "The Theory of Books Is Noble," *Queen's Quarterly*, 61 (Winter 1954–55), 498–512; rpt. in ed., *Writing in Canada: Proceedings of the Canadian Writer's Conference, Queen's University, 28–31 July, 1955*, introd. F.R. Scott, ed. George Whalley (Toronto: Macmillan, 1956), pp. 78–79. The questionnaire, responses, Webb's tabulation, and related correspondence are all in the Webb Collection.

³¹ Margaret Avison was also a panel member and participating poet at the University of British Columbia 1963 Poetry Conference. Tss. of Webb's interviews with Olson, Duncan, Ginsberg, Creeley, and Levertov are all in the Webb Collection.

³² "I didn't answer your question about how I became interested in anar-

chism and that was first of all by reading Paul Goodman's novel, *The Empire City*, in 1959. Paul Goodman was really one of the remarkable American anarchists of the twentieth century. . . . I thought I must go and find out more about anarchism and Kropotkin was often spoken of in the novel" (Interview with Phyllis Webb, CBC Radio, Sept. 1980, ts., p. 7). See also notes to *Wilson's Bowl*, p. 87. Section V of "A Question of Questions" (*WB*, pp. 52–53) is dedicated to "*R.D.L.*" — R.D. Laing who thanks Phyllis Webb "for making everything as easy as possible" for him in his preparation of the 1969 Massey lectures, Introd., in his *The Politics of the Family* (Toronto: CBC, 1969). Webb acknowledges her debt to Laing "for the inspiration for this poem" (Section V of "A Question of Questions") in her notes to *Wilson's Bowl* (p. 88).

33 The talks on Proust and "The Question as an Instrument of Torture" are printed, in revised forms, in *Talking*, pp. 18–30, 31–45. The scripts of both "Calamities and Crystals" and the Christopher Smart program are in the Webb Collection.

34 "Socrates," "Kropotkin," "For Fyodor," "Ezra Pound," "Treblinka Gas Chamber," "Solitary Confinement," and "from the Kropotkin Poems."

35 Phyllis Webb, "Protest in Paradise," *Maclean's*, June 1973, pp. 38–39, 73–77.

36 Phyllis Webb, letter to Robert Weaver, 7 Jan. 1974, Webb Collection.

37 Wilson Duff, *images: stone: b.c.: Thirty Centuries of Northwest Coast Indian Sculpture*, photographs and drawings by Hilary Stewart, exhibition originating at the Art Gallery of Greater Victoria; Richard Simmins, Director (Saanichton, B.C.: Hancock, 1975), originally the catalogue to the exhibition.

38 See Duff, pp. 162–67.

39 H.J. Kirchhoff, "She's Calling It Quits, But Still 'Hatching' Poems," *The Globe and Mail* [Toronto], 18 Feb. 1989, p. C14.

40 Joe Plaskett's famous double-portrait of Webb, painted in Paris, emphasizes Webb's fragility of appearance. She struck me as rather frail when I first met her, in 1961. I have, of course, revised my view radically. I have not, however, been compelled to revise many of the opinions I expressed in the Introduction to the 1971 *Selected Poems* in which I do not, at any point (though I have been accused of doing so) label Webb's work "neurotic."

41 The grounds on which to compare Webb with Woolf are too many and too extensive to be discussed here. That they exist, however, should be noted; and future Webb scholars would do well to examine them carefully.

42 When *Wilson's Bowl* was not even nominated for a Governor General's Award, "a group calling itself the Writers' Network, spearheaded by Michael Ondaatje, Margaret Atwood, bpNichol, and P.K. Page, sent Webb a cheque for

$2,300, a bouquet of flowers, and a card: 'All of us felt that your poetry has meant a great deal to us . . . [and] continues to move us and surprise us with its heart and craft. We want to emphasize that this gesture is a response to your whole body of work as well as to your presence as a touchstone of true, good writing in Canada, which we all know is beyond awards and prizes' " (Wachtel, p. 8).

[43] One of the most significant signals of this feminist-prompted re-evaluation of Webb's works is Eleanor Wachtel's interview-article, to which I have frequently referred. See also my review article, " 'Bird song in the apparatus': Webb's New Selected Poems," Essays on Canadian Writing, No. 30 (Winter 1984–85), pp. 359–70; Cecelia Frey's "The Left Hand of Webb," Prairie Fire: A Celebration of Writing by Canadian Women, 7 (Autumn 1986), 37–48; and Laurie Ricou's "Phyllis Webb, Daphne Marlatt and Similitude: Journal Entries from a Capitalist Bourgeois Patriarchal Anglo-Saxon Mainstream Critic," in A Mazing Space: Writing Canadian Women Writing, ed. Shirley Neuman and Smaro Kamboureli (Edmonton: NeWest, 1986), pp. 205–15.

[44] The reference is to Jakobson's distinction in "Two Aspects of Language and Two Types of Aphasic Disturbances," first published in Fundamentals of Language (The Hague: Mouton, 1956), by Roman Jakobson and Morris Halle.

[45] Northrop Frye, Anatomy of Criticism: Four Essays (Princeton: Princeton Univ. Press, 1957), p. 118. See also pp. 105–12.

[46] " 'You talk to me of nationality, language, religion. I shall try to fly by those nets,' " James Joyce, A Portrait of the Artist as a Young Man (Harmondsworth, Eng.: Penguin, 1960), p. 203. In 1962, Webb contributed to producer John Merritt's CBC Radio series, My Favourite Character in English Fiction. She spoke on Stephen Dedalus. The ts. is in the Webb Collection.

D.G. Jones (1929–)

E.D. BLODGETT

DOUGLAS GORDON JONES was born on New Year's Day, 1929, in Bancroft, Ontario, where his father ran a lumber and pulpwood business. After his early education in Bancroft, Jones enrolled in the Grove (now Lakefield) Preparatory College. After a period of a few years during which he considered careers as either an architect or an engineer, he graduated in honours English from McGill University in 1952. Subsequently, he went to Queen's University, where he completed an M.A. thesis on Ezra Pound's *Cantos* under the direction of George Whalley in 1954. No matter how propitious a choice Pound was for the development of Jones's poetic, his father remarked simply: "Pound. I heard that bastard from Italy during the Second World War."[1]

During the year 1954–55, Jones held a temporary position at the Royal Military College in Kingston; he then moved to the Ontario Agricultural College in Guelph, where he taught English literature until 1961. Although not a primary cause, one of the catalysts of

Jones's departure from the college was a talk to the women's literary society, highlighted by a reading of Irving Layton's poem "Beauty." Jones next assumed a new position at Bishop's University in Lennoxville, Quebec. His appointment at Bishop's was of rather short duration, and its termination may be attributed to another unhappy speech, this time to a group of nurses in neighbouring Sherbrooke, after which he was accused by doctors as being a hippy and communist masquerading in a Sunday suit. In 1963 he took a position as professor of English at the Université de Sherbrooke, where he continues to teach and direct a number of dissertations in comparative Canadian literature. This final change was significant for it marked the beginning of his serious study of the francophone poets of Quebec, which issued in an important translation of Paul-Marie Lapointe[2] as well as the founding of the literary review *ellipse* (1969–), devoted to the mutual translation and elucidation of francophone and anglophone poets.

Jones's marriage in 1950 to Betty Jane "Kim" Kimbark, a dedicatee of *The Sun Is Axeman* and mother of his four children (Stephen, Skyler, Tory Joanne, North), dissolved sometime after the move to Sherbrooke. In 1969 he married Sheila Fischman, a translator of Québécois fiction. That marriage was of short duration, and Jones subsequently married Monique Baril in December 1976, the year that saw the completion of "The Lampman Poems" and the poems set in Saint Lucia, all of which appeared in *Under the Thunder the Flowers Light Up the Earth*.

Jones first gained recognition as a poet while an undergraduate at McGill, where he won a number of prizes in creative writing. This early verse won the approval of Louis Dudek and Raymond Souster, who began publishing his poetry in *Contact*, civ/n, and *Poets '56*. Somewhat predictably, his first book, *Frost on the Sun*, was published by Contact Press in 1957, edited by both Dudek and Souster. This was followed by *The Sun Is Axeman* (1961); *Phrases from Orpheus* (1967); *Under the Thunder the Flowers Light Up the Earth* (1977), which was awarded both the Governor General's Award for Poetry in English and the President's Medal of the University of Western Ontario (for "The Lampman Poems"); *A Throw of Particles: Selected and New Poems* (1983); and *Balthazar and Other Poems* (1988), which was awarded the QSPELL prize for Quebec poetry in the English language in 1989.

Because of their effect on his poetry, it cannot be overlooked that Jones's hobbies are painting and gardening. He is also one of Canada's most astute critics of Canadian literature. Besides a number of papers and articles, he published *Butterfly on Rock: A Study of Themes and Images in Canadian Literature* in 1970, a fundamental examination of the mythopoeic dimensions of Canadian literature. While its mythopoeic stance and the themes it identifies — particularly that of the "garrison mentality" — immediately suggest Northrop Frye as one of Jones's mentors, one may also detect attitudes more consonant with the thinking of John Sutherland and Frank Davey.[3]

In 1978, the year in which he was awarded the President's Medal, he was elected Fellow of the Royal Society of Canada. With some small measure of irony, perhaps, he was awarded a doctorate (*honoris causa*) in 1982 from the University of Guelph, formerly the Ontario Agricultural College.

NOTES

[1] D.G. Jones, letter to E.D. Blodgett, 13 June 1982.

[2] D.G. Jones, trans., *The Terror of the Snows: Selected Poems*, by Paul-Marie Lapointe (Pittsburgh: Univ. of Pittsburgh Press, 1976).

[3] See Malcolm Ross, "Critical Theory: Some Trends," in *Literary History of Canada: Canadian Literature in English*, 2nd ed., gen. ed. and introd. Carl F. Klinck, III (Toronto: Univ. of Toronto Press, 1976), 169.

Jay Macpherson (1931–)

LORRAINE WEIR

BORN IN LONDON, England, on 13 June 1931, Jean Jay Macpherson moved at the age of nine to St. John's, Newfoundland, where she lived as a "war guest" until 1944. She attended Bishop Spencer College in St. John's and, after moving to Ottawa, continued her studies at Glebe Collegiate. In 1951 she received her B.A. from Carleton College and spent the next year studying literature at University College, London. Returning to Canada in 1952, Macpherson took a B.L.S. degree at McGill University, Montreal, and then moved to Toronto to take up studies in English literature at Victoria College, University of Toronto, graduating in 1955 with an M.A. Her thesis, "Milton and the Pastoral Tradition," was supervised by Northrop Frye. In 1957 Macpherson joined the Department of English at Victoria College while continuing her studies there, receiving her Ph.D. in 1964 with a dissertation entitled "Narcissus, or the Pastoral of Solitude; Some Conventions of Nineteenth-Century Romance," supervised from 1955 to 1959 by Northrop Frye and later, from 1960 to 1964, by Milton Wilson. She is now a professor of English at Victoria College.

Alan Crawley, founder and editor of *Contemporary Verse*, was the first to encourage Macpherson, responding warmly to poems that she began at the age of sixteen to send him for critical commentary. The first six poems to be published ("Ordinary People in the Last Days," "Concert," "Objective Correlative: Poor Child," "A Sentimental Journey," "Seasons," "Seascape") were judged to be the best group of poems by a contributor making her first appearance in *Contemporary Verse* in 1948 and were awarded a modest prize of twenty-five dollars. Several months later, Macpherson wrote to Crawley that she would "never have ventured into print last spring if it had not been for your constant encouragement."[1]

Robert Graves was the next to give encouragement and support, publishing Macpherson's first collection, *Nineteen Poems*, at the Seizin Press, Mallorca, in 1952. Her second booklet, *O Earth Return*, was first published in 1954 and was substantially reprinted as the first section of *The Boatman* (1957), the volume that first gained for the poet a wide reputation in Canada and which received the Governor General's Award for Poetry in English in 1958. In the previous year, she was awarded both the Levinson Prize from *Poetry* [Chicago] and the President's Medal from the University of Western Ontario. During the 1960s, while working on her doctoral dissertation, Macpherson was also occupied with the preparation of a rendering of classical mythology for young readers. Entitled *Four Ages of Man: The Classical Myths* (1962), this volume reveals not only its author's vast store of knowledge on her subject but also her commitment to the sharing of knowledge and her interest in the application of myth to modern life.

Macpherson's interest in Christian mythology has been similarly extensive, as we can see not only in *The Boatman* with its intricate use of Christian typology but also in the verse that the Canadian composer John Beckwith commissioned Macpherson to write for his cantata "Jonah," first published in James Reaney's magazine *Alphabet* in June 1964. The hymn that Macpherson also composed for Beckwith was, however, only the beginning of her liturgical work. In 1972 the revised *Hymn Book* of the Anglican and United Churches of Canada appeared, in part the product of Macpherson's work as chairperson of the Words Committee responsible for this revision of traditional hymns. Two years later, *Welcoming Disaster*, her major work to date, appeared in privately published form from Saannes Publications, Toronto. It was republished in 1981 together with the 1968 revised edition of *The Boatman* as *Poems Twice Told* by Oxford University Press. In 1982 her doctoral dissertation appeared in slightly revised form from Yale University Press as *The Spirit of Solitude: Conventions and Continuities in Late Romance.*

Margaret Atwood has written of Macpherson that she is not, in the conventional sense, "career-minded": "There's nowhere she wants to get, in the sense of 'getting somewhere.' She reminds us that poetry is not a career but a vocation, something to which one is called, or not, as the case may be."[2] In fact, this sense of vocation has coloured Macpherson's academic life as well, no doubt in part resulting in her considerable reputation as a teacher at the University of Toronto. The commitment of time and energy evident in her teaching have been reciprocated by the exemplary loyalty and affection of her students, not the least of them Atwood herself. In turn, Macpherson has long been associated as student and colleague with Northrop Frye, to whom *The Boatman* and *Poems Twice Told* are dedicated and who is identified as the "Best of Readers" of *Welcoming Disaster.*[3] A passage in Frye's first major work, *Fearful Symmetry: A Study of William Blake*, was "one of the starting points" for *The Spirit of Solitude*,[4] and clearly Frye during his years as principal was Macpherson's mentor at Victoria College.

In addition to her long friendship with Atwood, Macpherson has also been associated with the poet and classicist Daryl Hine, who dedicated *The Carnal and the Crane* (1957) to her.[5] James Reaney has been another kindred spirit, publishing in *Alphabet* a preliminary survey of the "territory" that Macpherson was to claim in her doctoral thesis and, perhaps more importantly, publishing Macpherson's illustrations to *The Boatman*, which were not included in the text until the *Poems Twice Told* version appeared.[6]

An intensely private person, Macpherson has been reluctant to associate herself with any one school or critical or political approach, preferring to set out her own, very individual course, one in which solitude has had its place. But, as she has said, ". . . one needs one's community to fend off the ghosts . . ."[7] — a community which, it seems, has been defined for Macpherson as

much by Victoria College and environs as by the hermeneutic circle
of poet, poem, and reader. As she remarked in 1955, "Anything
. . . that brings home to us the sense of our community as a lively
reacting organism, to be pleased or thwarted or argued with or
transfigured, gives us something of which most of us [writers] stand
in continuing need."⁸ Far from being reductive, this microcosm has
been a model of the relationship between poet and "other self, the
reader"⁹ — ideally one of sacramental transformation and nour-
ishment possible only within a community where the word is
spoken, enacted, every day.

NOTES

¹ Jay Macpherson, quoted in Joan McCullagh, *Alan Crawley and* Contem-
porary Verse (Vancouver: Univ. of British Columbia Press, 1976), p. 43. See
also pp. 32, 37–38.

² Margaret Atwood, "Into the Fields of Light," rev. of *Poems Twice Told*,
Books in Canada, April 1982, p. 15.

³ Jay Macpherson, "Notes and Acknowledgements," in her *Poems Twice
Told: The Boatman and Welcoming Disaster* (Toronto: Oxford Univ. Press,
1981), p. 96.

⁴ Jay Macpherson, *The Spirit of Solitude: Conventions and Continuities in
Late Romance* (New Haven, Conn.: Yale Univ. Press, 1982), p. 279, n. 3.
Macpherson also notes the influence of Frye — and of Frye's course in Canadian
literature at Victoria College, a course which Macpherson "inherited" from
him — on the last chapter of this book, the Epilogue devoted to Canadian
pastoral (p. 321, n. 3).

⁵ Hine's first published poems, like Macpherson's, appeared in *Contem-
porary Verse* (No. 37 [Winter–Spring 1951–52], in which two poems by
Macpherson also appeared). See McCullagh, pp. 32, 54.

⁶ See Jay Macpherson, "Narcissus: Some Uncertain Reflections," *Alphabet*,
No. 1 (Sept. 1960), pp. 41–57; "Narcissus: Some Uncertain Reflections; or,
From 'Lycidas' to *Donovan's Brain*," *Alphabet*, No. 2 (July 1961), pp. 65–71;
and "Emblem Drawings for *The Boatman*," *Alphabet*, No. 10 (July 1965),
pp. 51–57.

⁷ Macpherson, *The Spirit of Solitude*, p. xv.

⁸ Jay Macpherson, "Report on the Poetry Readings," in *Writing in Canada:
Proceedings of the Canadian Writer's Conference, Queen's University, 28–31
July, 1955*, ed. George Whalley (Toronto: Macmillan, 1956), p. 138.

⁹ Macpherson, "Report on the Poetry Readings," p. 138.

Alden Nowlan (1933–83)

MICHAEL OLIVER

ALDEN NOWLAN was born in Stanley, Nova Scotia, near Windsor, on 25 January 1933. His mother, Grace Reese, was of Welsh descent; his father, Freeman Nowlan, was of Irish ancestry. The Nowlans emigrated from Newtown-Barry, County Wexford, in the early nineteenth century and settled in King's County, Nova Scotia. "I think of myself as an elective Irishman," Nowlan told Robert Cockburn; ". . . a feeling of loyalty to a race enables you to project yourself into the infinite past."[1] By the early twentieth century his forebears were living in Hants County on the edge of the Annapolis Valley. Although he sometimes named Stanley his native place, Nowlan actually grew up in "one of the houses scattered along a three-mile-long stretch of dirt road."[2] In an important autobiographical essay, Nowlan calls his village Katpesa Creek,[3] and that mythical name — taken from the Micmac word for smelt, the only fish found in the local Kennetcook River — is perhaps as good as any, although he sometimes called it — with grim humour — Desolation Creek.

Unlike the Annapolis Valley, Hants County is mostly infertile land. During Nowlan's youth — the Depression or "The Hard Times" as his father called it (*DE*, p. 16) and later the Second World War — most of the people earned their meagre living by subsistence farming or through seasonal employment cutting pulpwood or working in sawmills. Nowlan's father, though he was more than willing, never held a permanent, year-round job in more than fifty years of hard labour. Freeman Nowlan was an expert with the axe, but the call for such workers vanished in the early twentieth century with the rapid decline of the shipping industry in the Maritime provinces. One of the results of this historic shift in Canadian economic affairs was that Alden Nowlan grew up poor.

Yet his childhood was not as troubled as many middle-class city-dwellers might think. More than once Nowlan likened his formative years to those of Huck Finn — the *real* Huck Finn, he always hastened to add: the boy Mark Twain describes moving through a world at once beautiful and grotesque, not the boy sentimentalized by the North American popular imagination. In Nowlan's words:

I possessed a degree of freedom that few middleclass children, even in these permissive times, would dare to dream about. Nobody ever told me when to go to bed or when to be home at night. Nobody ever told me to brush my teeth, wash my hands or comb my hair. During the summer I ran around in nothing but a pair of denim shorts, a young savage, exploring the woods, swamps, heaths and meadows, picking mush-rooms, strawberries, blueberries, and raspberries, building rafts and treehouses, making bows and arrows and whistles, surrounded by animals, birds and wildflowers. I was the kind of small boy that respectable mothers warn their sons and especially their daughters against. I started smoking when I was eight and got drunk for the first time when I was 12. On homebrew: I collapsed beside the road and when I looked up the stars were whirling all over the sky; at first I thought I was dying and then I decided this was the end of the world. (*DE*, p. 19)

Like Huck Finn, young Alden Nowlan was a truant from school as well as from the other forms of respectability. Although he had taught himself to read when he was five — and by ten he was reading everything from translations of Greek classics to contemporary comic books — Nowlan quit school after thirty-seven days in grade five. Much has been made of this ironic fact, and of his childhood poverty in general, by the people who read his poems, but Nowlan himself put it in its proper perspective:

> I didn't *feel* particularly poor, ignorant and isolated until I was about fifteen and the outside world, that until then had seemed half-mythical, began to be wholly real to me. Hundreds of thousands, perhaps even the majority, of Canadians lived much as we did in those days. . . . It wasn't unusual for a working class boy to leave school, as I did, without finishing Grade v. The only extraordinary thing is that I became a writer.[4]

It is interesting to note that Nowlan always gave eleven as the age at which he began writing — the same age, or very nearly so, at which he quit school. The reason he began to write at all — doggerel and diaries and detective stories — he attributes, in several places, to a desire to be a biblical prophet. Literally: " 'the words that the Lord God of Abraham and of Isaac and of Jacob spake unto His servant, Alden' " (*STWA*, p. 8). Elsewhere he adds, sardonically yet truthfully, "It wasn't piety that motivated me but the will to power" (*DE*, p. 156). Nowlan also gives three other reasons for beginning to write: the desire to create imaginary playmates, the desire for emotional release, and the desire to attain personal recognition.[5] At one point he even says, "I'm always embarrassed when people ask me what prompted me to start writing; because I really don't know the answer" ("Alden Nowlan," p. 20). In his earliest published interview, Nowlan tells of seeing a movie, when he was eleven, about Jack London and being very impressed by the image of someone lifting himself out of poverty by his writing and subsequently becoming a celebrity and a millionaire.[6] All things considered, it is tempting to think of the youthful Alden Nowlan beginning to write because he was a poor, lonely, backwoods boy affected almost equally by the biblical fanaticism of his heritage and the celluloid daydreams of his time.

But this would not be true. Wanting to be a prophet and wanting to be a celebrity were only the forms by which the poetic spirit chose to manifest itself to eleven-year-old Alden Nowlan. The truth is, he began to write for the same reason any writer begins to write: "There was a time when I wanted to be a Prophet . . . and there was a time when I wanted to be a King or an Emperor, but there was never a time when I 'wanted to be a writer.' Subjectively, it was always something I was, rather than something I aspired to become" (*STWA*, p. 8).

But being a writer in Hants County, Nova Scotia, in the 1940s was, by definition, a secret occupation. "My father would as soon have seen me wear lipstick," writes Nowlan, and that is probably not an exaggeration. It was a tough, puritanical masculine world that the eleven-year-old dropout entered, a world where literacy — let along literature — was next to useless. Offsetting the harshness of the outdoors world of work in the woods, the fields, and the sawmill was the gentler life of the house. Alden Nowlan was raised by his two grandmothers: Grammie Reese, who died when he was five, and Old Em, "an Irish peasant woman who, despite a lifetime of abysmal poverty, was as richly alive as anyone I've ever known" (*DE*, p. 28). This is the woman Nowlan celebrates in "There Was an Old Woman from Wexford," the story that won the President's Medal of the University of Western Ontario for the best Canadian short story of 1972, and which was subsequently incorporated into his "fictional memoir" *Various Persons Named Kevin O'Brien*. Nowlan's sister Harriet, who also appears as Stephanie in *Various Persons* and in several poems, was an important companion during his childhood and his youth, and she, more than his mother — whose people were "natural brigands and gypsies" ("Alden Nowlan," p. 19) and who separated from his father when Nowlan was still a boy — provided the young writer with his image of femininity. As Nowlan says in *Various Persons*, his — that is, Kevin's — childhood was "a time when there existed an entity known as Kevin-and-Stephanie."[7] The sensual yet innocent girl-child offered a natural contrast in Kevin's developing imagination to the practical and prosaic father, and she remained to haunt many of his mature poems. In later years, however, she was replaced by Nowlan's younger cousin Sylvia — his adopted sister — who sometimes played the role of muse to him.

When he was sixteen, Alden Nowlan discovered the regional library in Windsor, and this opened up the "half-mythical" outside world more than even the Bible or Hollywood movies had previously been able to do. Jack London, H.G. Wells, Rupert Brooke, Darwin, Shaw, Lawrence — Nowlan's adolescent reading, like any intelligent adolescent's reading, was eclectic to say the least. And it remained so up until his death in 1983. In one of his finest short stories, "The Girl Who Went to Mexico," Nowlan says of the main character: "His reading was a kind of dreaming. He was not a convert or a student, but an adventurer."[8] The same could be said of Nowlan's own reading; his knowledge extended over vast and varied terrains. At any rate, he was a unique visitor to the Windsor Regional Library in 1949 — in fact, the librarian, Eleanor Geary, often gave special considerations to him — so it is only fitting that thirty years later this modest but proud institution was formally dedicated to its most famous alumnus.

During his teens Alden Nowlan worked in the woods with his father cutting pulpwood and pit props; he worked for the Nova Scotia Department of Highways maintaining the roads; and — what he enjoyed most — he worked as a night watchman at the sawmill, where he spent most of his time reading and writing. He sent away to a mail-order house for a typewriter — the first one he had ever seen — and taught himself how to use it. In 1950, when he was seventeen, his first acceptance of a poem by a magazine came from *The Bridge*, published in Eagle Creek, Oregon. In 1952, having answered an advertisement placed by a weekly newspaper in northwestern New Brunswick, Alden Nowlan left Katpesa Creek to seek his fortune. He said of this: "I've often thought that my arrival in Hartland, New Brunswick, can't have been so very different from a raw Highlands youth coming down to the dour but safe Lowlands in the Scotland of, say, 1785" (*DE*, p. 24).

I have written at such length, and in considerable detail, about Alden Nowlan's childhood and youth for two reasons: first, it was the source, in one way or another, of much of his poetry; and second, it has also been the target of a fair amount of critical nonsense that has been written about his poetry. It is essential for the reader to understand what Nowlan meant when he said that the "predominant emotion" of his growing up in Katpesa Creek was "a sort of desperation" to escape (Cockburn, p. 7). Yet it is equally important for the reader to understand what Nowlan meant when he said: "Looking back as objectively as I can, I see my own childhood as a pilgrimage through hell. And yet I was seldom desperately unhappy and there can't have been many days when I didn't laugh" (*DE*, p. 15). The significance of this paradox seems to have eluded many readers, especially those who did not grow up in the Maritimes.

From 1952 until 1957 Alden Nowlan was, by his own description, an American little-magazine poet. There were very few literary magazines operating in Canada during those years. Nowlan published some three hundred poems in the United States before he ever saw one published in Canada. "For me," he writes, "it was like living in two worlds, working for a weekly newspaper in Hartland, N.B., and publishing verses in New York, San Francisco, Mexico City, and Lamoni, Iowa, or was it Lamoni, Idaho?"[9] Besides writing poetry and short stories and working for *The Hartland Observer*, Nowlan also managed a country and western band — George Shaw and the Green Valley Ranch Boys — which toured throughout the Maritimes and the state of Maine. He once said, "The main problem with the band was keeping them sober enough to play" (Cockburn, p. 7).

In 1957 Alden Nowlan met Fred Cogswell, and this proved to be a turning point in his life, for the simple reason that Cogswell was the first poet — indeed, the first person who read poetry — with whom Nowlan had ever spoken. Cogswell, besides being a professor of English at the University of New Brunswick, was also an American little-magazine poet at that time, and the two poets first learned of each other's existence through the notes on contributors in *Miscellaneous Man*, a literary magazine published in San Francisco. Nowlan describes their first meeting at his boarding house in Hartland: "The day Fred Cogswell and I introduced ourselves to one another he wore a belt six or eight inches too long for him. Instead of being tucked into a loop, the end of it swung free like a bull's pizzle. His necktie — I kiss the Book — bore a picture of a bubble dancer."[10] The effect on Alden Nowlan of meeting, for the first time in his life, at the age of twenty-five, another real live poet is difficult to imagine. Yet we must if we are ever to understand the intense personal isolation of his youth.

Nowlan's first chapbook to appear in print was *The Rose and the Puritan*, a pamphlet containing sixteen poems and which Cogswell published through Fiddlehead Poetry Books in 1958. His first more substantial work was *A Darkness in the Earth*, which was published by Hearse Press of Eureka, California, in 1959. Reading them today, one can see that *The Rose and the Puritan* marks a sudden and distinct development from Nowlan's literary-magazine poetry. Several of the poems in this book resulted from a trip Nowlan took back to his village in Nova Scotia in the summer of 1957. This, like meeting Fred Cogswell, proved to be a turning point in his life: "[F]or the first time I saw the people and landscape of my native place as entities separate from myself. . . . I looked around me and tried to write down what I sensed, intuited and thought about it" (*STWA*, p. 10). By 1961 Nowlan had published two more books: *Wind in a Rocky Country*, a chapbook put out by Emblem Books of Toronto, and *Under the Ice*, his first full-length book, published by Ryerson Press. That same year Nowlan received a Canada Council Junior Arts Fellowship, and in 1962 Contact Press published *The Things Which Are*, marking the end of his stay in Hartland.

In 1963 Alden Nowlan moved to Saint John, New Brunswick, to work on the daily *Telegraph-Journal*, first as a reporter, then as provincial editor, and finally as night news editor. He kept writing poetry and short stories, of course, and things began to look very promising for him and his wife Claudine (Orser), whom he had met in Hartland, and their son Johnnie. But in 1966 he was stricken with cancer of the throat and had to undergo three serious operations. Fortunately he recovered, and in 1967 he published *Bread, Wine and Salt* with Clarke, Irwin. This book won the Governor General's Gold Medal for Poetry. Alden Nowlan also received a Guggenheim Fellowship in 1967, and he and his family travelled to Ireland and England. In 1968 *Miracle at Indian River*, a collection of his short stories, was published by Clarke, Irwin, and during that same year he became writer-in-residence at the University of New Brunswick in Fredericton, a position he held until his death.

In 1969 Alden Nowlan published *The Mysterious Naked Man*, and throughout the 1970s and into the 1980s he was recognized as one of Canada's finest poets. An American edition of his selected poems, *Playing the Jesus Game*, was published in 1970, and three more collections appeared in the 1970s: *Between Tears and Laugh-*

ter in 1971, *I'm a Stranger Here Myself* in 1974, and *Smoked Glass* in 1977. In 1973 his fictional memoir, *Various Persons Named Kevin O'Brien*, was published. This and *Double Exposure*, a collection of his essays published by Brunswick Press in 1978, are essential reading for the serious Nowlan scholar. Nowlan also wrote four plays in collaboration with Walter Learning: *Franken-stein: The Man Who Became God*, *The Dollar Woman*, *The Incredible Murder of Cardinal Tosca*, and *A City to Last*. In addition, he wrote television scripts for the CBC and continued to write a weekly column for the *Telegraph-Journal* [Saint John] and a monthly column for *The Atlantic Advocate*, as well as frequently contributing articles to *Atlantic Insight* and other magazines until his death in 1983. In 1971 he received an honorary D.Litt. from the University of New Brunswick, and in 1976 he received an honorary LL.D. from Dalhousie University. In 1977 he was awarded the Queen's Silver Jubilee Medal. On 27 June 1983, Alden Nowlan died — not from cancer, but from respiratory failure. His death was noticed in the media from coast to coast, but in the Maritimes — especially in Fredericton — the sense of public grief surpassed by far the recognition normally afforded poets in this country when they die. Professor Robert Gibbs of the University of New Brunswick, himself a writer and long-time friend of Nowlan's, summarized this very well:

> To the community of readers and writers in a given place, the death of a writer brings a particular sense of loss. The dimin-ishing we feel is neither just general nor just personal, it is communal. We are less because he has gone, just as we were more because he was here. Alden Nowlan's death has brought such a sense of loss to this community. I speak locally, of Fredericton, of his friends, fellow writers, readers, neighbours, of politicians, doctors, farmers, taxi-drivers, and professors. I think I speak too of the country, the larger community of writers and readers who knew him, some personally, some only through his words.[11]

Alden Nowlan's burial and wake — with diverse dignitaries in attendance, bagpipes skirling in the summer breeze, and Irish whiskey passed around the grave — suggested a Gaelic hero had been laid to rest: a fitting tribute by Claudine and Johnnie and by many writers, many readers, many friends. And now, each year, on Forest Hill in Fredericton, behind the monolithic marker of Bliss Carman in the cemetery, many strangers pause before the simple Celtic cross that marks the grave of Alden Nowlan.

Since his death two major books of Alden Nowlan's poems have been published: *Early Poems* gives the reader every verse he published in his first five works — indeed a powerful collection; *An Exchange of Gifts* presents a generous selection from the total body of his poetry, including twenty-one "New Poems" he left in manuscript. A book of stories called *Will Ye Let the Mummers In?* and a novel called *The Wanton Troopers* have also been released. Both of these present important semi-autobiographical material.

NOTES

[1] Robert Cockburn, "An Interview with Alden Nowlan," *The Fiddlehead*, No. 81 (Aug.–Sept. 1969), p. 9. Further references to this interview appear in the text.

[2] Alden Nowlan, "Alden Nowlan: Autobiographical Sketch," *Yes*, No. 16 (Oct. 1967), p. 19. Further references to this work ("Alden Nowlan") appear in the text.

[3] Alden Nowlan, "Growing Up in Katpesa Creek," in his *Double Exposure* (Fredericton: Brunswick, 1978), p. 17. Further references to this work (*DE*) appear in the text.

[4] Alden Nowlan, "Something To Write About," *Canadian Literature*, Nos. 68–69 (Spring–Summer 1976), p. 7. Further references to this work (*STWA*) appear in the text.

[5] See Nowlan, "Something To Write About," p. 8, and *Double Exposure*, p. 23. Also see Gregory Cook, "An Interview with Alden Nowlan," *Amethyst*, 2, No. 4 (Summer 1963), 16–25.

[6] See Cook, p. 17.

[7] Alden Nowlan, *Various Persons Named Kevin O'Brien: A Fictional Memoir* (Toronto: Clarke, Irwin, 1973), p. 67.

[8] Alden Nowlan, *Miracle at Indian River/Stories by Alden Nowlan* (Toronto: Clarke, Irwin, 1968), p. 84.

[9] Alden Nowlan, "A Bubble Dancer and the Wickedest Man in Carleton County," *The Fiddlehead*, No. 125 (Spring 1980), p. 77.

[10] Nowlan, "A Bubble Dancer," p. 75.

[11] Robert Gibbs, "Alden Nowlan, 1933–1983," *Books in Canada*, Aug.–Sept. 1983, p. 21.

Joe Rosenblatt (1933–)

ED JEWINSKI

JOE ROSENBLATT was born on 26 December 1933 in the Kensington Market district of Toronto.[1] He attended Lansdowne Public School and, afterwards, Central Technical High School. Dissatisfied with the routine and monotonous discipline, he dropped out of grade ten. During the years that followed, Rosenblatt restlessly moved from job to job: initially he became a plumber's assistant, then a busboy, then a labourer in a battery factory, then a rubber worker, then a sheet-metal worker. He even went back to school in search of a suitable trade, attending the Provincial Institute of Trades (now George Brown College) to become a welder-fitter. Not content with this training, he joined the Canadian Pacific Railway as a freight handler and held this job for seven years.

During his years as a freight handler, Rosenblatt turned to writing poetry. His initial efforts dealt either with nature, far removed from his work for the CPR, or with social injustice, of which he had seen and experienced a great deal while shifting from menial job to menial job. These dual concerns are striking in Rosenblatt's first chapbook of poems, *Voyage of the Mood* (1963). Since his interests at the time leaned towards socialism and political change, Rosenblatt attended socialist meetings. It was at one of these gatherings that he first met the poet Milton Acorn. Acorn read Rosenblatt's early efforts at verse and offered strong encouragement and support. He also showed the young poet's work to others, thereby actively introducing Rosenblatt to Canadian poetry and poets. Al Purdy, a friend of Acorn's, also recognized Rosenblatt's talent and sponsored him for a short-term Canada Council grant in 1963.

From this time on, Rosenblatt was determined to make his living as a writer. He quit his job as a freight handler and left for Vancouver, a city which would, he felt, be conducive to his writing. In fact, many of the poems in *The LSD Leacock* (1966) and *Winter of the Luna Moth* (1968) were inspired by his people-watching in Stanley Park. Since his initial move to Vancouver, Rosenblatt has lived either in Toronto (from 1968 to 1980) or in British Columbia. He now resides in Qualicum Beach, Vancouver Island, with his wife, Faye, and son, Eliot.

During the ten years following the initial Canada Council grant, Rosenblatt published six new books of poetry — *Bumblebee Dithyramb* (1972), *Blind Photographer* (1972), *Dream Craters* (1974), *Virgins and Vampires* (1975), *Loosely Tied Hands: An Experiment in Punk* (1978), and *The Sleeping Lady* (1979) — as well as the selected *Top Soil* (1976). This output is staggering, especially when one considers that, during the same period, he also began to take himself seriously as a visual artist. His drawings illustrate most of his own books, including a story for children (*Tommy Fry and the Ant Colony* [1979]), and his artwork has been collected in three separate publications: *Greenbaum* (1970), *Dr. Anaconda's Solar Fun Club* (1978), and *Drawings by Joe Rosenblatt* (1979). The first two of these collections are books unaccompanied by text. The third is a series of loose prints held together in a green leather folder tied with a ribbon. Many of the india-ink drawings of these collections are of interest because they offer a visual account of Rosenblatt's animal and insect world.

After moving to Vancouver Island in August of 1980, Rosenblatt continued to draw, but he increasingly turned back to writing, publishing *Brides of the Stream* (1983), *Escape from the Glue Factory: A Memoir of a Paranormal Toronto Childhood in the Late Forties* (1985), and *The Kissing Goldfish of Siam* (1989). Unlike his earlier works, these new books show Rosenblatt as gradually moving from predominantly free-verse forms to narrative and prose poems. *Poetry Hotel: Selected Poems 1963–1985*, dedicated to Barry Callaghan and published in 1985, is largely a republishing of earlier material, but one that illustrates well the difference between the poetic experiments Rosenblatt explored during his years in Toronto and those he turned to once he took up residence in Qualicum Beach. *Poetry Hotel* begins with the free verse of "Top Soil" and ends with "Life Notes," a section that explores in prose Rosenblatt's approach to autobiographical writing.

Since a poet can rarely make his living exclusively from his writing, Rosenblatt took up the teaching of creative writing. He has taught this subject at Three Schools of Art in Toronto, at summer writers' workshops in Toronto and Collingwood, Ontario, and as writer-in-residence at the University of Western Ontario (1979–80), the University of Victoria (1980–81), and the Saskatoon public library (1984–85). He was the senior editor of *Jewish Di'al-og* from 1972 to 1983 and poetry editor for *The Malahat Review* from 1982 to 1983.

The work of Joe Rosenblatt has not gone unnoticed. He has been included in over fifteen anthologies and featured on several radio and television programs. He has twice been the recipient of Canada Council Senior Arts Awards. More importantly, two of his books have achieved special recognition: *Winter of the Luna Moth* was nominated for the Governor General's Award for Poetry in English, and *Top Soil* won that award in 1976. Finally, Rosenblatt's work has also gained recognition outside Canada. An Italian translation of a selected edition of Rosenblatt's prose and poetry is being prepared by Alfredo Rizzardi of the University of Bologna in Italy.

NOTE

[1] I wish to express my appreciation to Joe Rosenblatt for providing me with biographical information.

Leonard Cohen (1934–)

LINDA HUTCHEON

IN 1967 George Bowering wrote that "Leonard Cohen could become the Jewish Kahlil Gibran."[1] And, certainly, with McClelland and Stewart printing or reprinting a half-dozen of his books in the mid-1960s, Cohen's popular success as a poet of the times seemed assured. His early background was probably appropriate, though perhaps less exotic than these somewhat dubious accolades might have suggested. Born into a comfortable Jewish family, Cohen attended McGill University and later, briefly, Columbia University. His interest and skill in poetry writing were manifest early: McGill awarded him the McNaughton Prize in creative writing, and Louis Dudek published *Let Us Compare Mythologies* as the first book of his McGill Poetry Series in 1956. After graduation from McGill, Cohen edited a New York literary magazine called *The Phoenix*, where, in 1957, many of the poems later published in *The Spice-Box of Earth* (1961) appeared. In his early years, Cohen frequently published individual poems in literary journals — *civ/n* (1953–54), *Forge* [McGill Univ.] (1954–56), *Prism* [Sir George Williams College] (1958), *The Tamarack Review* (1958), and *Queen's Quarterly* (1959).

Freed by a small inheritance, Cohen left North America for the Greek island of Hydra in the late 1950s. Here he lived with a Norwegian woman named Marianne and her son, and here he wrote the poems of *Flowers for Hitler* (1964) and *Parasites of Heaven* (1966). He also tried his hand at two novels: *The Favorite Game* (1963) and *Beautiful Losers* (1966). The *succès de scandale* of the latter coincided with the beginning of Cohen's career as a popular singer and songwriter. At one point, a *Melody Maker* poll listed Cohen as second only to Bob Dylan in popularity. With the help of Judy Collins and brief appearances at concerts (Newport Folk Festival and Central Park, New York) and on television (CBS's *Camera Three*), Cohen soon became the darling of the pop music promoters. The publication of his *Selected Poems 1956–1968* (1968) coincided with the release of his first album, *Songs of Leonard Cohen* (1968), followed shortly by *Songs from a Room* (1969).

Leaving a quiet life in Hydra with Marianne, Cohen began both a new career and life-style — as a concert performer — and a new relationship. His new companion, Suzanne Elrod, was to be the mother of his two children (Adam Nathan and Lorca Sarah) and the "Lady" celebrated, lost, mourned, and scorned in his later *Death of a Lady's Man* (1978). With Cohen's public career came the press cult of the Cohen personality and the spate of articles on, and interviews of, the various newsworthy personae of the lonely rebel drop-out artist; the ironic, sardonic poet-lover; the vegetarian, mystic seer. As a poet, too, Cohen was at the height of his success in the late 1960s, winning the Quebec Award (1964) and the Governor General's Award for Poetry in English (1968), which he refused with predictable irony, claiming that, while much in him strove for the honour, the poems themselves forbade it absolutely. In 1962 Cohen had announced that he would seek his audience in *Esquire* and *Playboy* — which *people* read — rather than literary magazines that only *poets* read. Nevertheless the poetic and academic establishment did not turn its back on its rebel son. In 1971 Dalhousie University awarded him an honorary Litt. D., and the next year the University of Toronto purchased his papers.

Cohen's energy in these years, however, was primarily devoted to his singing and songwriting. In 1971 Columbia Records released *Songs of Love and Hate*, and Robert Altman used Cohen's music as the score for his film *McCabe and Mrs. Miller*. In 1972 Cohen published his first new book of poems in six years — *The Energy of Slaves* — and perhaps it was the generally unfavourable reviews that confirmed Cohen in his choice of a stage career. In Europe in particular, his concerts were major cultural events, and as a result, his poems were translated into French, German, Spanish, Danish, Swedish, and Dutch. The Royal Winnipeg Ballet took *The Shining People of Leonard Cohen* on its European tour. In the next few years Cohen released three more albums: *Live Songs* (1973), *New Skin for the Old Ceremony* (1974), and *The Best of Leonard Cohen* (1975). The show *Sisters of Mercy* was a hit at the 1973 Shaw Festival in Niagara-on-the-Lake, Ontario.

The later 1970s saw a change in Cohen's life and work. After spending some time at a Zen centre in California, Cohen, now separated from Suzanne Elrod, began to write and record the album *Death of a Ladies' Man* (1977) with the help of Phil Spector (note the plural "Ladies' "; the book title is in the singular). The new sound that was born of this odd professional collaboration was greeted with mixed reactions, as was his publication of the book *Death of a Lady's Man* (1978).

When not on the road or recording in Nashville or New York for his albums *Recent Songs* (1979), *Various Positions* (1984), *I'm Your Man* (1988), and *The Future* (1992), Cohen seems to have spent much of his time either in a Saint Dominique Street flat in Montreal's immigrant district or at his upper duplex near Los Angeles. The publication of *Book of Mercy* (1984), a book of "contemporary psalms," consolidated a renewal of Cohen's interest in devotional traditions dating from his earliest verse and clear in the recent songs, presented here in a prose (and quasi-narrative) form. As both Don Owen in his NFB film *Ladies and Gentlemen . . . Mr. Leonard Cohen* (1965) and, later, Harry Rasky in his CBC film *The Song of Leonard Cohen* (1980) learned, Cohen's power as a performer and personality is strong and easily (and entertainingly) documentable. The *enfant terrible* of Canadian poetry may no longer be an *enfant*, but the old desire to shock, to play, to "con," is still strong and appealing as his first video, *I Am a Hotel* (1984), suggested. His European following seems to have remained faithful, as the figures of his sales attest: as early as 1978, his book sales were already estimated at two million and his records at ten million — not bad for a former member of the Buckskin Boys who began playing the guitar to impress the girls at summer camp.

NOTE

[1] George Bowering, "Inside Leonard Cohen," rev. of *Parasites of Heaven*, *Canadian Literature*, No. 33 (Summer 1967), p. 71.

George Bowering (1935–)

JOHN HARRIS

GEORGE BOWERING is wise and witty, and he does everything —
and that includes teaching, editing, analyzing, and writing poetry
— with energy and flair. He's done a lot of work as both publisher
and editor that has resulted in significant changes on the literary
landscape. He's made a lot of loyal friends in the course of this
work and these people have helped to spread his ideas and influ-
ence. He's produced a body of literary work that is massive, varied,
and often admired. Many people think of him as a poet's poet, a
leader.

Bowering has adopted the practice of seeking society among his
own kind. He's gone much further than accumulating a small circle
of writer-friends; he's become a dedicated bohemian. He dresses
(the famous bobby's cape and assorted fedoras and unusual t-
shirts), acts (his "Granville Grange Zephyrs" writer's baseball
team, and his love of cigarillos and assorted series of unusual café

and bar hangouts), and talks like a poet. His locale is Vancouver and he has celebrated that city's bars, streets, cafés, bookstores, and writers in some of his best poetry and fiction. His network of relationships extends into the United States and Eastern Canada where old friends like John Newlove and Frank Davey now live and where Coach House Press has become a second home.[1] Vancouver and George Bowering came of age during the "hippie" movement of the 1960s, and that energy and optimism, though matured and perhaps also changed to suit the fashion of the times, are still very much alive in both the place and the man.

The fashion of the times includes creative-writing departments and subsidies. Certainly The Canada Council and the universities can be considered to be within reasonable limits. And while Bowering has profited from the system, he has not done so selfishly. And the activities that he engages in through the universities and cultural agencies profit other writers. Here again, his sense of community is dominant. Bowering has published his own small magazines, written articles and reviews about his favourite writers, joined organizations, edited collections, worked for The Canada Council, and made his best insights available in books, conferences, and writing seminars. He has done these things for salary, subsidy, or for free. Throughout, he has shown that his concern is for poetry in general and the welfare of poets as much as it is for his own poetry and welfare in particular.

Apart from his achievements as a poet-novelist-critic, Bowering is also noteworthy for his friendship with Red Lane and as the recipient of *Letters from Geeksville*. By the time of Red Lane's death, Purdy was starting to take over as Bowering's "romantic conscience." The two poets have since corresponded and carried the debate into the public forum. Bowering and Lane met in 1955, in the RCAF, in Manitoba. They were attracted to one another because they were both from the Okanagan. Lane was from the North Okanagan (Vernon) and Bowering from the South (born in Penticton and raised there and in Peachland and finally further South in Oliver where he finished high school). Bowering spent one year at the University of Victoria and then enlisted for three years of service, and there he met Lane.

After quitting the airforce in 1957, Bowering went to the University of British Columbia to study poetry. Here, he teamed up with classmates Frank Davey and Fred Wah to start *TISH*. Thus, Bowering is considered an innovator and a co-founder of a "school." In an interview taped by Barry McKinnon in May, 1976, Bowering says,

> I knew Lionel Kearns because he was in a couple of classes of mine (Spanish and something else). I heard about Gladys Hindmarch. She had apparently moved . . . into the house of this English professor and his wife (which turned out to be Warren and Ellen Tallman). . . . I was never in a class of his. I was following Earle Birney around and Gladys. . . . Then all of a sudden there was Frank Davey, Fred Wah, Jamie Ried, David Dawson and all those other guys; and it happened because of Warren Tallman. . . . I found out about Irving Layton and Souster and Dudek, largely . . . Lionel and I were the only ones who knew about them. . . . So for me there were two contiguous lines developing in the things I was reading and being influenced by. . . . I was mainly in charge of stuff from the east until Frank began to know the people from the east and Frank opened the door to the east.[2]

Davey and Bowering can hardly be said to have promulgated the idea that Canada is an indistinguishable part of the North American whole. Indeed, their subsequent work has had quite the opposite significance. It seems obvious now that *TISH* was very good for Canadian poetry. It sparked a literary renaissance on the West Coast. Its "spin-offs" include *Iron*, *B.C. Monthly*, blewointmentpress, Talonbooks, *Georgia Straight*, and NMFG. It influenced the work of prominent Eastern writers like David McFadden, bpNichol, and Victor Coleman. Since *TISH*, West Coast writers are being heard all across the country.

In 1963, Bowering left the University of British Columbia to teach English in Calgary. In 1966–67 he was at Western on a Canada Council fellowship, to study for a Ph.D. on Shelley.[3] He gave up on this idea and went to Sir George Williams (now Concordia) as writer-in-residence and later as professor of English. In 1971 he returned to British Columbia as a professor at Simon Fraser University, where he has since remained. At Calgary, Bowering started *Imago*, which he edited until 1974, through twenty issues, publishing along the way eight titles in the Beaver Kosmos Folio Series. Bowering's editorial policy in *Imago* followed in the tradition of TISH, though he was more nationalistic.

On his return to Vancouver in 1971, Bowering became an important figure for the poets who had gathered around Robin Blaser at Simon Fraser University. This group included Brian Fawcett, Stan Persky, Sharon Thesen, and George Stanley, writers who are now becoming prominent. His editing projects since *Imago* include work on the editorial board of *Open Letter* and *B.C. Monthly* and books like *Fiction of Contemporary Canada*, *The Story So Far*, and *Great Canadian Sports Stories*.

Bowering's poetry is, as he himself has said, "romantic." The poems that have generally received the most critical acclaim, *Autobiology*, *Curious*, the "Summer Solstice" and "Desert Elm" sequences, and some of the shorter poems like "Grandfather," "Family," and "The Egg," deal with his family history, his childhood, his daughter, the Okanagan area where he grew up, and the Vancouver poetry scene. They are all autobiographical.

Bowering was labelled a prodigy after the appearance of his first book, *Points on the Grid*, published by Contact Press in 1964. His next three books, *The Man in Yellow Boots* (1965), *Sitting in Mexico* (in *Imago* 12, 1965), and *The Silver Wire* (1966) add another dozen good poems to Bowering's canon. *Baseball: A Poem in the Magic Number 9* (1967), as well as *Two Police Poems* (1969), *The Sensible* (1972), *Layers 1–13*, *At War with the U.S.* (1974), "Stab" and "In the Beginning" (in *In the Flesh* [1974]), *Allophanes* (1976), *The Concrete Island* (1977), and the poem sequences and travel poems in *Another Mouth* (1979), can only be regarded as unsuccessful experiments in the long poem. Some (*Allophanes* in particular) are more promising than others. None are significant departures from the traditional lyric-sequence, and Bowering at this time was developing possibilities in prose that interested him more. Bowering's first novel, *Mirror on the Floor* (1967), opened up this more promising territory.

Rocky Mountain Foot and *Gangs of the Kosmos*, both published in 1969, won Bowering the Governor General's Award for Poetry in English in 1970. *George, Vancouver* (1970) develops Bowering's interest, first exhibited in "Spanish B.C." in *Points on the Grid*, in the history of the West Coast.

In 1971, Bowering published *Al Purdy*, his only book to date on a single author. In the same year, Bowering published *Touch: Selected Poems*, wrapping up his work in the 1960s. The book is dedicated to Olson, Duncan, and Creeley, a declaration of Bowering's major allegiance during the period.

Genève, also published in 1971, is a good companion piece to *Autobiology* (1972),[4] which is Bowering's masterpiece, the best book of poems by an English Canadian in the 1970s, the only successful book-length lyric ever produced in this country. *Curious* (1973) is another companion piece for *Autobiology*.

In the Flesh (1974) contains magazine verse published between 1964 and 1971. *Flycatcher and Other Stories* (also 1974) shows that Bowering had not let his interest in fiction lapse entirely in the years since *Mirror on the Floor*. But these are conventionally written stories. In general, *Flycatcher* is one of the better short story collections of the 1970s. For Bowering, it shows consolidation but not development.

The Catch (1976) is Bowering's best poetry book. It reprints *George, Vancouver* and *Autobiology*. *Allophanes* (also 1976), Bowering tells us, was written between September and December 1974 and "seems to bridge the gap between the politics of *At War with the U.S.* and the cultural narrative of *A Short, Sad Book*."[5] It also, along with *A Short, Sad Book*, represents Bowering's first move towards a new theory of writing. Bowering's new theory is postlyrical (in poetry), post-realist (in fiction), and postmodern (overall). The operative word in this theory is "process" (rather than "product").

A Short, Sad Book (1977) is a humorous series of still-life portraits of prominent Canadian literary and historical figures and situations that are tied together by an outrageous plot. *Protective Footwear* (1978) is not as good a collection as *Flycatcher*; it includes a number of old stories held out of *Flycatcher* for revision. The newer stories are better. Bowering's second novel, *Burning Water* (1980), has had a mixed reception, but won Bowering his second Governor General's Award, this time for Fiction in English. *Caprice* (1987) is a follow-up to *Burning Water* but lacks the earlier book's seriousness. It is a farce — light entertainment.

Particular Accidents: Selected Poems, edited by Robin Blaser and published in 1980, is a good collection of Bowering's work. In

1982, Bowering published two more collections of poetry. *Smoking Mirror* contains all new work. *West Window: The Selected Poetry of George Bowering* (1980) is a major collection, reprinting *Curious*, *At War with the U.S.*, *Allophanes*, and *Uncle Louis*, and presenting a new poem sequence "Between the Sheets." Two collections of Bowering's critical articles, *A Way with Words* and *The Mask in Place*, also appeared in 1982. Most of these articles had appeared before in various periodicals, some as early as 1975.

In 1983, Bowering published his third collection of short stories, *A Place to Die*. In 1984 Bowering switches back to poetry with *Kerrisdale Elegies*, which is a variation on a theme, echoing Rilke in *Duino Elegies*.

Craft Slices (1985) is pleasant reading. It includes old reviews, introductions to forgotten books and anthologies, and new material. Bowering continues in this mode, even more formally, in *Errata* (1988).

Seventy-One Poems for People (1985) proved again that Bowering cannot write poetry about politics. *Delayed Mercy and Other Poems* (1986) continues the theme of *Kerrisdale Elegies* — that "art is life."

Imaginary Hand (1988) is a strong book of critical essays. Bowering is no longer an apologist for postmodernism; he is redefining postmodernism in terms of T.S. Eliot. He is, as editor, critic, and theorist, the acknowledged leader of the "new forces" in contemporary Canadian poetry.

NOTES

[1] George Bowering, "Random Access Coach House," *Capilano Review*, 2, No. 5 (Summer 1991), 99–105.

[2] Barry McKinnon, "George Bowering," in his *Poets and Print: Barry McKinnon Talks with 10 British Columbia Poet Publishers* [*Open Letter*, 7, Nos. 2–3 (Summer–Fall 1988)], 12–13.

[3] Robin Blaser, "George Bowering's Plain Song," in *Particular Accidents: Selected Poems*, by George Bowering (Vancouver: Talonbooks, 1980), p. 17. See also Ted Ferguson's "George Bowering, Resident Writer," *The Montrealer*, 42 (Feb. 1968), 8–9; and Bowering's Acknowledgements, in his *The Catch* (Toronto: McClelland and Stewart, 1976).

[4] The title is a Pogo joke. See Walt Kelley, *Pogo* (New York: Simon and

Schuster, 1951), p. 82. In the cartoon, the character Pogo remarks, in connec-
tion with a witticism that he has just heard, that he will remember it when he
writes his "Autobiology." Of course, Bowering is quite capable of thinking the
title up on his own.

5 George Bowering, *Craft Slices* (Ottawa: Oberon, 1985), p. 68.

John Newlove (1938–   )

DOUGLAS BARBOUR

JOHN NEWLOVE was born to Thomas Harold and Mary Constant Newlove on 13 June 1938 in Regina, Saskatchewan. His father was a lawyer, his mother a teacher. Since the family moved quite often, Newlove lived in many districts of Saskatchewan during his childhood, and, although not simply a poet of landscape, he has made the Prairies he knew as a young boy an icon of imaginative possibilities in his work. At one point, his mother taught school in the Doukhobor community of Veregin, the focus of many of his poems of childhood experience.

He went to primary and secondary school in Kamsack, Saskatchewan, near the Manitoba border. After one year of university, he worked during 1957–58 as a high-school English teacher in Birtle, Manitoba, as a Saskatchewan government public-assistance social worker during 1958–59, and as a radio copywriter, music and news announcer, and news editor for CFSL in Weyburn, CJME in Regina, and CKSW in Swift Current during 1959–60.

In 1960, at the age of twenty-two, Newlove left the Prairies for the West Coast. Although he often hitchhiked back and forth across the country, British Columbia was his home for the next ten years, except for a period on the opposite coast in Portuguese Cove, Nova Scotia. In Vancouver he befriended a number of artists: Brian Fisher (another *émigré* from Saskatchewan), Robert Reid, Takao Tanabe, and Roy Kiyooka. In the early years, Newlove dedicated himself to learning his craft and spent much of his time in the Vancouver Public Library, reading poetry, but also studying history and mythology, especially the history of the exploration of Canada. Although the TISH group of poets was busy at the University of British Columbia, and although he knew most of them and eventually had some poems published in TISH in 1963, Newlove was not a member of that group. Nevertheless, his early published poems indicate that he was learning from some of the same masters as they were.

In 1962 Reid and Tanabe privately published Newlove's first collection, *Grave Sirs*, in a limited edition of three hundred copies, of which fewer than half were bound. Only a couple of its poems ever appeared in later Newlove collections, which is perhaps an indication of his own evaluation of this early work. In 1962, as well, Newlove's poems began appearing in various little magazines. In the following years, his poems graced the pages of periodicals in Canada, the United States, and Great Britain. Almost all of them are remarkably good, and carefully crafted. It is obvious that Newlove served most of his apprenticeship in private, not attempting to publish until he was writing poems of high quality. As a result, he has little early published work to be ashamed of.

In a profile in *Books in Canada*, Newlove talks about his first big break:

> It's such an accidental life. I'd been in a few little mags in the early 1960s. What really set me off from small private-press books was that I was doing my laundry in a laundromat on Fourth Avenue in Vancouver when George Bowering walked in to do his laundry and said there's some guy out East named Colombo who's putting together an anthology for Ryerson. Why don't you send him some of your crap?
>
> So I did and he took 10 or 12, and he was then also connected

with *Tamarack* so he took six or seven for *Tamarack*. You get
into a few good magazines, an anthology or two, one full-size
book, and suddenly you're an "arrived" poet.[1]

The anthology was *Poésie/Poetry '64*, and the poems included are
still judged by some to be among Newlove's finest. In 1964
Newlove was also awarded his first Canada Council writing grant,
a sign that his work was receiving critical attention.

In 1966, he married Susan Mary Phillips, a graphic artist and
professional organizer for the NDP, who had two children, Jeremy
Charles and Tamsin Elizabeth, by a previous marriage. As his
poetic reputation grew, Newlove came in contact with poets across
Canada, including Al Purdy, who had become a McClelland and
Stewart poet in 1965. In 1968 McClelland and Stewart published
Newlove's sixth collection, *Black Night Window*, and in 1970, *The
Cave*. In 1970, as well, Newlove moved to Toronto and joined the
publishing firm as a senior editor, continuing in that position until
1974. In 1973, he won the Governor General's Award for Poetry
in English for *Lies* (1972). In 1974 he became writer-in-residence
at Concordia University in Montreal, a sure sign of his eminence
in Canadian literary circles. He followed that appointment with
two more residencies, at the University of Western Ontario (1975–
76) and at Massey College, University of Toronto (1976–77). In
1977 he was awarded a Senior Arts Grant from the Canada
Council, and, in the same year, McClelland and Stewart published
The Fat Man: Selected Poems 1962–1972, a fitting summation of
his extraordinary first decade as a published poet.

In 1979 Newlove returned to Saskatchewan to take up the
position of writer-in-residence at the Regina Public Library. He
remained in Regina, where his wife worked for the NDP, until the
summer of 1982, when he moved to Nelson, British Columbia, to
take up a teaching position in the writing program at David
Thompson University Centre. When the British Columbia govern-
ment closed the writing program at David Thompson in the early
1980s, Newlove moved to Ottawa, where he works as an editor
for the federal government.

During the latter half of the 1970s, Newlove published little in
comparison to his prolific first decade. One longer poem, "The
Green Plain," appeared in a privately printed volume, *Dreams*

Surround Us, which he and John Metcalf produced in 1977. That year he also edited an anthology of verse, *Canadian Poetry: The Modern Era*, for McClelland and Stewart. He has continued to work as a freelance editor, one of his projects being *The Collected Poems of F.R. Scott* (1981). In 1981 Oolichan Books published *The Green Plain*, and in 1986 ECW PRESS brought out *The Night the Dog Smiled*, his first collection of new poems since *Lies*. Newlove's poetry is the work of a unique and significant voice in Canadian literature.

NOTE

[1] John Newlove, quoted in A.F. Moritz, "The Man from Vaudeville, Sask.," *Books in Canada*, Jan. 1978, p. 12.

Margaret Atwood (1939–)

JEAN MALLINSON

FOR A LYRIC POET like Margaret Atwood, a close relation between the poet's life as lived and the poetry as written is, with some justification and despite the poet's disclaimers, often assumed. An interested reader could piece together a minimal life story from evidence in the poems, but it would be intermittent, largely geographical, and entirely devoid of the names of persons, even her own. But if the poems cannot be construed as evidence for events in the life, it remains true that some elements of biography are important to the poems; by her own admission and in the shared view of critics, some of the circumstances of Margaret Atwood's life are crucial to her poetry.[1] Her experience, as a child up to the age of twelve, of living for eight months of each year in the Quebec or Ontario bush, with resourceful parents and one male sibling for company; the entomologist father, the absence of doctrinal religious training, the family atmosphere of looking things up, finding out facts, how things worked, how to make things; the years at Victoria College, of the University of Toronto, including her friendship while there and after with Jay Macpherson and Dennis Lee; the early formed and lasting friendship with Charles Pachter, graphic artist and sometimes collaborator with the poet; her time with House of Anansi Press; her spell as a graduate student at Harvard; her teaching at Sir George Williams University, Montreal, and at the University of British Columbia; her marriage to and subsequent divorce from an American, Jim Polk, a fellow graduate student at Harvard; her *de facto* marriage to Graeme Gibson and the birth of their daughter, Jess; her involvement with the Writers Union of Canada and with Amnesty International — all these are some of the markers in her life, though not its substance.

The fact that on both her mother's and her father's side there is a family history of habitation in North America going back to the seventeenth century is probably of momentous importance in terms of her sense of the past and the land and her sense of the legitimacy of her claims on life and literature; she does not have the uncertain stance of the newcomer, whether it be expressed as diffidence or bravado. Certainly her personal presence, combining strength and a beauty that is both sharply contemporary and pre-Raphaelite, has had something to do with the astonishing amount of attention paid, not only to her work, but to her life. In interviews, she is candid about what she wishes to discuss, reticent about what she prefers to keep private.

A poet, any poet, as she appears in her poems, is an invention, part of a poetic fiction. The lines of power that link the image of the self in the poem, or speaker of the poem, with the creaturely self composing the poem must be there, but they may be invisible, to be surmised but not ascertained. In Margaret Atwood's poetry, the pattern that emerges is a movement from near invisibility, with a sense of high risk and vulnerability, through mask lyrics in which the poet speaks through the personae of Susanna Moodie, Circe, and others, to poems in which the poet speaks *in propria persona*, making formal arrangements of words that render her sense of being where she is. If her later poems are closer to what Wallace Stevens calls "The poem of pure reality, untouched / By trope or deviation . . . ,"[2] it remains true that in any poem, the actual candle blazes with artifice.[3]

NOTES

¹ Margaret Eleanor Atwood was born on 18 November 1939, in Ottawa, Ontario, to Margaret (Killam) Atwood and Carl Edmund Atwood, a professional entomologist. Besides Margaret, there is a brother and a younger sister. She attended Leaside High School, Toronto, and later, Victoria College, University of Toronto, where she received her B.A. in 1961. She met Charles Pachter, now a well-known graphic artist, at Camp White Pine, Ontario, and what began as, and remained, a friendship also developed into an artistic collaboration. In 1961 her first collection of poems, *Double Persephone*, was published and was awarded the E.J. Pratt Medal. She studied at Radcliffe College, Harvard, receiving her M.A. in 1962. During 1964–65 she lectured in English at the University of British Columbia, where she began writing *The Edible Woman*, her first published novel (1969). In the mid-1960s she married Jim Polk, whom she subsequently divorced. During 1967–68 she was an instructor in English at Sir George Williams University, Montreal. In 1967 her first full-length book of poems, *The Circle Game*, won a Governor General's Award for Poetry in English. In 1967 she also received a Centennial Commission Prize and, in 1969, the Union League Civic and Arts Foundation Prize from *Poetry* [Chicago]. She has received honorary doctorates from Trent University, Queen's University, Concordia University, Smith College, the universities of Toronto, Waterloo, and Guelph, Mount Holyoke College, and the Université de Montréal. From 1971 to 1973, she was an editor and a member of the board of directors at House of Anansi Press, Toronto. She has been awarded many prizes, including the Bess Hopkins Prize by *Poetry* [Chicago] in 1974, the City of Toronto Book Award in 1977, the Radcliffe Medal in 1980, the City of Toronto Book Award in 1989, and the Order of Ontario in 1990. She was made a Fellow of the Royal Society of Canada in 1987. She lived for a number of years on her farm near Alliston, Ontario, with the novelist Graeme Gibson. A daughter, Jess, was born to them in 1976. They now reside in Toronto. Atwood is an active member of the Writers Union of Canada, of Amnesty International, and of the Canadian Civil Liberties Association, of which she was a member of the board of directors during 1973–75. She is a contributing editor of *This Magazine*.

² Wallace Stevens, "An Ordinary Evening in New Haven," in his *The Collected Poems of Wallace Stevens* (New York: Knopf, 1954), p. 471.

³ Stevens, p. 523. I have adapted the line "But his actual candle blazed with artifice" from Stevens' poem "A Quiet Normal Life."

bill bissett (1939–   )

KARL JIRGENS

. . . i think art is the bridge to life . . .
—bill bissett, 1980[1]

BILL BISSETT has appeared in numerous poetry festivals in Canada
and across Europe. His work is recognized throughout North and
South America, Western Europe, and in some of the Eastern Bloc
countries. He has prepared hours of audio material on tape and
record, painted miles of canvas, and published a continuous stream
of books featuring lyric poetry, collage, sound-poem notation,
concrete poems, and narrative poems. In his spare time he has
appeared in a number of films including *Strange Grey Day This*
(CBC), *In Search of Innocence* (NFB), and *Poets of the Late Sixties*
(with bpNichol and Phyllis Webb).[2] More recently (1985), he was
the writer-in-residence at the University of Western Ontario. At
present he is working on a new book and yet another series of
paintings.

By his own account, bissett was born in 1939 in Halifax, Nova Scotia, weighing in at a healthy twelve pounds, eight ounces. He was born on the cusp of Scorpio and Sagittarius with a Gemini rising. He has lived in the Vancouver region since the late 1950s, having made much of his living washing dishes and on the welfare line. At other times he has earned money as a fence builder, ditch digger, and co-op art-gallery partner.[3] This hand-to-mouth existence has happily been spiced up by occasional writers' grants from The Canada Council. Over the years he has supplemented his poverty-bracket income by selling his paintings and doing Council-sponsored readings. bissett occasionally spends time in the northland wilderness of the British Columbia interior, about three hundred miles north of Vancouver around William's Lake. While there, he chops wood when he isn't writing poetry or painting.[4] Since his engagement as writer-in-residence at the University of Western Ontario, he has revisited London, Ontario, for extended periods, often stopping in for a meal at the Prince Albert diner where he once held a room. He currently divides his time between London, Ontario, Vancouver, and Toronto.

His family background is as interesting as his unusual life, which is apparent from an interview held in Toronto in 1985:

For a long time, my parents wouldn't tell me that a third of my family was American [i.e., U.S. citizens]; they wouldn't tell me my father was born in Newfoundland. It was a deep dark secret. And I could never find out where my father's family had come from either. Now, I've finally found out. Just before he died, he [my father] wrote me while I was doing a reading in Scotland. I wrote him a postcard and he wrote me a letter saying I'd find lots of my relatives in Scotland. There's something like eight pages of "Bissetts" in the Glasgow white pages. His dad came from Inverness, north of Edinburgh. He had [merchant] sailing vessels and used to sail them to Portugal. At one time, there used to be a "Bissett" wharf in Halifax that was named after him. The other parts of the family who are in Nova Scotia now, will tell you [about it]. There's competing parts of the family. Some have two "t's" some have one "t," some have two "t's" and an "e," others one "t" and an "e."[5]

bissett claims a wide heritage. In his poem "bisett or bissette is a trade name," he discusses his lineage as well as the etymology of the family name, mentioning that the bissetts were originally brought to Scotland and England from Normandy.[6] They were skilled in the martial art of placing arrow-tips on arrows. Historical records of the Bissett clan can be traced back as far as 1198, when they served as witnesses to charters established by William the Lion-Hearted. Although they eventually lost their tartan due to rivalry with other, stronger clans, their numbers increased. In the poem referred to above, bissett goes on to explain that in Old French the name "Bissett" means "rock dove." The image seems singularly suited to bissett, who as a poet and artist has been advocating peace on earth. All of bissett's claims to ancestors may not be verifiable, such as his purported kinship to the Italian composer Bizet; however, there is no denying that the Bissett name has ancient historical and mythic roots. As his poetry ultimately reveals, bissett claims kinship to everyman.

While it is true that bissett has read widely, he is largely a self-taught writer. He acknowledges a number of influences, perhaps the most important being Gertrude Stein. He attended the University of British Columbia for three years during which time he completed courses in English and Political Philosophy, but failed to complete other courses that he found less interesting. Among his English courses was one on poetry taught by writer Warren Tallman. While at the University of British Columbia he attended slide lectures delivered by Earle Birney, who is well-known for his lyric and concrete poetry. Although he received high grades in the subjects that held his interest, he has always remained rebellious towards what he perceived to be restrictive rules of academia (Interview, Oct. 1986).

bill bissett began drawing and painting even before he began writing, but he has always felt a strong correspondence between the two media. Perhaps his sound-poetry roots lie partly in "Mandan Massacre"— the Vancouver-area musical ensemble that he did vocals with. With them he produced *Awake in th Red Desert*. He has never given up his interest in collaboration with musical groups and currently is a member of Sonic Horses, along with Dermot Foley, in Vancouver. He also collaborates with a band called the Luddites during his stays in London, Ontario. Near the beginning of his artistic career, he carried out textual/visual explorations with friends Lance Farrell and Martina Clinton. During the early to mid-1960s he established a liaison with other writers in the Vancouver region who had similar sensibilities. Soon after, bissett encountered and befriended artists such as Judith Copithorne, Gerry Gilbert, Maxine Gadd, and bpNichol. bissett's blewointmentpress eventually published many of these writers during the 1970s.[7]

bissett's first book, *we sleep inside each other all*, was published by his cohort and friend bpNichol. Like many of the more than fifty books that follow, it displays an emphasis on both visual presentation and metaphysical subject grounded in street-level reality.

bissett firmly believes that the artist must control the means of production if he is to retain his own integrity and the integrity of his statement. With this belief driving him, he started *blewointment* magazine in 1963. Nearly all of his early books have a personal touch. They contain inserts, or inserted drawings, or are coloured in by hand. In 1967 he founded blewointmentpress. In the years since, his most consistent collaboration has been with his long-time friend Allan Rosen, who carried out a lot of behind-the-scenes work for blewointmentpress. It is Rosen who has almost single-handedly photographically documented bissett throughout the years, as is evident by the photographic cover-images on nearly every book written by bissett.

bill bissett's life has not been an easy one. A poet-rebel, part of what was called the "hippie" generation, he has lived in near poverty all of his life. He has also had a number of skirmishes with the law. As his autobiographical poems testify, and as he himself admits, bissett has been incarcerated a number of times on drug-related charges. His health has also been a major concern. He had a near-fatal accident in the late 1960s that required brain surgery and several years of rehabilitation in order for him to regain motor-control of the left side of his body. During the crisis that resulted from the accident, he had a near-death experience that he claims has altered his perception of life (Interview, June 1985). He is a deeply spiritual individual with egalitarian values whose politics might be considered left-wing. He is both an idealist and an egalitarian.

In 1979 he was the runner-up in the CBC poetry contest and although he has yet to win a Governor General's Award, he holds another distinction along with writing and publishing colleague and long-time friend, bpNichol: he has been denounced in the House of Commons as a pornographer (Interview, Oct. 1986).

bissett is an enlightened internationalist who despises the borders, controls, and rules that impede the flow and freedom of our daily lives. More importantly, he is deeply committed to identifying and living up to our global social responsibilities. bill bissett has no qualms about barbecuing sacred cows in order to feed the poor and the underprivileged. He holds an ironic mirror up to ugly fact and, for some, asks too many embarrassing, seemingly naïve questions. In this sense, he is a revolutionary as well as a romantic. His belief that humanity can and must be saved from itself may be considered alternately mad or inspired. Nonetheless, unlike many of his peers who seem to find comfort by meandering into a middle period of self-centred individualism, bissett continues in his daily quest for a harmonic cosmic vision that may gradually calm a raging planet. While the outcome has yet to be decided, it is certain that through his art, bill bissett will continue to log the passage of what he calls the "soul-ship" of life.

NOTES

[1] Karl Jirgens, "Chopping Wood: An Excerpt from a Talk with bill bissett in a Toronto Restaurant during the Spring of 1980," *Rampike*, 1, Nos. 2–3 (1980), 23.

[2] "Biographies: Bill Bissett," in *Sound Poetry: A Catalogue for the Eleventh International Sound Poetry Festival, Toronto, Canada, October 14 to 21, 1978*, ed. Steve McCaffery and bpNichol (Toronto: Underwhich Editions, 1978), p. 92.

[3] bill bissett, "bare bones biography what els shudint i remembr," in NOBODY OWNS TH EARTH (Toronto: House of Anansi, 1971), n. pag.

[4] Jirgens, "Chopping Wood," p. 23.

[5] Karl Jirgens, Audio-taped interviews with bill bissett, June 1985 and Oct. 1986. Further references to these interviews will be cited in the text with the dates.

[6] bill bissett, *Canada Gees Mate for Life* (Vancouver: Talonbooks, 1985), p. 38.

[7] bissett, "bare bones biography," n. pag.

Patrick Lane (1939–)

GEORGE WOODCOCK

PATRICK LANE was born in Nelson, in the Kootenay district of inland British Columbia, on 26 March 1939. His elder brother was the poet Red Lane, who died in 1964 at the age of twenty-eight. Early in Patrick's life, the Lane family moved to Vernon in the Okanagan Valley. Here he was educated, leaving school in the late 1950s and not going on to the university. Instead, he worked as an unskilled labourer in construction, sawmilling, logging, and, as he remarked in a letter to the writer of this essay, "a variety of jobs from fruit-picking to first aid, house-building to hopelessness."[1] He married twice in those early years and had five children by the two marriages, both of which broke up. He lived in poverty among the poor, in a world that — as he remarked in an interview with Stephen Dale that was published in *Books in Canada* — "in a very odd way, I was a slave to. I accepted that world intrinsically, the world of labouring. I didn't know there was another way. I was mindlessly accepting my poverty and my struggle. I had no intellectual detachment."[2]

Yet beneath this acceptance, there must have been an urge to break free. Lane's brother Red had begun to publish his poems and to associate with other poets in Vancouver, and, in the interview with Dale, Lane himself admitted that writing became for him "a way out of poverty" (p. 33). He can hardly have meant that in a material way since he chose the worst-paid kind of writing, poetry, and never attempted to support himself by journalism, literary or any other form of writing. Indeed, he continued to live by labouring, including work on the building of the Rogers Pass Highway, even after he had started to write poetry, and it was not until the mid-1970s, more than a decade after he had begun to write and publish his verse, that he found the means to escape from the labouring life.

Many of the experiences of that working life and peripheral incidents — spending nights in jail, living the life of the city streets and slums and the lonely road — have entered deeply into Lane's poetry and helped to create its characteristically plebeian tone. They have also led him to evolve the concept of the poet as outlaw that has influenced his life, the way he looks at the world, and the kind of poetry he writes. In an essay entitled "To the Outlaw," printed in *New: American and Canadian Poetry* in the spring of 1971, he elaborated that concept of the Nietzschean role of the poet:

Outside the law is a place that is beyond even freedom, for to be free you must be free of something or someone and no-one is free that *must* live. Beyond freedom, beyond all temporal boundaries of ethics and morality is a place called beauty where the outlaw resides in bondage and in that beauty is a burning beyond all knowledge and understanding. It is from there that the poem comes. It is there the outlaw lives.[3]

Lane did not begin writing poetry until the early 1960s, although, in the interview with Stephen Dale already quoted, he claimed that he had felt the urge towards a creative life even in his early childhood:

I do remember when I was a child we had one of those Christmas recording things, one of those huge machines that makes little plastic discs. And somebody asked me what I wanted to be when I grew up. I was six years old and I said I wanted to be an artist. Now how did I know when I was six years old that this is what I'd spend the rest of my life at? I didn't even start writing until I was 23 or 24. (pp. 32–33)

After Patrick Lane began to write poetry, his brother, Red Lane, induced him to move to Vancouver, where he associated with Earle Birney and Milton Acorn, who were then both living in the city. Eventually, with two other young poets, Seymour Mayne and bill bissett, he founded the little press Very Stone House, which began in 1966 and published as one of its first releases Lane's *Letters from the Savage Mind* (1966). Already he had gained a degree of acceptance, not only in Western Canada, where his poems had been published in *blewointment*, *West Coast Review*, and *Talon*, but also in the more easterly provinces, where his work had appeared in *The Canadian Forum*, *The Fiddlehead*, and *Quarry* and had been printed by James Reaney in *Alphabet*.

Lane continued to run Very Stone House from Vancouver until 1970. Then his life resumed its wandering course, and the publishing house, never completely abandoned and still run by Lane, was renamed Very Stone House in Transit, issuing its occasional publications from places as far apart as Vernon, Winnipeg, and Montreal. It came to an end in 1980.

In the meantime, Lane published books, pamphlets, and broadsheets of his poems at fairly regular intervals, amassing more than twenty-five titles by 1990. Most of these were little-press publications in small editions that quickly went out of print, and, in biographical terms, the most important volumes were probably those that were brought out by established publishers and which tended to be selections of poems already issued in more ephemeral form. They are *Beware the Months of Fire*, published by House of Anansi in 1974; *Poems New and Selected*, which was published by the Oxford University Press in 1978 and won the Governor General's Award for Poetry in English in that year; and *Old Mother* (1982), also published by Oxford. For another reason, a fourth collection has a special biographical significance. This is *Unborn*

Things: South American Poems, issued by Harbour Publishing in 1975 and inspired by the travels Lane made shortly beforehand in Peru, Ecuador, and Colombia — his first major journey outside North America. *Old Mother* contains a cycle of poems written on a journey to China in 1971. Lane's most recent books are *Blue Windows: New and Selected Poems* (1988), which won the Canadian Authors Association Award for poetry, *Winter* (1990), and *How Do You Spell Beautiful and Other Stories* (1992).

Lane's work has appeared in most of the Canadian literary journals, from fugitive little magazines to mandarin journals like *The Tamarack Review*, *The Malahat Review*, and *Canadian Literature*, and in magazines abroad like *The Chicago Review* and *The Times Literary Supplement*. He has read his poems often on CBC Radio and other stations, and the double-voiced poem sequence *No Longer Two People*, which he wrote with Lorna Uher, was read by the two poets as a special program on CBC *Anthology* before it was published in 1979 by Turnstone Press.

Unlike many poets, Lane has written little prose, and that in the form of rare reviews. But he has often supplemented his poems by drawings, which have been used to illustrate some of his books, notably *Separations* (1969) and *Unborn Things*. Eight pages of his drawings were also published in the spring 1971 issue of *Prism International*.

In his 1971 manifesto, "To the Outlaw," Lane remarked that poetry "is not having tenure in a university with a guarantee of $15,000 a year and all the coeds you can fuck."⁴ But, in fact, his liberation from the labouring life he had felt "a slave to" was achieved largely through the help of institutions like the universities and the arts councils. He has held Junior Canada Council Arts Awards in 1966 and 1970 and Senior Awards in 1973 and 1976, Ontario Arts Council grants in 1974, 1975, and 1978, and a Manitoba Arts Council Senior Grant in 1979, while, in addition to the Governor General's Award, he received in 1971 the York University Poet's Award.

"I'm on the writer-in-residence thing now, until that dries up," Lane said to Stephen Dale as he was explaining the economics of the modern poet's life in the *Books in Canada* interview (p. 33). And since 1978, he has in fact been continuously a poet-in-residence or special lecturer at the University of Manitoba to begin with, then at the University of Ottawa, the University of Alberta, the Saskatoon Public Library, and most recently at the University of Saskatchewan. Lane now lives in Victoria.

His work with universities has not halted Lane's steady production of poems that show great care in the writing, and it is appropriate to end this biography with one of the rare glimpses that Lane gives — again it is part of the *Books in Canada* interview — of himself at work as a poet:

> I have to have my cup of coffee and my cigarette burning and the typewriter just right. I could spend three hours in the morning, which is when I write, going through all the rituals and never getting anything done. Those games every writer goes through. One of the hardest things is to sit down and actually start writing. . . . When the poem comes, it's great. It's marvellous. It's one of the most beautiful sensations in the world. The act of creation, I think for any artist — and there's an artist in all of us — is one of the most profound experiences a person can go through. As human beings that kind of entrance is a very special one. When the good poem comes, — and you know it's good, that's marvellous. (p. 33)

NOTES

[1] Patrick Lane, letter to George Woodcock, n.d.

[2] Stephen Dale, interview with Patrick Lane, *Books in Canada*, Dec. 1981, p. 33. Further references to this work appear in the text.

[3] Patrick Lane, "To the Outlaw," *New: American and Canadian Poetry*, No. 15 (April–March 1971), p. 58.

[4] Lane, "To the Outlaw," p. 57.

Dennis Lee (1939–)

T.G. MIDDLEBRO'

DENNIS LEE was born in Toronto on 31 August 1939 and attended Kingsway Lambton Public School, Etobicoke, and the University of Toronto Schools. In 1957 he enrolled in honours English at Victoria College of the University of Toronto. As an undergraduate, he was active with the Student Christian Movement, with the Victoria College literary review *Acta Victoriana*, and in theatre. Lee published one short story and fifteen poems in *Acta Victoriana* between 1959 and 1964 and, in addition, collaborated with Margaret Atwood in writing a humorous column with the signature "Shakesbeat Latweed." In theatre, he wrote the lyrics to accompany the music of Peter Grant for two productions of the annual college review, *The Bob*. His interest in this field was to lead later to his writing the libretto for John Beckwith's cantata *Place of Meeting*, a work commissioned by the Toronto Mendelssohn Choir for premier performance in 1967.

Lee graduated in 1962. After spending a year in England, he returned to the University of Toronto for graduate work and received an M.A. in 1964. His thesis was on the American fascist[1] poet Ezra Pound. He taught English literature at Victoria College, then at Rochdale Cooperative and York University. His interest in literature and education led him to coedit, with Roberta Charlesworth, two secondary-school verse anthologies, *An Anthology of Verse* (1964; revised edition 1989) and *The Second Century Anthologies of Verse* (2 vols., 1967–69), both published by Oxford University Press.

In 1967 Dennis Lee and Dave Godfrey founded the House of Anansi Press. The first volume published was Lee's collection of irregular sonnets, *Kingdom of Absence*. Individual poems by Lee had begun to appear in various periodicals late in 1963, and in April 1966 a sequence of sixteen sonnets was published in *The Canadian Forum* under the title "Kingdom of Absence." The book with that title contains forty-three sonnets. In 1968 the House of Anansi published the first version of Lee's *Civil Elegies*. The revised version of 1972 won the Governor General's Award for Poetry in English.

Lee worked as chief editor with Anansi for six years. The press published mainly prose; however, in 1968 it published *T.O. Now: The Young Toronto Poets*, an anthology of thirteen young poets with an introduction by Lee. In it he wrote,

> . . . the city's aesthetic puritanism, which surfaced in many of its writers as an inability to write convincingly of the *polis*, as gaucherie in any sphere between the private and the metaphysical — that puritanism is becoming something of an asset as it recedes. For while many of these poets now write with an unforced sense of their own time and place as a public arena, they seem to retain the sense that decisions about starting-point and direction originate in the space that they occupy as private men and women.[2]

Whatever its applicability to the anthologized poets, the statement does give Lee's own goal as a poet.

During his time at Anansi, Lee wrote a number of brief prose articles, such as a review of Al Purdy's poetry, "Running and

Dwelling: Homage to Al Purdy," published in the July 1972 issue of *Saturday Night*, and the essay "Modern Poetry" for *Read Canadian: A Book about Canadian Books* (1972), edited by Robert Fulford, Dave Godfrey, and Abraham Rotstein. His major prose work was the autobiographical essay "Cadence, Country, Silence," first published in *Liberté* in 1972, then republished, slightly revised throughout and with an altered conclusion, as "Cadence, Country, Silence: Writing in a Colonial Space," in the Fall 1973 issue of *Open Letter*. Later, after leaving Anansi, Lee published his most important critical essay to date, *Savage Fields: An Essay in Literature and Cosmology* (1977). It is a study of Michael Ondaatje's *The Collected Works of Billy the Kid: Left Handed Poems* and Leonard Cohen's *Beautiful Losers* and has been as important to its time as John Sutherland's critical book on E.J. Pratt was to his. Like Sutherland's work, Lee's study is open to the charge that it is a thesis statement and that the thesis predetermines the critical literary analyses. Lee responded to this and other criticisms (by Godfrey and others) in the essay "Reading *Savage Fields*," which first appeared in the Summer 1979 issue of *Canadian Journal of Political and Social Theory*. It was reprinted, with some of the debate with Godfrey's criticism omitted, in the Fall 1981 issue of *Brick*. A subsequent essay, "Polyphony, Enacting a Meditation," first published as an interview in 1979 and then revised as a sequence of aphorisms on some themes from the earlier "Cadence, Country, Silence," appeared in *Tasks of Passion: Dennis Lee at Mid-Career* (1982).

In 1970 Lee published the first of his books of children's verse, *Wiggle to the Laundromat*. There were three immensely popular successors: *Alligator Pie* (1974), *Nicholas Knock and Other People* (1974), and *Garbage Delight* (1977), all published by Macmillan, with illustrations by Frank Newfeld. *Jelly Belly* (1983) was illustrated by Juan Wijngaard. A book of adult poetry, *The Gods*, appeared in 1979. *Lizzy's Lion* was published in 1984, *The Difficulty of Living on Other Planets* in 1987, and, most recently, *The Ice-Cream Store* in 1991. From 1982 to 1986 Lee was a songwriter for the children's series *Fraggle Rock*, a co-production of CBC–TV and Henson Associates. Lee is currently preparing a volume of new and selected poems.

Lee continued to work actively in publishing until the mid-1980s, first with Macmillan of Canada, then as a poetry consultant with McClelland and Stewart between 1981 and 1984. In 1961 he married Donna Youngblut, and the couple had two children before being divorced in 1976. Lee married Susan Perly in 1985.

NOTES

¹ See *Dk/Some Letters of Ezra Pound*, ed. Louis Dudek (Montreal: DC Books, 1974), especially letters 20–27, pp. 45–56.

² Dennis Lee, "A Warning Against This Kind of Anthology: Being an Introduction Which Discusses the Reader," *T.O. Now: The Young Toronto Poets*, ed. Dennis Lee (Toronto: House of Anansi, 1968), p. iii.

Gwendolyn MacEwen (1941–87)

JAN BARTLEY

GWENDOLYN MACEWEN was born on 1 September 1941, in Toronto. She attended Western Technical High School in Toronto from 1955 to 1959 but left school at the age of eighteen to write. At age seventeen, she published her first poems in *The Canadian Forum*, and she completed three novels before the appearance of *Julian the Magician*, published when she was only twenty-two. One of the first three efforts became the short story "Day of Twelve Princes." MacEwen herself has said, "I can't trace where the original impulse came from, but I always wanted to write."[1]

MacEwen spent a short time in Montreal editing the little magazine *Moment* from 1960 to 1962, with Al Purdy and Milton Acorn. She later married Acorn, divorced, and in 1971 married Nikos Tsingos. Her second marriage lasted six years. Some of her poetry and, later, her novels reflect her travelling experiences in Israel in 1962, Egypt in 1966, and Greece in 1971 and 1976. Although she enjoyed a personal friendship with Margaret Atwood and was involved in the 1980s in the Toronto theatre scene, MacEwen was never formally aligned with any particular group of poets. In fact, her own view of literature and experience seemed to be stamped by a very personal sensibility:

> In my poetry I am concerned with finding the relationships between what we call the "real" world and that other world which consists of dream, fantasy and myth. I've never felt that these "two worlds" are as separate as one might think, and in fact my poetry as well as my life seems to occupy a place — you might call it a kind of no-man's land — between the two. Very often experiences or observations which are immediate take on grand or universal significance for me, because they seem to capsulize and give new force to the age-old wonders, mysteries and fears which have always delighted and bewildered mankind. In my attempt to describe a world which is for me both miraculous and terrible, I make abundant use of myth, metaphor and symbol; these are as much a part of my language as the alphabet I use.[2]

The shaping of MacEwen's myth sustained a prolific career that spanned more than twenty years: two pamphlets of poetry, *The Drunken Clock* (1961) and *Selah* (1961); and seven collections of poetry, *The Rising Fire* (1963), *A Breakfast for Barbarians* (1966), *The Shadow-Maker* (1969), *The Armies of the Moon* (1972), *The Fire-Eaters* (1976), *The T.E. Laurence Poems* (1982), and *Afterworlds* (1987). Her selected poems appear in *Magic Animals* (1974), together with a cycle of new poems, "Part Two: Magic Animals, 1972–74." *Earth-Light* (1982) contains selected poems from 1963 to 1982. In addition, she published two novels, *Julian the Magician* (1963) and *King of Egypt, King of Dreams* (1971), a collection of short stories, *Noman* (1972), and two children's books, *The Chocolate Moose* (1979) and *The Honey Drum* (1983). *Mermaids and Ikons: A Greek Summer* (1978) is a whimsical travel book that MacEwen claimed to have written more for fun than with any serious literary intent.[3] She wrote several radio plays and documentary programs. One verse-play, *Terror and Erebus*, was published in *The Tamarack Review* (1974). She also published an adaptation of Euripides' *The Trojan Women* (1979 and 1981), which was performed at the Saint Lawrence Centre in Toronto in 1978. During her career MacEwen received several Canada Council awards, including Senior Arts Awards. In 1965 she was the winner of the CBC New Canadian Writing Contest. In 1969 she was the recipient of the Governor General's Award for Poetry in English for *The Shadow-Maker* and, in 1973, recipient of the A.J.M. Smith Award. She received the Governor General's Award for Poetry in English posthumously in 1988 for *Afterworlds*. MacEwen died at her home on 30 November 1987.

NOTES

[1] Jan Bartley, personal interview with Gwendolyn MacEwen, 1 May 1979.

[2] Gwendolyn MacEwen, *Rhymes and Reasons: Nine Canadian Poets Discuss Their Work*, ed. John Robert Colombo (Toronto: Holt, Rinehart and Winston, 1971), p. 65.

[3] Bartley, interview, 1 May 1979.

Daphne Marlatt (1942–   )

DOUGLAS BARBOUR

DAPHNE MARLATT was born Daphne Buckle in Melbourne, Australia, in 1942. Her family moved to the island of Penang in Northern Malaysia when she was three; she spent the next six years of her life there, after which the family "spent nine months in England saying goodbye to all the relatives and emigrated . . . to Vancouver"[1] in 1951. The family settled in North Vancouver, at the edge of the forest, and the presence of the coastal landscape came to have a central importance for her. Despite a number of moves to other locales over the years, and a number of writings set in such "exotic" places as Mexico, Penang, and England, not to mention other parts of Canada, Vancouver has remained the creative "ground" of her writing, to which she always returns.

Marlatt studied English and Creative Writing at the University of British Columbia from 1960 to 1964. Her first major publication, the story "The Sea Haven," was written for Earle Birney's class in 1962. Although not a member of the editorial board for the first series of *TISH*, she participated in it and supported its general poetics. She has listed Warren Tallman, Robert Creeley, Earle Birney, and in the summer school of 1963, Charles Olson and Robert Duncan, as her major teachers. Following that summer, which included the Vancouver Poetry Conference, she joined the second wave of *TISH* editors. And with various members of that group and others of her generation, she appeared in Raymond Souster's landmark anthology, *New Wave Canada*, in 1966. In 1964, she and her then husband, Alan Marlatt, spent the summer in Spain and then moved to Bloomington, Indiana, where they both pursued graduate studies. Marlatt's M.A. Thesis in Comparative Literature consisted of translations of Francis Ponge's *Le Parti pris des choses* and a critical essay comparing his work with that of William Carlos Williams. She also began working on the manuscript of what would become her first book, *Frames of a story*. While working on this text, she met D. Alexander, a young poet and linguist who made her listen more carefully to her natural speech patterns and to tighten up her line. The results of this effort can be seen in *leaf leaf/s*, published by Black Sparrow Press in 1969. Marlatt herself can best describe the next few years of her life:

In 1968, my husband Al & i were living in the Napa Valley in California, each of us having finished several years of graduate work at Indiana University & supposedly heading for home, Vancouver, B.C. He was finishing the last requirement for his doctorate in clinical psychology — an internship at Napa State Hospital. I was doing a little teaching & some writing. In the fall of that year a job came through for him from the Psychiatry & Psychology Departments at U.B.C. We returned home as we always knew or imagined we would. Our child was born there but the job didn't fit & by the fall of 1969 we were back in the States, in Wisconsin, where he was teaching in the Psychology Department at UW. I was writing about Vancouver, watching our son grow, & wondering what i was doing on a tobacco farm in the American Midwest. By the end of 1970 i had come home to Vancouver with Kit for good (as it has since been).[2]

During the 1970s, Marlatt lived mostly in Vancouver. She taught creative writing, English literature, and composition courses at Capilano College, where she was also the poetry editor for *The Capilano Review* from 1973 to 1976. In the fall of 1972, Marlatt began work on what would become *Steveston Recollected: A Japanese-Canadian History* (1975). This was an oral history of the Japanese fishermen and their families in Steveston, which Marlatt edited. One of her major works, *Steveston* (with photographer Robert Minden) also came out of this endeavour. From January 1978 to late 1979, Marlatt worked with Carole Itter, interviewing ethnic residents of Strathcona, Vancouver's oldest residential neighbourhood, for another oral history, *Opening Doors: Vancouver's East End* (1979). During this period, she also coedited, with Paul de Barros, *periodics*, a magazine for innovative prose writing. It existed from 1977 to 1981. She was contributing editor to *Island* from 1981 to 1985; in 1982–83 she joined Barbara Godard, Kathy Mezei, and Gail Scott to form the editorial collective for *Tessera*, a bilingual magazine of Quebec and Canadian feminist criticism whose first four issues appeared in host journals — *Room of One's Own* (1984), *la nouvelle barre du jour* (1985), *Canadian Fiction Magazine* (1986), and *Contemporary Verse* 2 (1987); since 1988, *Tessera* has appeared under its own imprint.

Although she left Capilano College in 1976, she returned to teach there in the fall of 1981. More important, she taught creative writing workshops at the Kootenay Lake Summer School of the Arts, David Thompson University Centre in Nelson, British Columbia, in 1980 and 1982, a course on "Keeping a Journal" through the Centre for Continuing Education at the University of British Columbia in 1983, a Writing Workshop at the Kootenay School of Writing in Vancouver in the fall of 1984, and a poetry workshop at Westword, the first summer school of writing for women in Canada, in August 1985. She was writer-in-residence at the University of Manitoba in the fall term, 1982, and writer-in-residenceat the University of Alberta in 1985–86.

During the 1970s and early 1980s, Marlatt has continued to write, producing more than ten full-length works of poetry and prose. As her writing has become better known and appreciated, she has been invited to participate in many major conferences and readings in Canada and the United States. These include the 1975

Writers' Tour of the Northwest Territories; the Poetry Festival at the College of New Caledonia, Prince George, 1975; the Writing in Our Time series in Vancouver, 1979; The Canadian Poetry Festival at the State University of New York at Buffalo, October 1980; The Coast Is Only a Line: Contemporary Poetry & Prose in B.C., at Simon Fraser University in the summer of 1981; Dialogue: a Conference on Feminist Criticism, at York University in October 1981; Words of Another Tribe: The Poetry of Women, at the University of Hawaii in April 1982; Words without Borders at the Gay Games in Vancouver, 1986; and she both helped to organize and participated in Women & Words / Les femmes et les mots, a conference for writers from Quebec and Canada held in Vancouver in the summer of 1983. She has also given readings all over Canada and in the United States.

For years Marlatt had to divide her time between teaching and writing and editing. In recent years, she has been able to concentrate on writing full time, with such teaching (creative writing, for example) and editing as does not really interfere with her creative work. Since 1983, she has been living with her companion, the writer Betsy Warland. Although she has already created a substantial body of work, much more will surely follow.

NOTES

[1] David Arnason, Dennis Cooley, and Robert Enright, "There's This and This Connexion," *CV/II*, 3, No. 1 (Spring 1977), 28.

[2] Daphne Marlatt, *What Matters: Writing 1968–70* (Toronto: Coach House, 1980), n. pag.

Michael Ondaatje (1943–   )

NELL WALDMAN

I had already planned the journey back. During quiet after-
noons I spread maps onto the floor and searched out possible
routes to Ceylon. . . . I realised I would be travelling back to
the family I had grown from — those relations from my
parents' generation who stood in my memory like frozen
opera. I wanted to touch them into words.[1]

THESE LINES, from the opening chapter of Michael Ondaatje's
fictionalized autobiography, describe the author's creative method
in the book, as well as his achievement. Though he terms it a
"perverse and solitary desire" (*RF*, p. 22), this touching of still
pictures into words, words which then evoke startlingly intense life,
is the stuff of Ondaatje's poetry and prose generally. *Running in
the Family* breathes this life into a word-portrait of Ceylon and
simultaneously into generations of Ondaatje forebears.

Ceylon, called Sri Lanka since 1972, is the tear-shaped pendant of an island that lies not far off the southeast coast of India. Fabled for centuries for its cinnamon, spices, fauna, pearls, and precious stones, Ceylon has been a favourite landfall for diverse seafarers: Greeks, Romans, Chinese, Arabs. Islamic legend has it that Adam and Eve, expelled from the Garden of Eden, consoled themselves in Ceylon, the second most paradisal spot on earth. Similarly, the island has served European writers as a symbol of beauty and romance. Milton refers to it in *Paradise Regained* as the "utmost *Indian* Isle *Taprobane*."[2] Ondaatje acknowledges the legendary fascination of his homeland in the autobiography:

> . . . the routes for invasion and trade, and the dark mad mind of travellers' tales appears throughout Arab and Chinese and medieval records. The island seduced all of Europe. The Portuguese. The Dutch. The English. And so its name changed, as well as its shape, — Serendip, Ratnapida ("island of gems"), Taprobane, Zeloan, Zeilan, Seyllan, Ceilon, and Ceylon — the wife of many marriages, courted by invaders who stepped ashore and claimed everything with the power of their sword or bible or language. (*RF*, p. 64)

The population of the island is a curious admixture of its long imperial history. The two largest groups are the Sinhalese and the Tamils. The Sinhalese are descendants of a northern Indian people who colonized the island in the sixth or fifth century B.C. Their language is an Indo-European one derived from Sanskrit; most Sinhalese practise Hinyana Buddhism. Concentrated in the north and east of Ceylon, Tamils descend from southern Indian peoples, speak a Dravidian language, and practise Hinduism. The island population also consists of a large number of Moslems as well as what are termed Burghers, descendants of Dutch, Portuguese, and other Europeans — many of whom intermarried with the Sinhalese. Naturally, this mix of peoples (much of which is reflected in Ondaatje's own heritage) enriches the island culture on one hand, while it has also ensured political, social, religious, linguistic, and cultural friction.

This ethnic diversity is an important factor in the pictures of his ancestors which Ondaatje touches into words. The family itself can be traced back to 1600 in Ceylon. *Running in the Family* recounts the writer's explorations in St. Thomas Church, Colombo, where he uncovers plaques and ledgers documenting a prominent string of doctor, lawyer, preacher, or botanist Ondaatjes back through the seventeenth, eighteenth, and nineteenth centuries:

> ... my own ancestor arriving in 1600, a doctor who cured the residing governor's daughter with a strange herb and was rewarded with land, a foreign wife, and a new name which was a Dutch spelling of his own. Ondaatje. A parody of the ruling language. And when his Dutch wife died, marrying a Sinhalese woman, having nine children, and remaining. (*RF*, p. 64)

Mainly, however, the autobiography is a search for self through parents and grandparents, to recreate the era immediately preceding that of the far-flung Ondaatje siblings exiled to England or to Canada, sundered from that time and place. Ondaatje's paternal grandfather, Philip, is remembered as a stern, reserved man, an immensely wealthy lawyer whose " 'empire' . . . to all purposes disappeared" (*RF*, p. 60) during the troubled life of his son, Michael's father Mervyn. The maternal grandmother, Lalla Gratiaen "who managed to persuade all those she met into chaos" (*RF*, p. 41), is lovingly recreated in the book as an eccentric who blithely gambled, drank, cavorted with lovers, and ravaged flower gardens until she made her grand exit, swept away in a monsoon flood at the age of 68.

The "frozen opera" of his parents' marriage Ondaatje touches into words as a passionate and turbulent relationship. Mervyn, who prided himself on Tamil ancestry, was charming, erratic, and irresponsible. He bounded through affairs, engagements, and an education at Cambridge that he never availed himself of — though his father footed the bills for three years. Mervyn's exploits in the élite social circles of Ceylonese society and in the Ceylon Light Infantry during the 1930s became legendary, fuelled increasingly by uncontrollable binge drinking.

In 1932 Mervyn married Doris Gratiaen, the beautiful, flamboyant daughter of an old Colombo family. She bore him four children: Christopher, Gillian, Janet, and in September 1943, the youngest

— Michael. The marriage seemed to flourish in periods of calm on the tea plantation in Kegalle where the family settled. Yet the family was eventually destroyed by Mervyn's recurrent alcoholic rampages when the otherwise respected, intensely quiet man became a dipsomaniac capable of hijacking trains or stranding children on mountain roads. In 1946 Doris left Mervyn and, in a characteristically theatrical gesture, refused to accept any financial support for herself or the four children. Mervyn was to marry again and have a second family, but he continued to be tortured by the alcohol-induced demons he could not exorcise. Doris supported her children in a succession of hotel housekeeper-manager positions in Ceylon and, after 1949, in England. They had "come a long way in fourteen years from being the products of two of the best known and wealthiest families in Ceylon: my father now owning only a chicken farm at Rock Hill, my mother working in a hotel" (*RF*, p. 172).

Michael and his sister Gillian stayed in Ceylon after their mother went to England; he attended St. Thomas College Boys' School and spent holidays at his father's chicken farm in Kegalle. He would not see his father again after his departure for England in 1954 to join his mother and attend Dulwich College. Ondaatje notes that his mother had been told by a fortune-teller in 1949, "that while she would continue to see each of her children often for the rest of her life, she would never see them all together again. This turned out to be true" (*RF*, p. 172).

In 1955 the eldest Ondaatje child, Christopher, emigrated from England to Canada where he has distinguished himself as a stockbroker and publisher. The sisters too were educated in England where Janet eventually settled, while Gillian subsequently returned to Sri Lanka. Michael, following the paths of his peripatetic siblings, joined his brother in Canada in 1962. Four years later he would become a Canadian citizen, taking legal root in the country that has been his home for all of his adult life.

It is important to note the centrality of Ondaatje's richly haunted and displaced childhood in Ceylon to his later work. The odyssey from the lush, tropical clime with its portents of violence and impinging family chaos to create a life in a northern land has likely not been an easy passage, yet it has been a singularly creative journey for the writer.

Ondaatje attended Bishop's University in Lennoxville, Quebec, where he arrived in Canada. Here, under the tutelage of various teachers — notably Governor General's Award winning poet D.G. Jones — Ondaatje turned his creative energies toward poetry. Jones was instrumental in introducing him into the Canadian literary milieu of the early 1960s. On the personal level, Ondaatje married Kim Jones (the poet's ex-wife), a painter and film maker fourteen years his senior, in 1964. The couple moved to Toronto where their daughter Quintin was born and where Michael finished his B.A. In 1967 their son Griffin was born. Ondaatje achieved a Master's degree at Queen's University with a thesis on Edwin Muir. A teaching position at the University of Western Ontario followed, though Ondaatje's refusal to sacrifice creative writing in pursuit of a Ph.D. cost him this job. York University in Toronto recognized the promise of the young poet who had won the Governor General's Award for Poetry in English in 1970, and he has taught English literature at Glendon College since 1971. He has also had a fruitful long-term relationship with Coach House Press where he is an editor. Through the 1970s, the Ondaatjes pursued their active artistic careers, alternating much of their time between life in Toronto and on a farm north of Kingston. However, in 1981, Michael and Kim Ondaatje divorced.

Ondaatje's creative work has spanned his years in Canada, and it has taken shape in an interesting mix of genres. His first collection of poems, *The Dainty Monsters*, was published by Coach House in 1967. It anthologized poems written between 1963 and 1966 including pieces for which he had won the Ralph Gustafson Award in 1965, the Norma Epstein Award and the E.J. Pratt Gold Medal for Poetry in 1966, and the President's Medal at Western in 1967. Coach House also published *the man with seven toes* in 1969, a long narrative poem that received dramatic readings in Vancouver and Stratford.

The Collected Works of Billy the Kid: Left Handed Poems burst through the literary scene into the popular culture in 1970. Ondaatje adapted this gripping multi-genre prose-poem for the stage, and it was produced in theatres across the continent, in Toronto, Halifax, Vancouver, New York, Los Angeles, and Montreal. *Billy the Kid* won the Governor General's Award for Poetry in English, as well as the Chalmer's Award in 1973.

Ondaatje's first novel, *Coming Through Slaughter*, weaves an intense fiction around the life of pioneer jazz cornetist Buddy Bolden. It was published in 1976 after five years of research on Ondaatje's part, and it promptly won the *Books in Canada* Award for First Novel. *There's a Trick with a Knife I'm Learning to Do*, published in New York by Norton and in Toronto by McClelland and Stewart in 1979, selects pieces from the earlier collections and adds poems written up to 1978. It won Ondaatje a second Governor General's Award for Poetry in English in 1979.

Then followed the period of travel and search for beginnings in Sri Lanka (1978 and 1980) that culminated in *Running in the Family* (1982), the spellbinding memoir discussed in the opening here. *Secular Love*, which includes several of the poetic set pieces from *Running in the Family*, is a collection of poems published by Coach House in 1984.

Ondaatje's long-awaited novel about an earlier Toronto made up largely of the voiceless immigrants whose labours built the city was published by McClelland and Stewart in 1987. *In the Skin of a Lion* brings Ondaatje's immigrant perspective to bear on the city and the country where he has lived his adult life. Another novel, *The English Patient*, published in 1992, won the Booker Prize and the Governor General's Award for Fiction.

Ondaatje's critical and editorial work includes *Leonard Cohen* (1970) in the McClelland and Stewart Canadian Writers Series; *The Broken Ark: A Book of Beasts* (1971); *Personal Fictions: Stories by Munro, Wiebe, Thomas, and Blaise* (1977); and *The Long Poem Anthology* (1979). His creative repertoire is rounded out by a serious interest in film. During the early 1970s he produced a thirty-five-minute film portrait of poet bpNichol, *Sons of Captain Poetry*, a comic short called *Carry on Crime and Punishment*, and a seventy-one-minute documentary entitled *The Clinton Special*. Ondaatje has also written screenplays for Robert Kroetsch's novel *Badlands* and his own *Coming Through Slaughter*. Ondaatje is compelled by the visual and editing possibilities in the film medium, yet the written word remains his métier. He notes humorously in an interview, "I love film, the end product, or editing; but my main image of making movies is still carrying heavy cans of film through railroad stations."[3]

What has been described here is the "so far," the origins, the journey, and the writing of Michael Ondaatje — an exile to Canada from a distant part of the world — who touches the lives of other people, other kinds of exiles, into words. Yet one cannot conclude the biographical outline of the life of an artist in full creative stride without hearing the echo of his own words on Leonard Cohen: "It is impossible to write a biography or a critical study on someone still halfway through his career without becoming out of date."[4] What will come to be can only enrich the literary culture of Ondaatje's adopted land.

NOTES

[1] Michael Ondaatje, *Running in the Family* (Toronto: McClelland and Stewart, 1982), p. 22. Further references to this work (*RF*) appear in the text.

[2] John Milton, *Paradise Regained*, IV, 1. 79.

[3] *Spider Blues: Essays on Michael Ondaatje*, ed. Sam Solecki (Montreal: Véhicule, 1985), p. 330.

[4] Michael Ondaatje, *Leonard Cohen* (Toronto: McClelland and Stewart, 1970), p. 3.

bpNichol (1944–88)

DOUGLAS BARBOUR

BPNICHOL WAS ONE OF THE MOST innovative and influential writers of his generation. Although much of his writing staked out ground on the frontiers of the new, he was a professional writer in the traditional sense, turning his hand to a wide range of forms and situations. Alongside one of the most challenging, complex, and original long poems of our time, he wrote novels and short fiction, essays, stage and radio plays, musicals, television scripts, comic-book narratives, popular verse for children, and concrete and performance poetry; as well, he taught creative writing and edited books and magazines with consummate insight and understanding. To few other writers can the phrase "a life in letters" be applied with so many rich connotations.

In 1986, fellow writers from Canada and around the world joined to pay Nichol the kind of homage few artists ever receive: a *festschrift* honouring the man and his work. As Paul Dutton and Steven Smith write in their Foreword,

There are numerous writers in Canada today . . . — older or
younger than bp, of like or unlike orientation in form, style,
or content — who have been nurtured in their work by his
encouragement, constructive criticism, enthusiastic interest,
and generous emotional support; who have learned from him,
collaborated with him, been championed, inspired, and
(often) published by him. The present collection is intended as
a response in kind and as a deeply felt "thank you."[1]

On 14 October 1986, writers from across Canada and as far
away as Britain gathered at Harbourfront in Toronto to present
the *festschrift* to Nichol and to celebrate in their readings and
performances an artist whose life and writing set an example they
all admired. Typically, despite his utter surprise at this celebration
in his honour, Nichol gave a superb reading of brilliant new work
at the end of the evening, graciously demonstrating once again how
fully he deserved the honour his fellow artists had given him.

Born in Vancouver, British Columbia, 30 September 1944, the
son of Glen Fuller and Avis Aileen (Workman), Nichol spent his
youth in various cities of Western Canada, for his parents, both
railway workers, moved around a lot. Eventually he earned an
elementary basic teaching certificate at the University of British
Columbia, taught grade school in Port Coquitlam for part of a year,
then, in late 1963, moved to Toronto, his home to the time of his
death in 1988.

Nichol at first worked in the University of Toronto Library,
where he met David Aylward, with whom he soon began editing
Ganglia. While meeting Joe Rosenblatt, Victor Coleman, David
McFadden, and other writers, he corresponded with bill bissett in
Vancouver, whose *blewointment* magazine, along with TISH and
Talon, kept him in contact with West Coast poetry. George Bower-
ing, knowing of his interest in concrete poetry, put him in touch
with Cavan McCarthy in Great Britain, through whom he was
soon corresponding with such major concrete poets as Bob Cob-
bing, who was to publish his first collection of concrete poetry in
Britain a few years later. In an ironic reversal of the usual situation,
Nichol established his international reputation in concrete poetry
before achieving recognition in Canada.[2]

Nichol had begun by writing traditionally conventional lyric poetry; but by 1964 he felt that he was "somehow simply plugging in. And I've always believed that content takes care of itself. If there are things you have to say, you will say them. So the question becomes one of form — how do I get that out as openly and as clinically as possible?"[3] For the next year and a half, Nichol worked at what he called "ideopomes" — various kinds of concrete poetry — wholly abandoning traditional lyric verse. When Margaret Avison told him about Raymond Souster's *New Wave Canada* anthology, he rewrote the early lyrics, using what he had learned about form: "My ear was better. I could hear better after that year. I had a much better sense of rhythm, of music. I was better able to listen to the words and less concerned with imposing some sort of preconceived notion of wisdom on the occasion of writing" (*Out-Posts*, p. 19). *New Wave Canada* (1966) introduced many of the poets who would expand the boundaries of Canadian poetry during the next two decades; Nichol became one of the most important and influential of them, a "language researcher" at the leading edge of contemporary writing.[4]

Having begun his lifelong "apprenticeship to language," Nichol also entered the lay therapeutic community of Therafields, where he lived and studied to become a therapist. Nichol's continuing dedication to the first five books of *The Martyrology*[5] signalled his indebtedness to Therafields' founder, Lea Hindley-Smith, with whom he began therapy in 1963. In 1966, Nichol became a practising theradramist, and both his work in theradrama and his life in the community influenced his writing and performance, especially as it led him towards various forms of collaborative art.[6] In 1967, Therafields' farm outside Toronto became a central landscape in large sections of *The Martyrology*, the first two books of which he had begun to write.

In 1967, the year Bob Cobbing published *KonfessIons of an ElizAbeThan Fan Dancer* in London, Coach House Press in Toronto brought out Nichol's first major work in Canada. The box titled *bp* contained a book, *JOURNEYING & the returns*, a record of sound poetry, *Borders*, *Wild Thing*, a flip poem, and an envelope of concrete poetry objects, *Letters Home*. It proved an auspicious beginning, and in the next few years he continued to publish widely. In 1970, he and Michael Ondaatje both won Governor General's Awards for Poetry in English, and Ondaatje was making his film about Nichol, *Sons of Captain Poetry*. Nichol won for four books: *The True Eventual Story of Billy the Kid*, a wickedly funny pamphlet, parodying the legend; *still water*, a lovely box of minimal language images; *Beach Head*, a small collection of early lyrics; and *The Cosmic Chef: An Evening of Concrete*, the first anthology of Canadian concrete poetry, which he edited. In 1970, as well, he joined Rafael Barreto-Rivera, Paul Dutton, and Steve McCaffery to form The Four Horsemen, the premier sound poetry group in Canada during the past two decades.

During the 1970s, Nichol pursued his various careers as therapist, writer, sound poet, and editor with immense energy. He published the more than usually fugitive *Ganglia* and *grOnk* pamphlets and cards; he joined the editorial collectives at Coach House Press and *Open Letter*, and at the end of the decade he founded Underwhich Editions with some other writers. He and Steve McCaffery joined critical forces to become The Toronto Research Group, which published its own and others' work in *Open Letter*. As both a solo artist and a member of The Four Horsemen, he performed his work across Canada and in the United States, Great Britain, and Europe. And he continued writing, most centrally the ongoing long poem, *The Martyrology*, the first four books of which appeared during the 1970s. Other important books of that period include *Monotones* (1971), *The Other Side of the Room* (1971), *love: a book of remembrances* (1974), *Craft Dinner* (1978), and *Journal* (1978), the latter two works in prose.

It's clear that whatever else *The Martyrology* is, it is an often intimate record of Nichol's life. For example, *Briefly: The Birth/ Death Cycle from The Book of Hours* in Book 6 of *The Martyrology*, commemorates the 1979 stillborn child to Nichol and his long time companion, Eleanor Hiebert, whom he married in 1980. Their daughter, Sarah, was born in 1981. That same year he ended his involvement with Therafields and after a six month hiatus began writing for children's television as a way of earning a living. Nichol's experiences as a parent obviously affected his writing: he explored the theme of familial descent, of both having and being parents, more fully in the later books of *The Martyrology*; he wrote books of verse for young children as well as scripts for *Fraggle Rock* and *The Racoons*, at least partly because of his new interest in the imaginative lives of the young.

In the 1980s, Nichol became a full-time professional writer, as his television work demonstrated. As well, in the fall of 1979, he began teaching creative writing at York University. A popular instructor, he sought to help others write the way they wished to. He also gave writing workshops in various parts of Canada. Most importantly, he continued to practise his craft, writing and performing those luminous works by which he is best known, living the writing life as fully and wholeheartedly as anyone could.

NOTES

[1] *Read the Way He Writes: A Festschrift for bpNichol*, ed. Paul Dutton and Steven Smith, *Open Letter*, 6, Nos. 5–6 (Summer–Fall 1986), 6.

[2] Nichol is the only Canadian contributor to Hansjorg Mayer's CONCRETE POETRY *Britain Canada United States* (Stuttgart: Editions Hansjorg Mayer, 1966), Emmett Williams's *An Anthology of Concrete Poetry* (New York: Something Else, 1967), and Mary Ellen Solt's *Concrete Poetry: A World View* (Bloomington: Indiana Univ. Press, 1968).

[3] Caroline Bayard and Jack David, "bpNichol," in *Out-Posts/Avant-Postes*, Three Solitudes: Contemporary Literary Criticism in Canada, Vol. IV (Erin, Ont.: Porcépic, 1978), p. 19.

[4] In an interview with Stephen Scobie and Douglas Barbour, Nichol said " 'I tend to avoid the word "experimental," because it's become a rather loaded term. I use the term "research" . . . .' " As Scobie points out, "Such terms as 'research' and 'apprenticeship' (which is Nichol's most frequently repeated description of his own work) imply an attitude of humility towards the medium being explored." Stephen Scobie, *bpNichol: What History Teaches*, The New Canadian Criticism Series (Vancouver: Talonbooks, 1984), p. 13.

[5] As it appears in *The Martyrology Books 1 & 2* (Toronto: Coach House, 1977) the dedication reads: "for lea / without whose act of friendship / quite literally none of this would have been written."

[6] Lea Hindley-Smith, Stan Kutz, Philip McKenna, and bpNichol, "Therafields," *The Canadian Forum*, Jan. 1973, pp. 12–17, provides a description of and a rationale for this experimental community and its socio-psychological philosophy of therapy.